ST. ANNES ON THE SEA PAINTINGS

BY

RONALD HABER

For
Lozo, Nicki,
Sienna & Lucy

I am a local artist from St. Annes on the Sea and I have spent many pleasant hours painting the views around the area. Some paintings are of the current times and some I have taken the liberty of trying to depict it in the past.

Hope you enjoy my works.

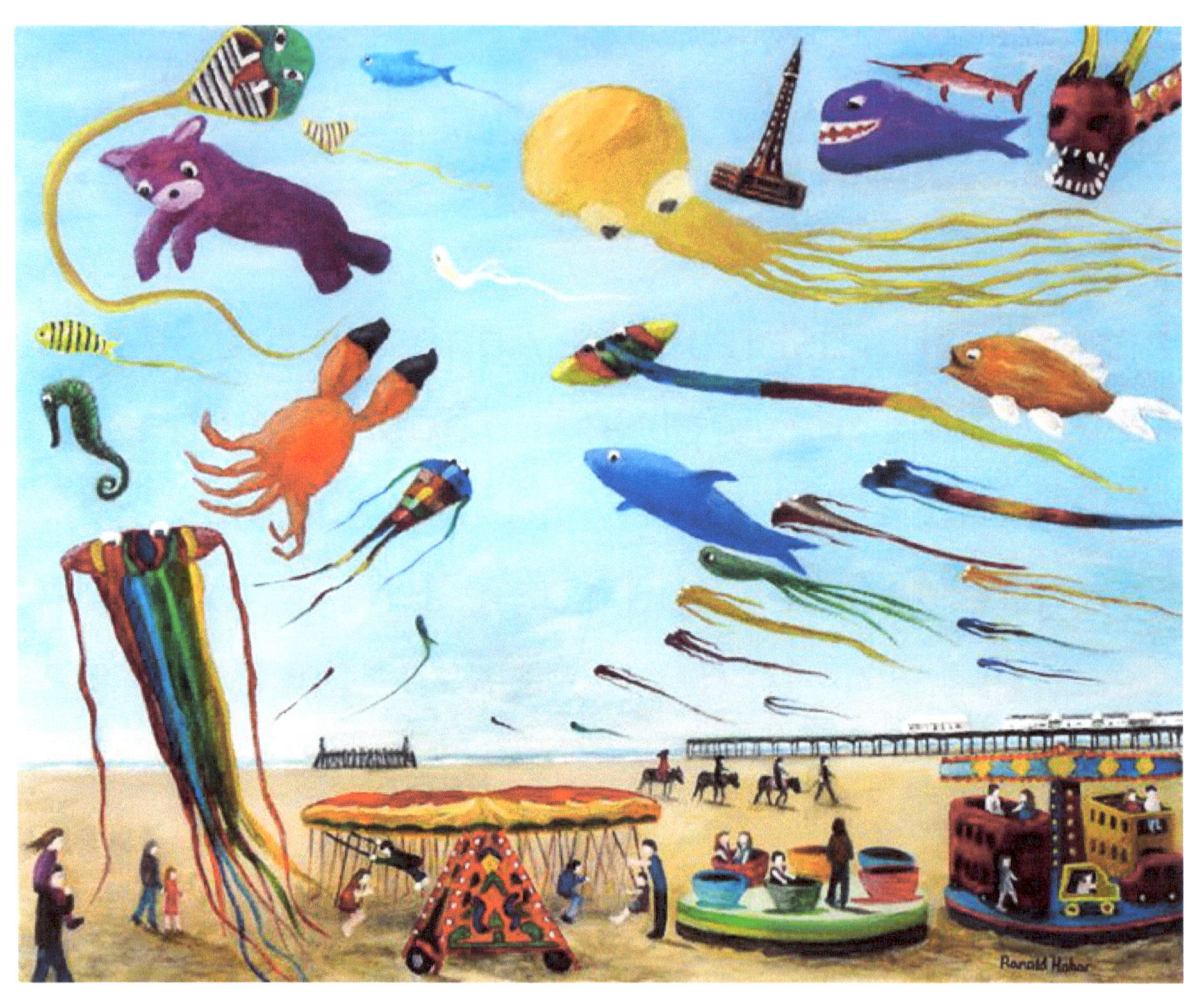

St. Annes on Sea International Kite Festival

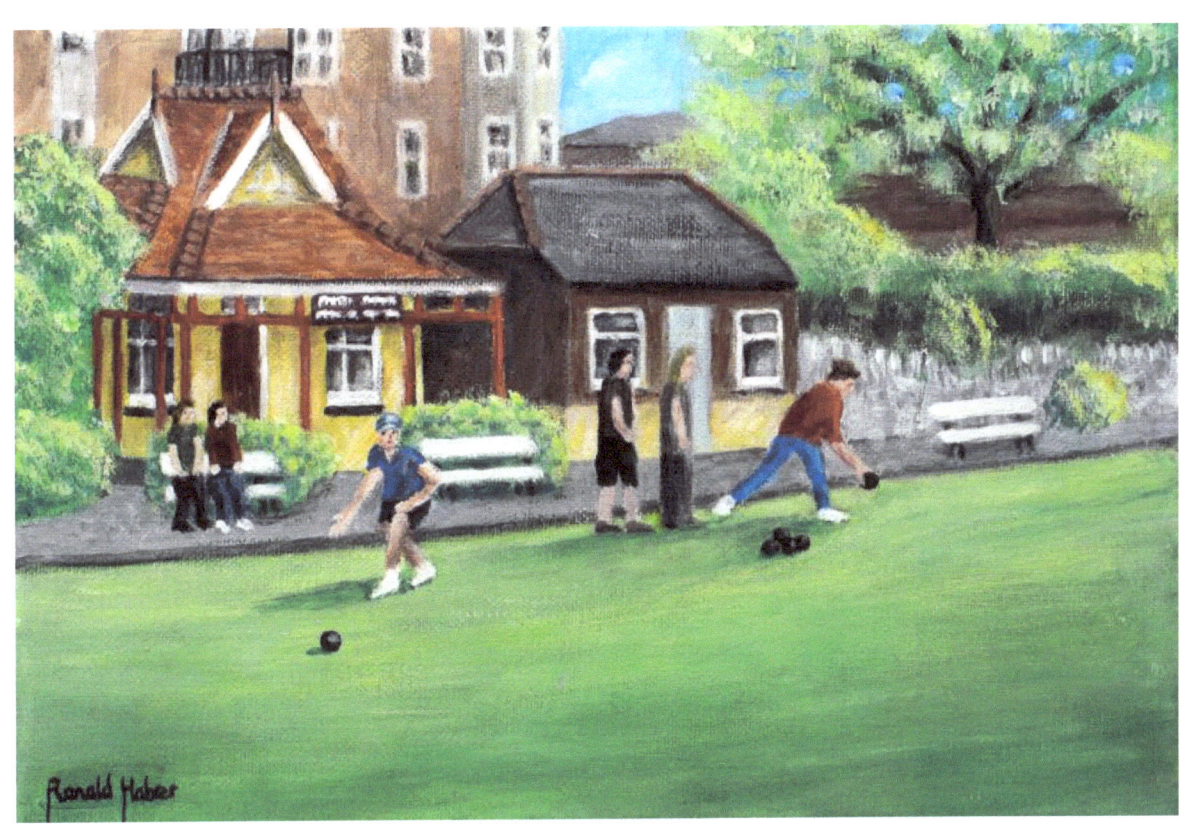

St. Annes on Sea Ashton Gardens Playing Bowls

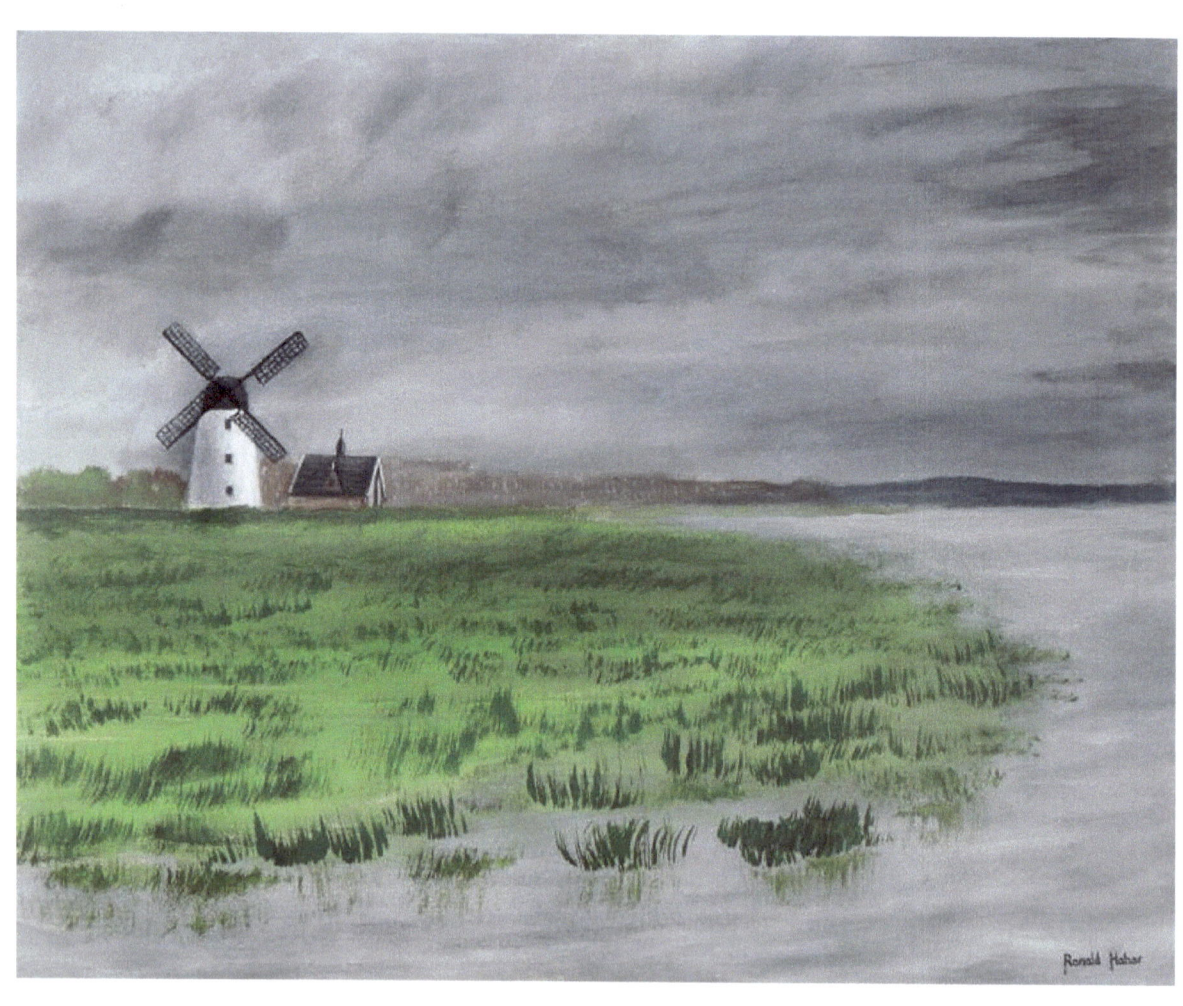

Lytham Windmill from the Jetty

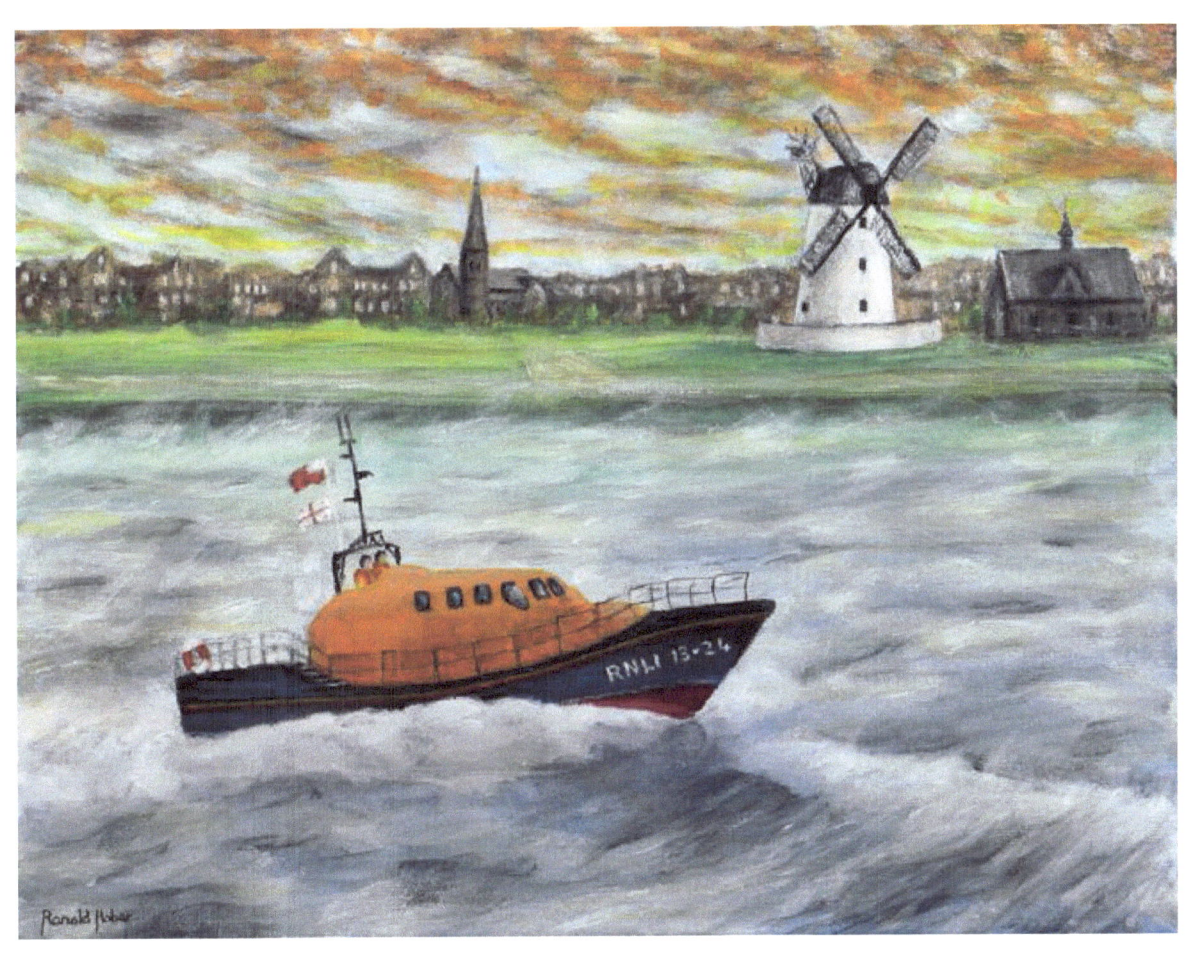

St. Annes on Sea Lifeboat

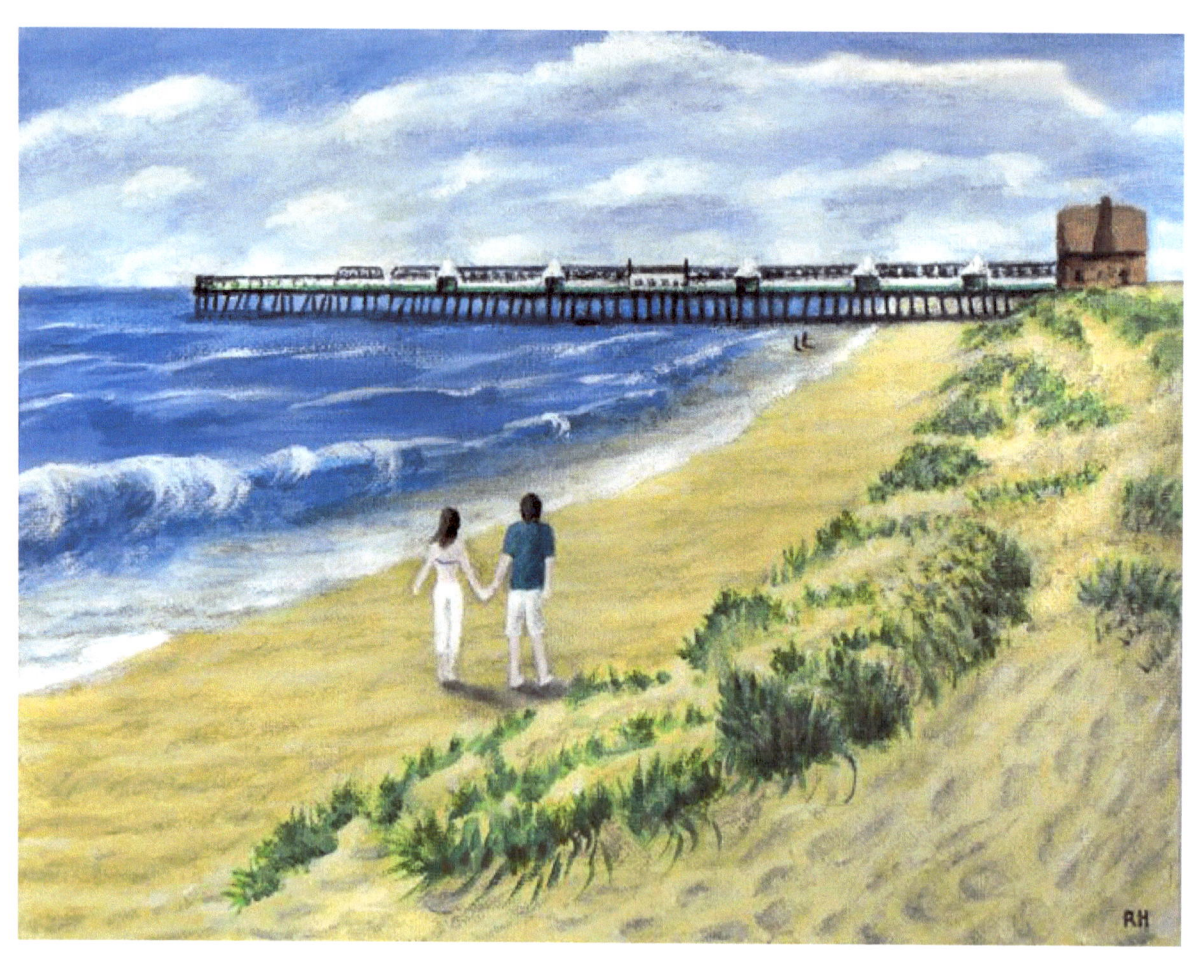

St. Annes on Sea Stroll along the Beach

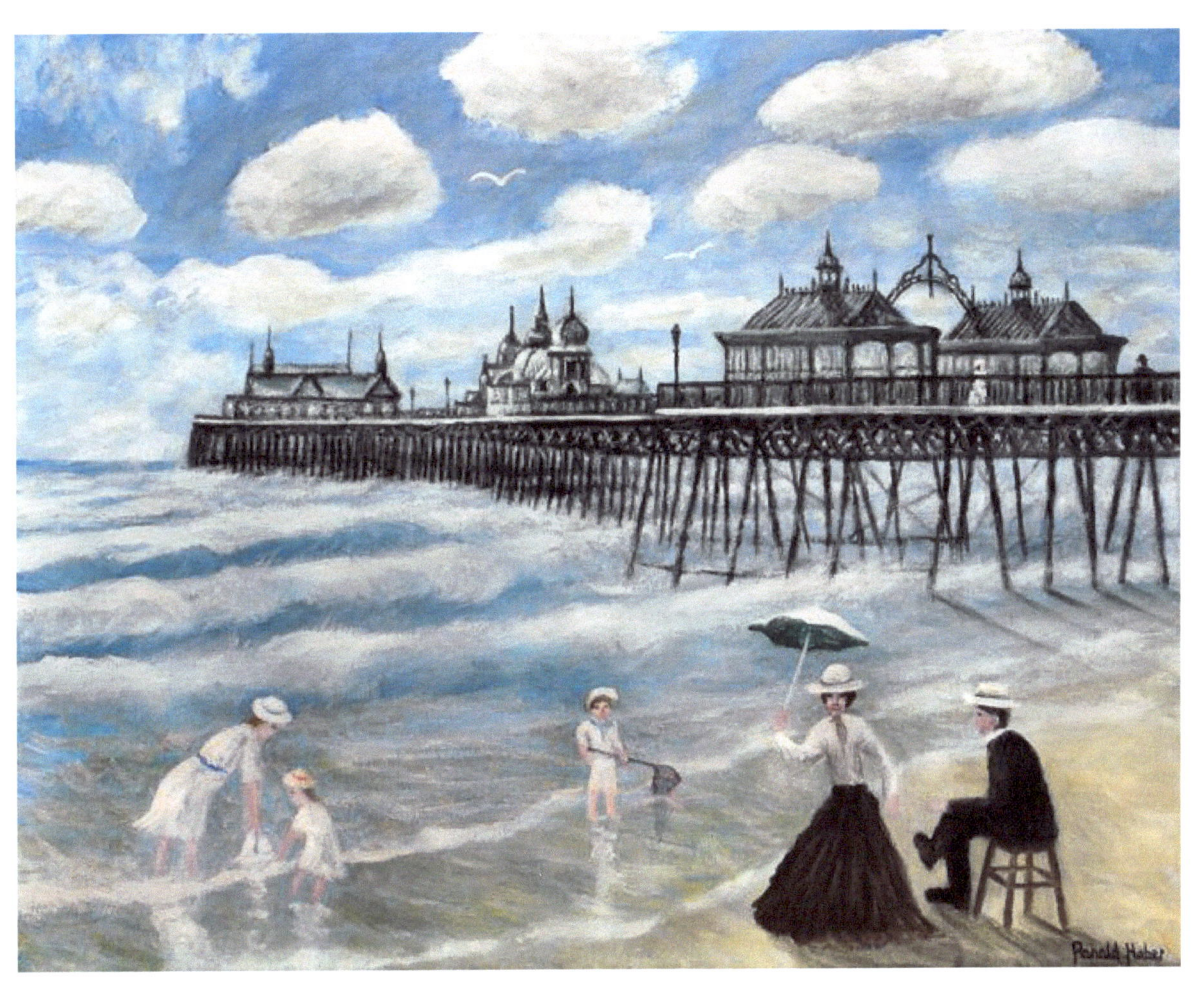

St. Annes on Sea Pier 1906

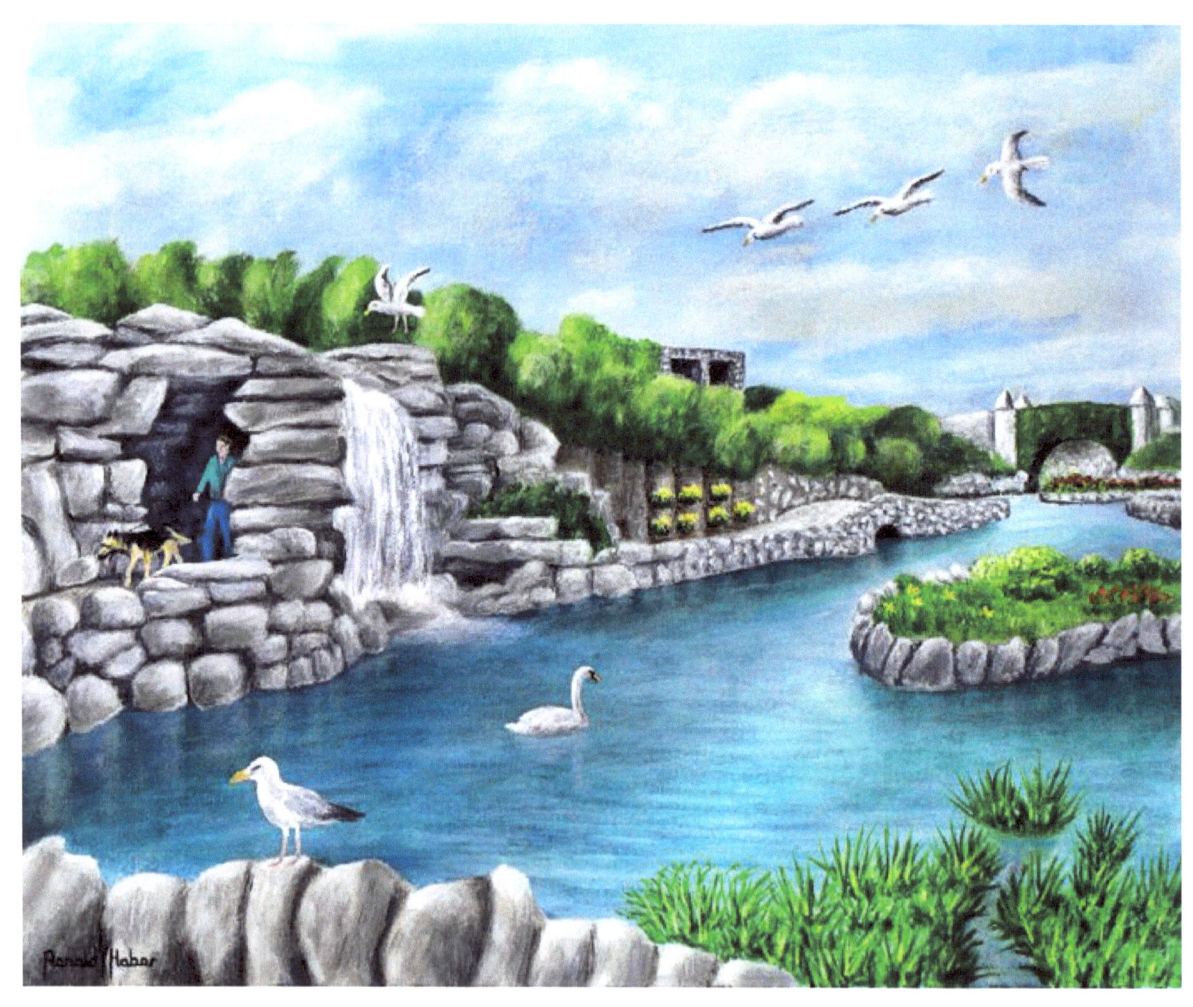

St. Annes on Sea Promenade Waterfall and Gardens

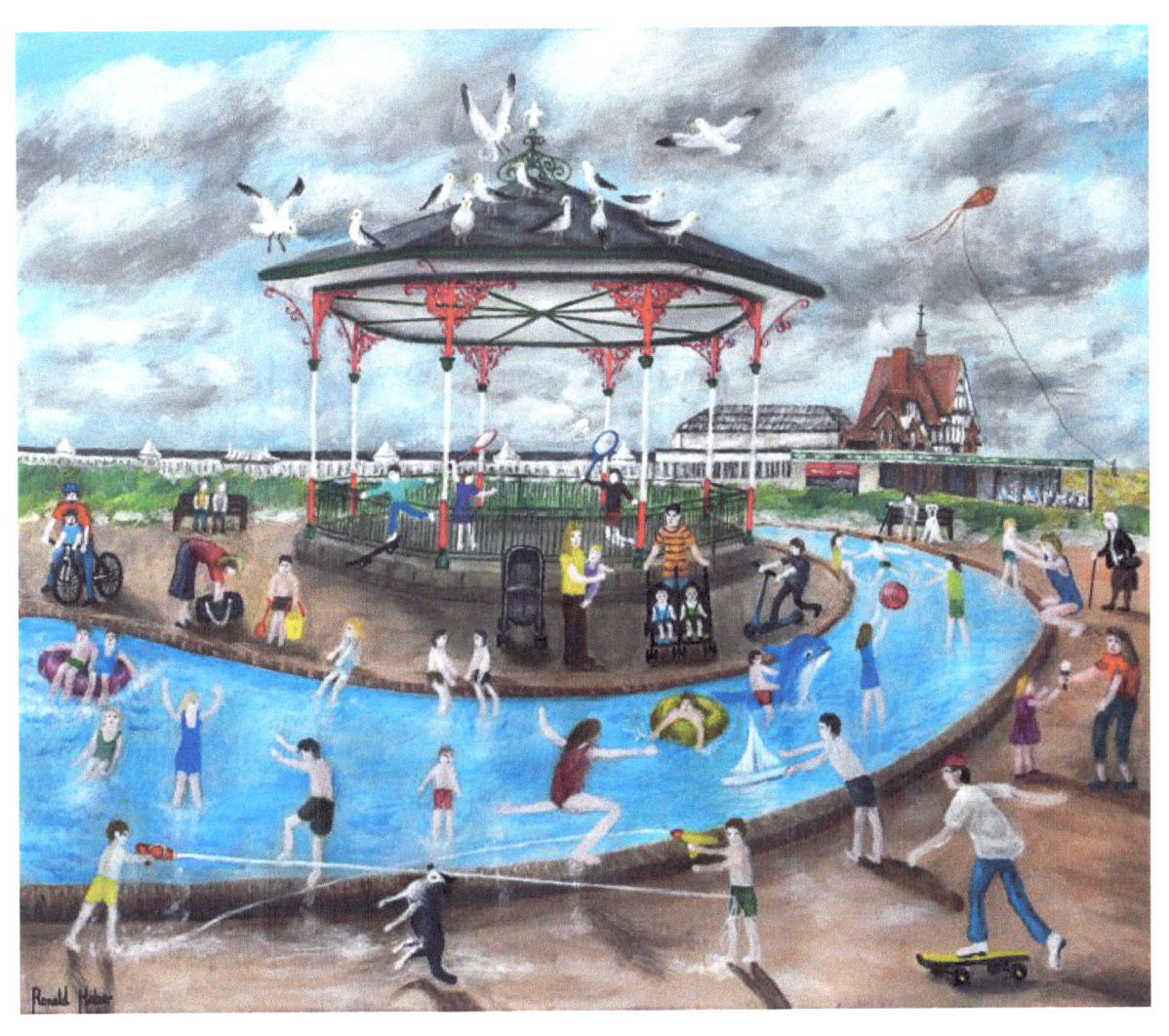

St. Annes on Sea Paddling Pool, Bandstand and Pier

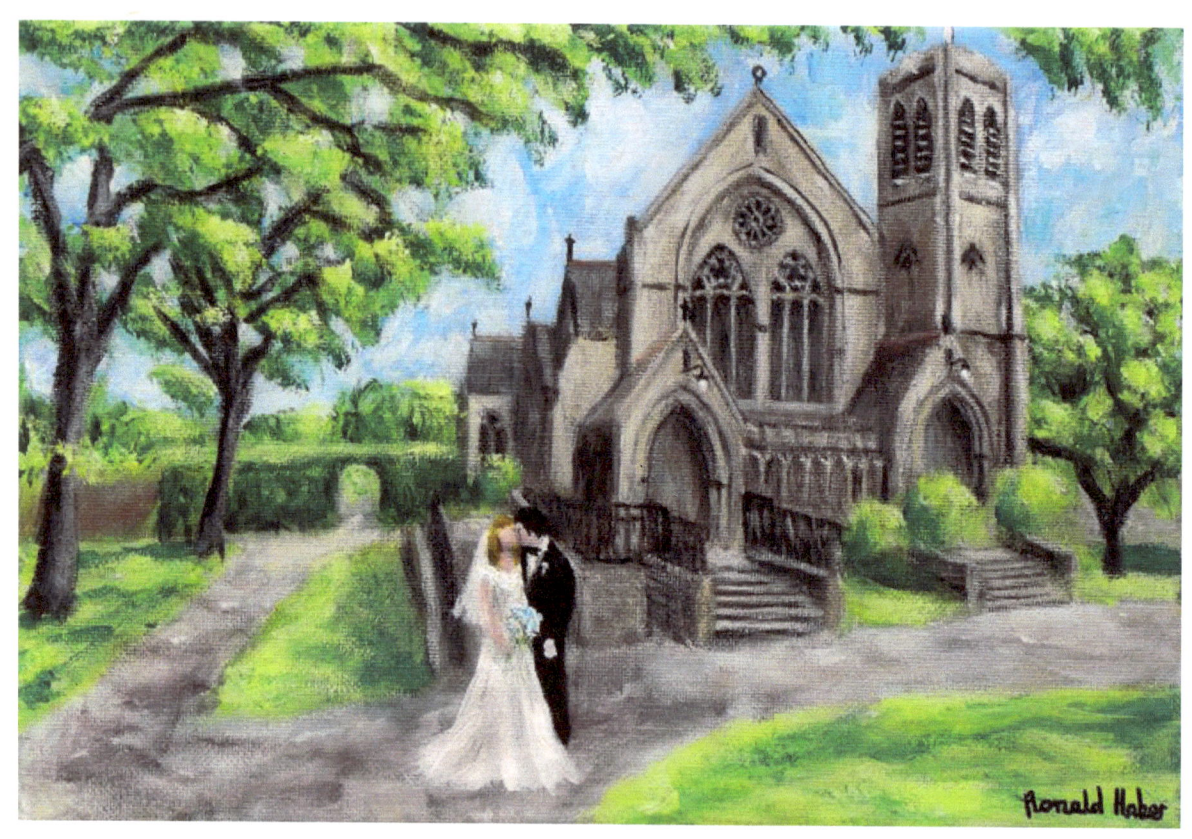

St. Annes on Sea United Reformed Church Wedding

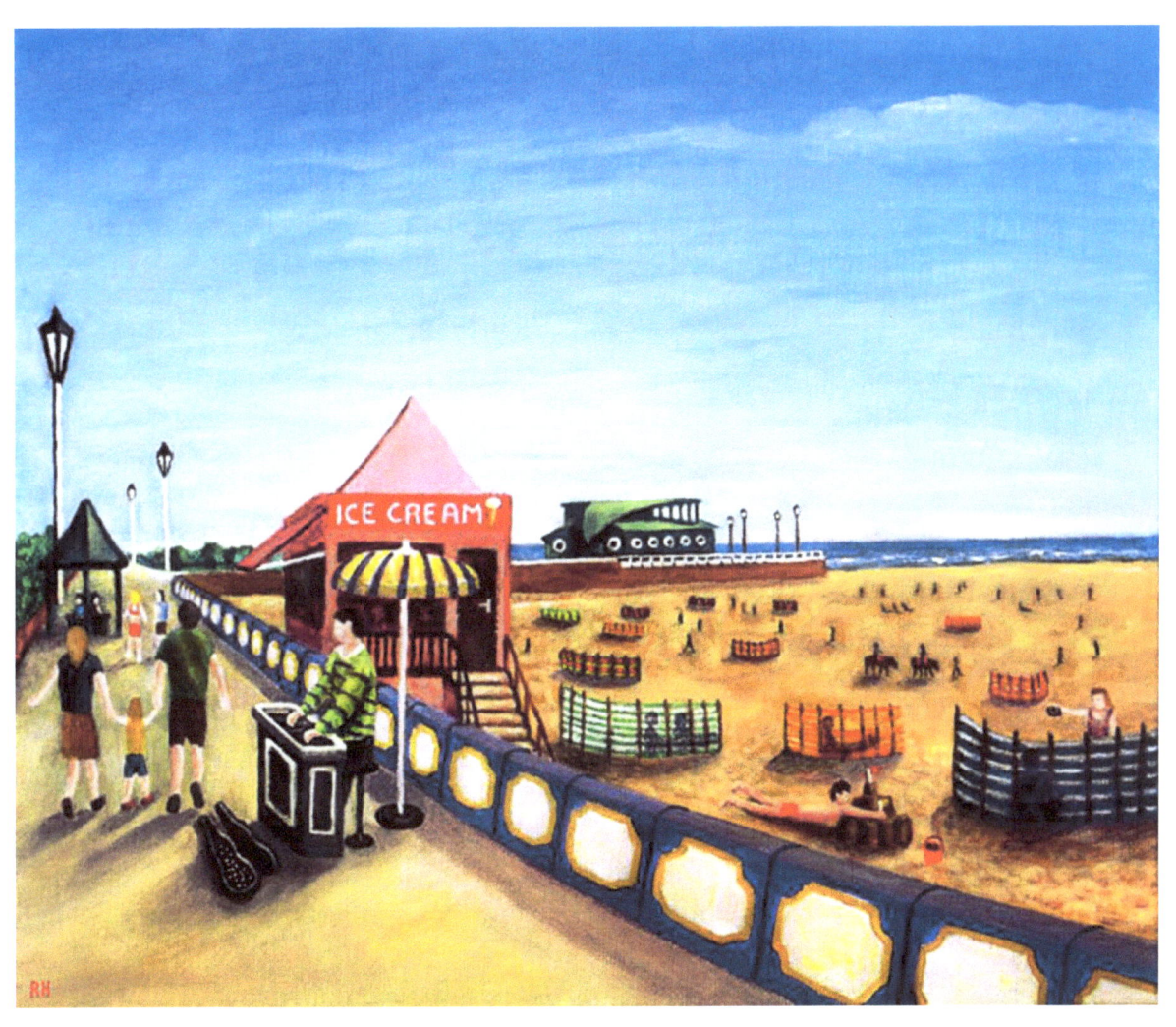

St. Annes on Sea Promenade Ice Cream Hut, Beach and Busker

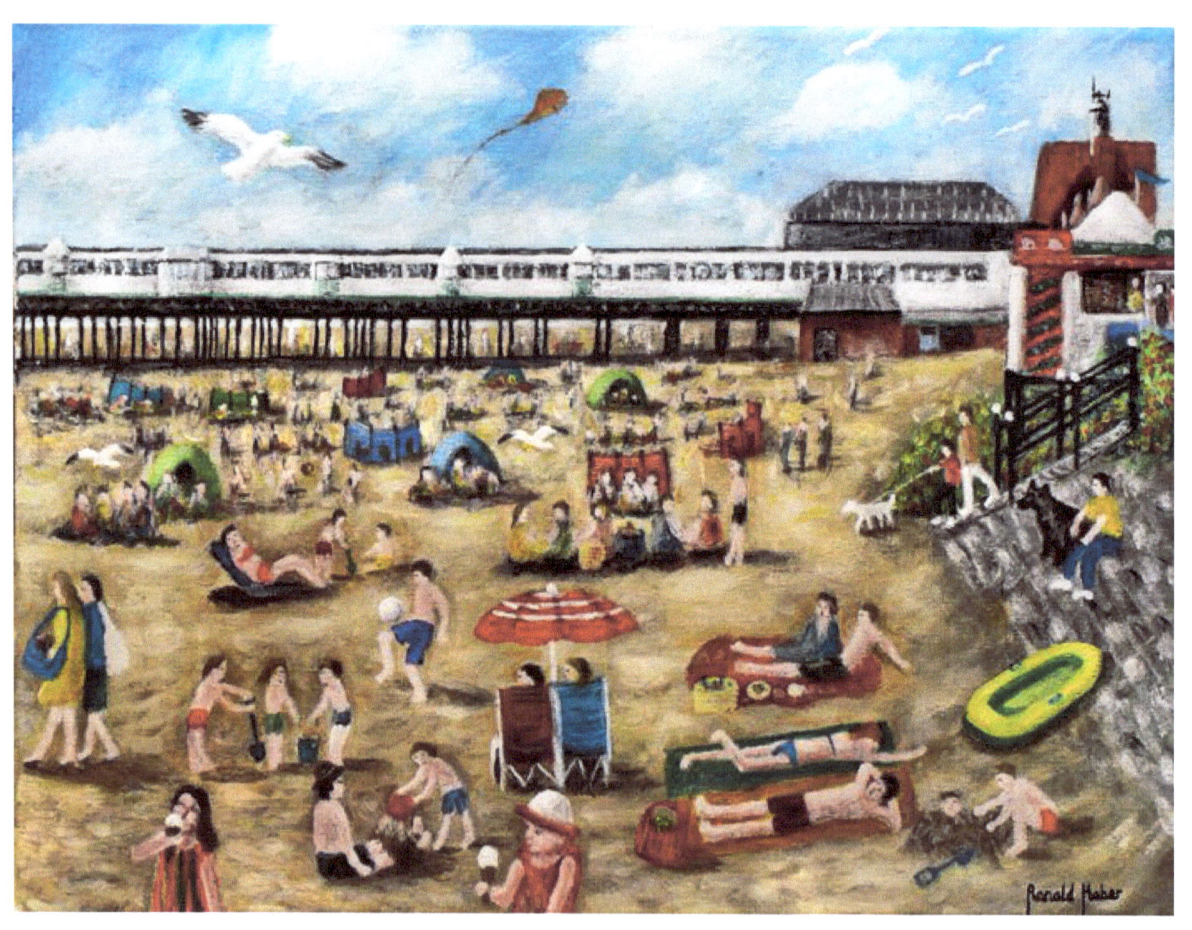

St. Annes on Sea Beach and Pier on a Summer's Day

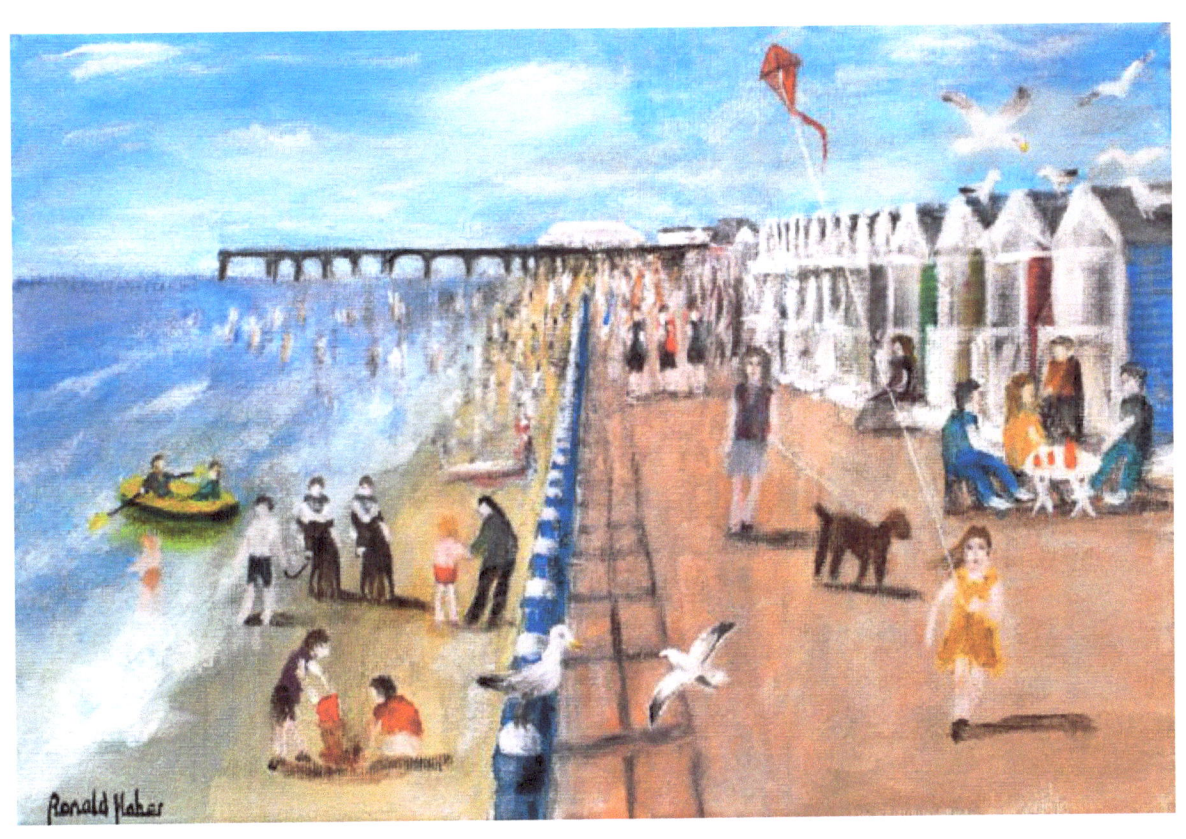

St. Annes on Sea Beach Huts

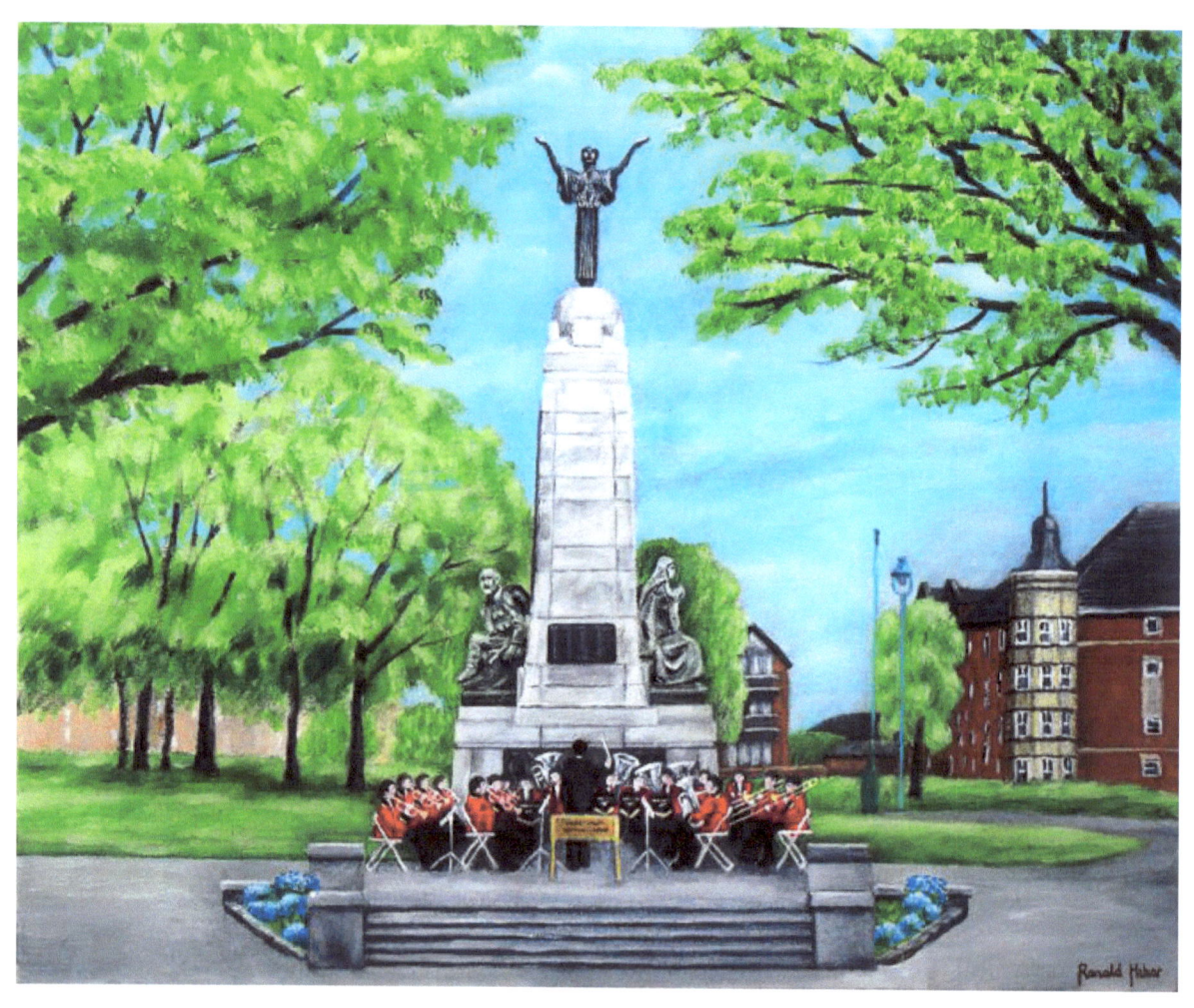

St. Annes on Sea Blackpool Brass Band in Ashton Gardens

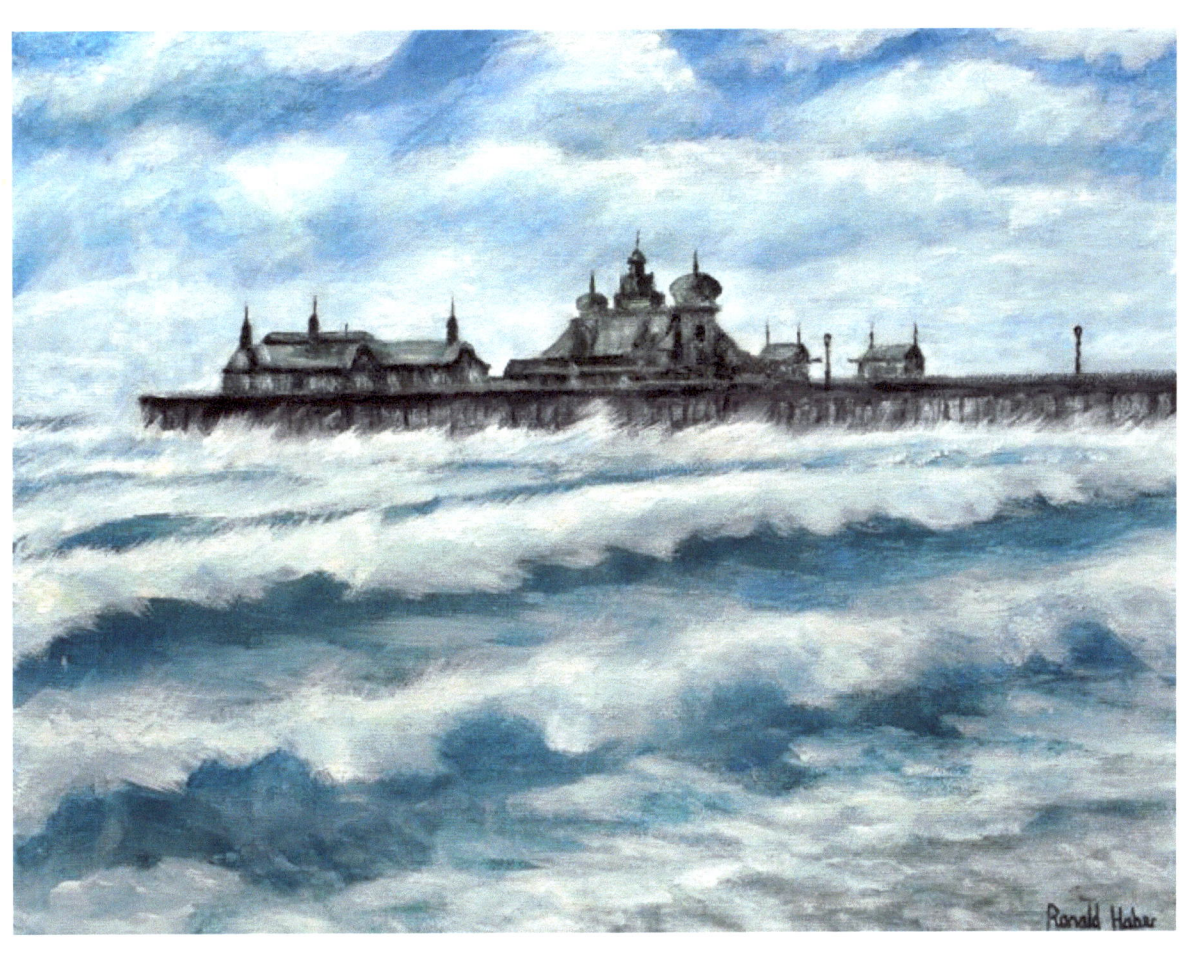

St. Annes on Sea Pier 1906 Stormy Seas

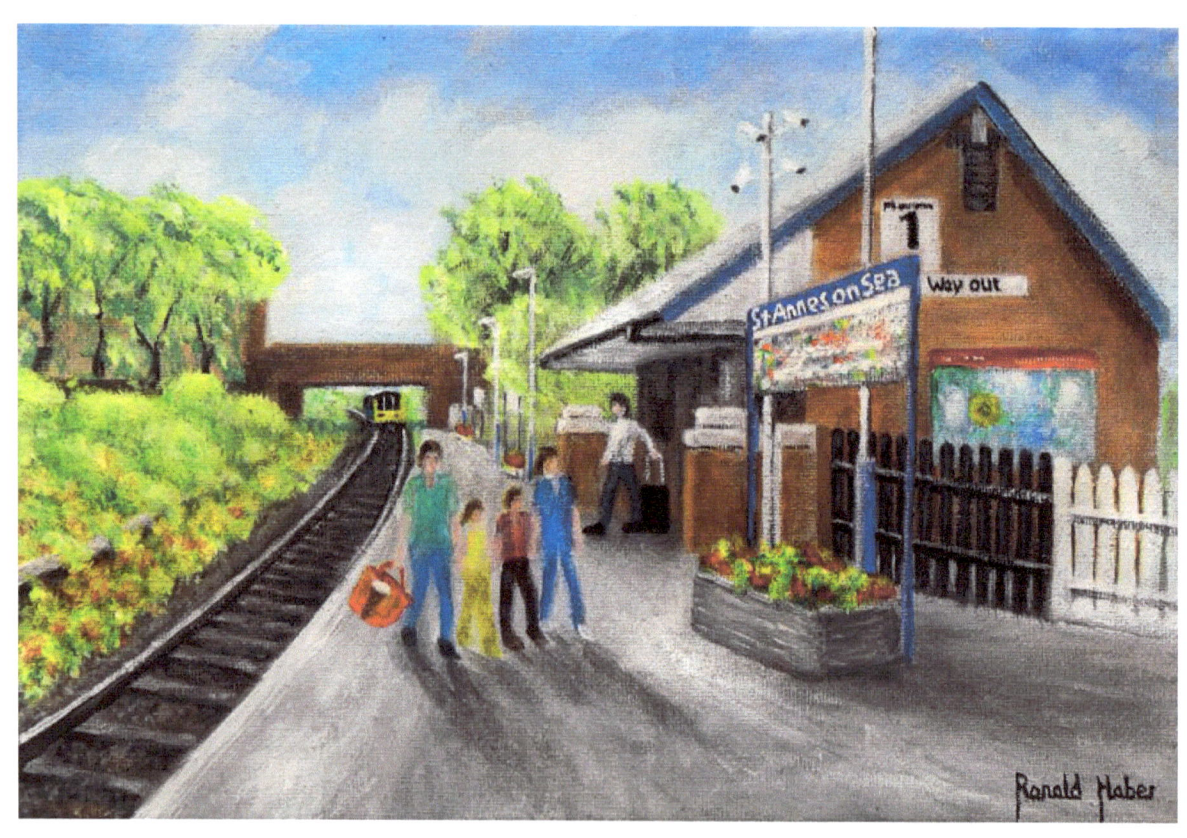

St. Annes on Sea Railway Station

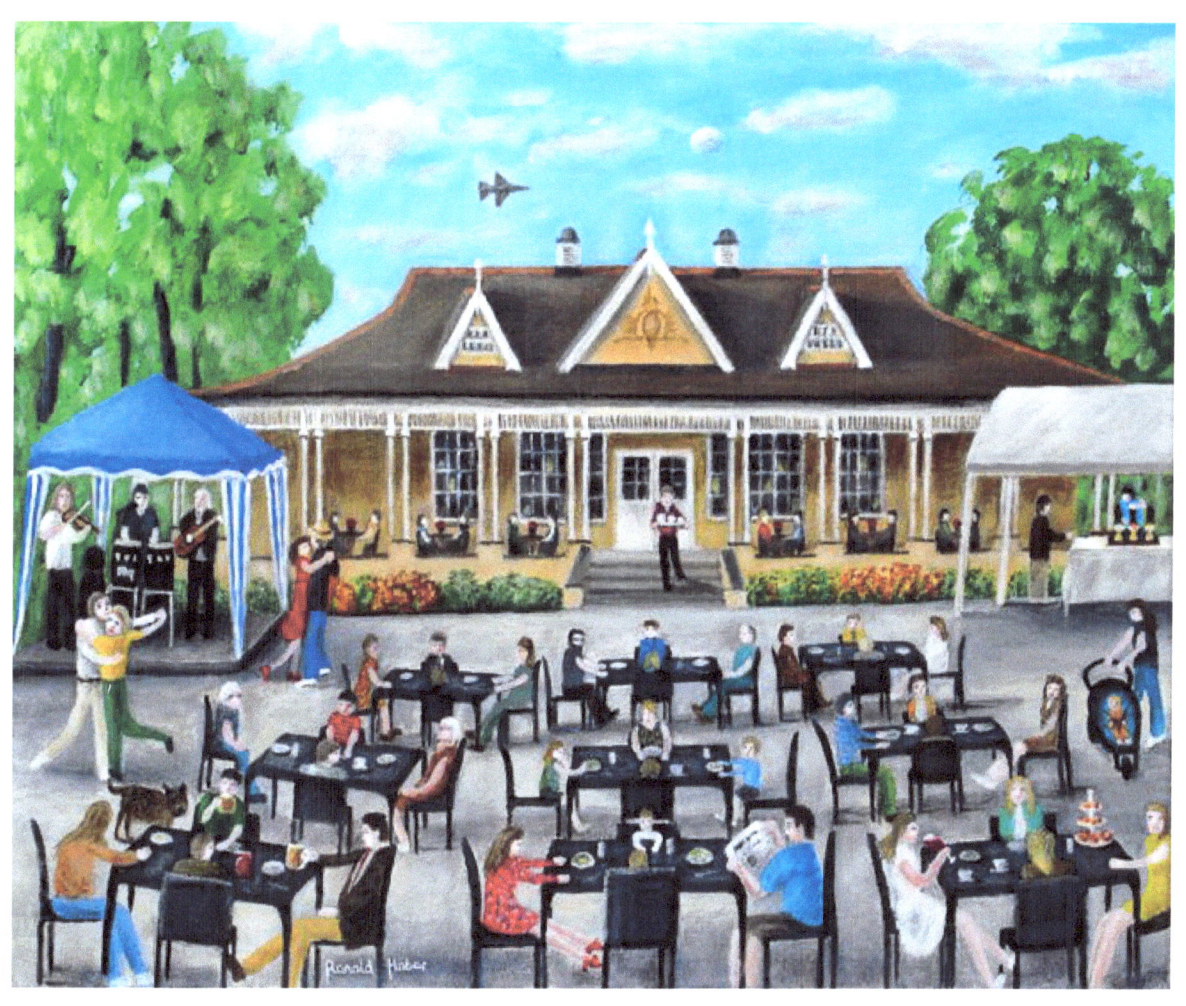

St. Annes on Sea Ashton Gardens Pavilion Cafe

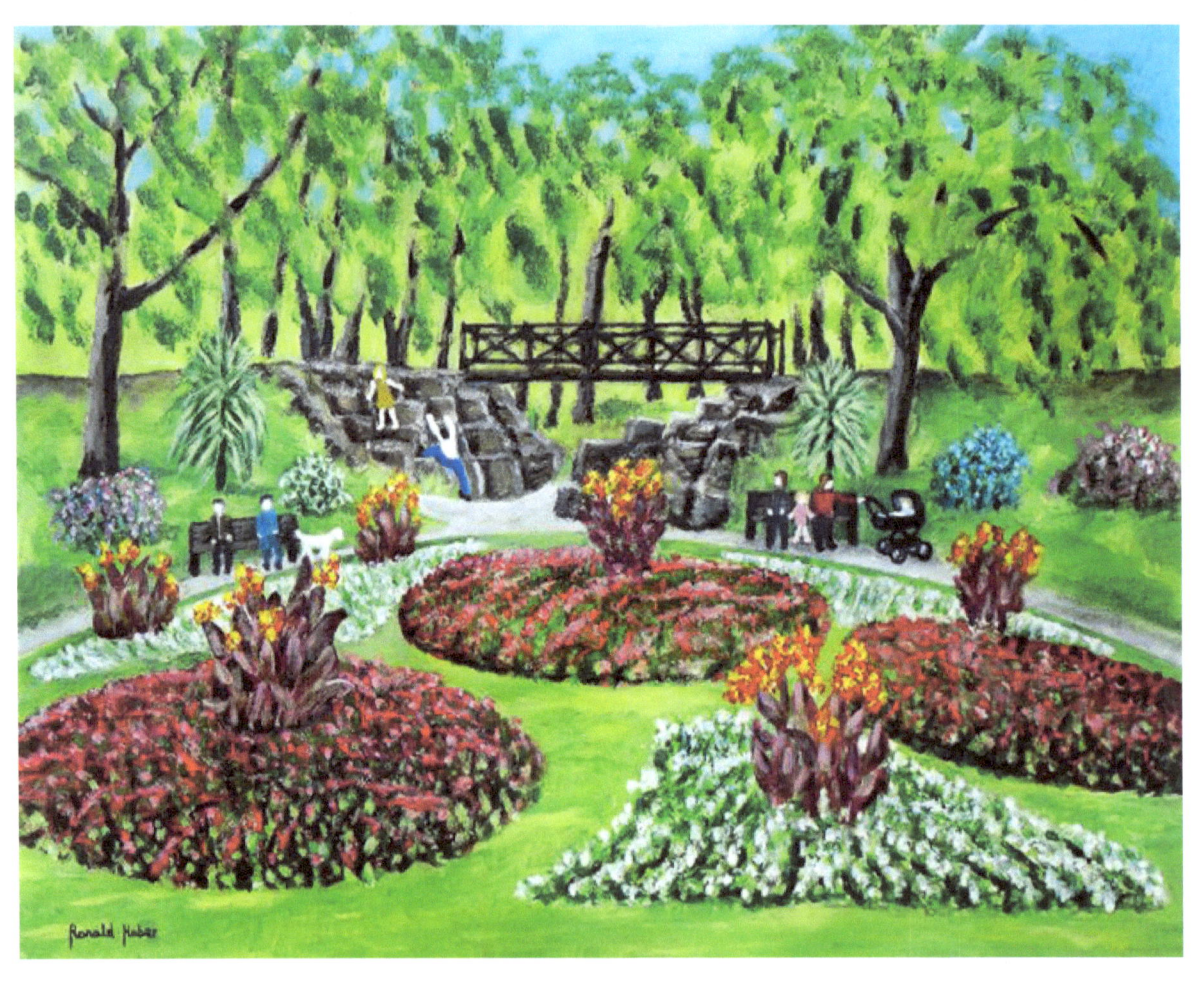

St. Annes on Sea Sunken Garden at Ashton Gardens

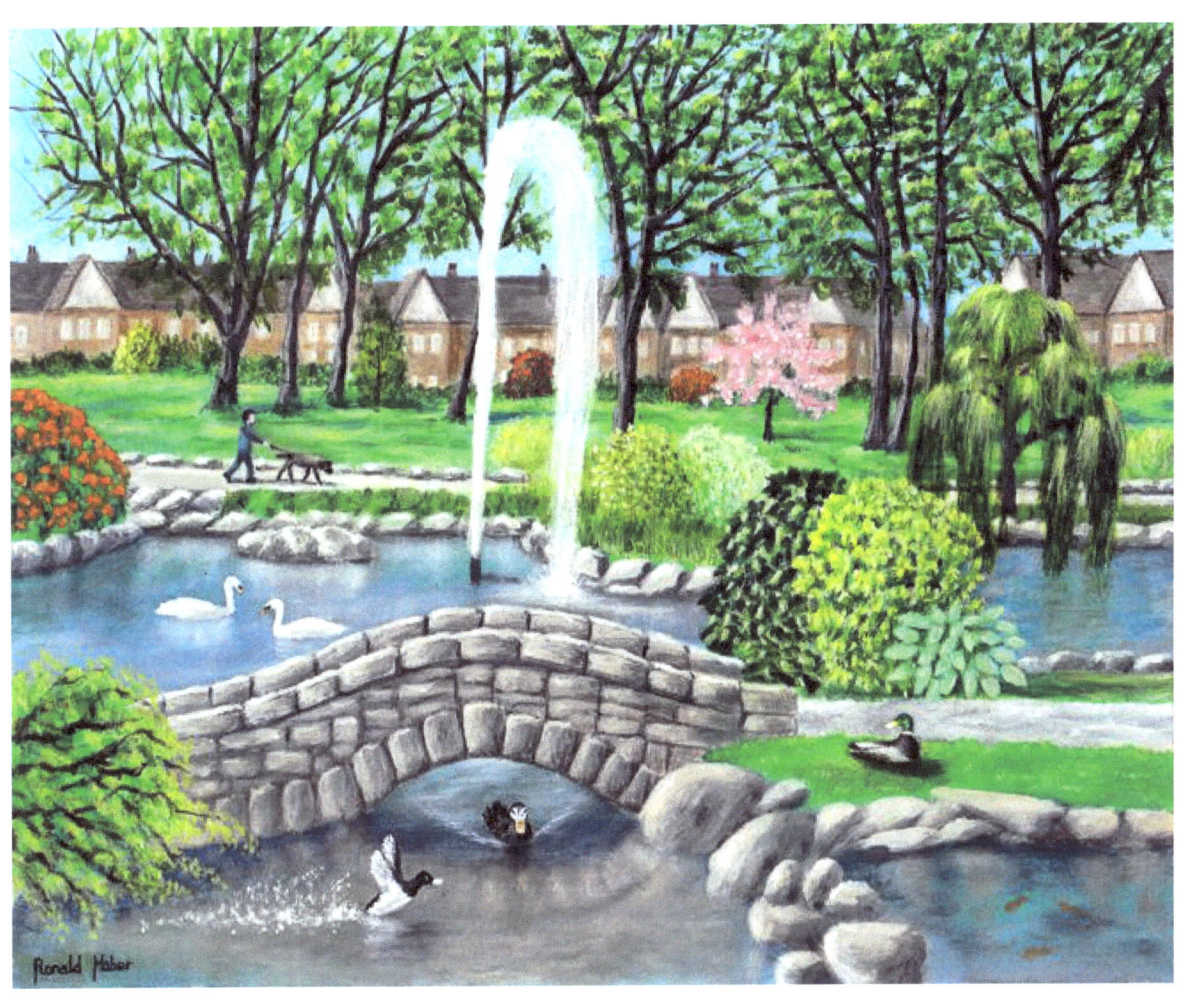

St. Annes on Sea Ashton Gardens Fountain and Bridge

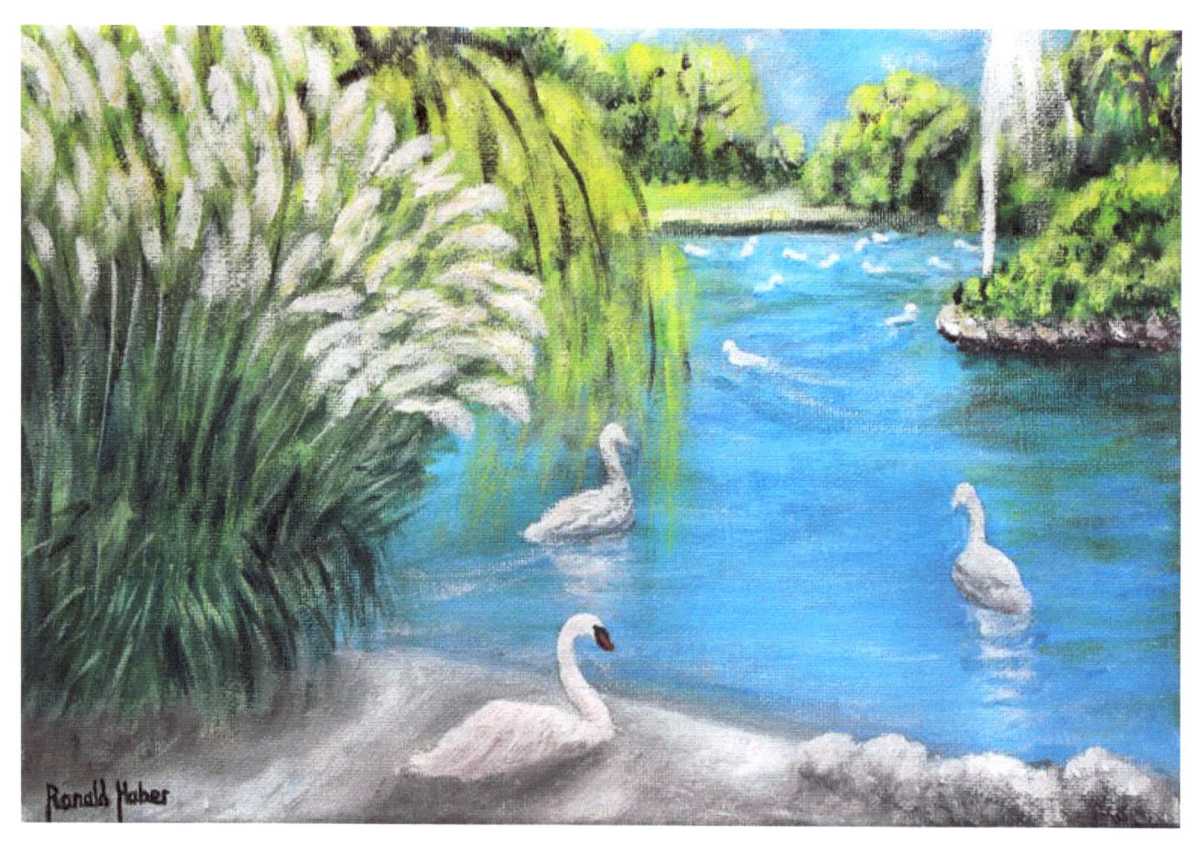

St. Annes on Sea Ashton Gardens Lake

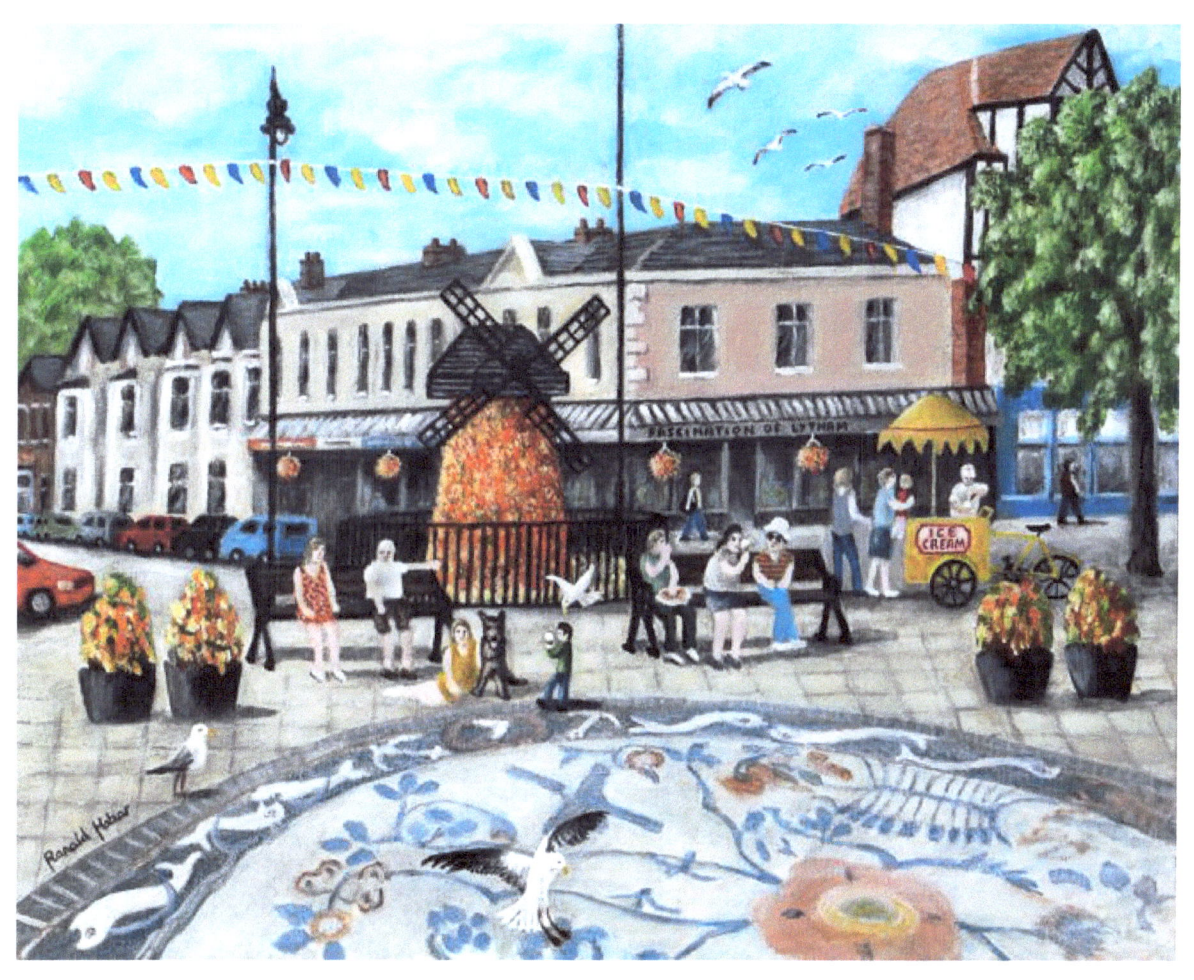

Lytham Square

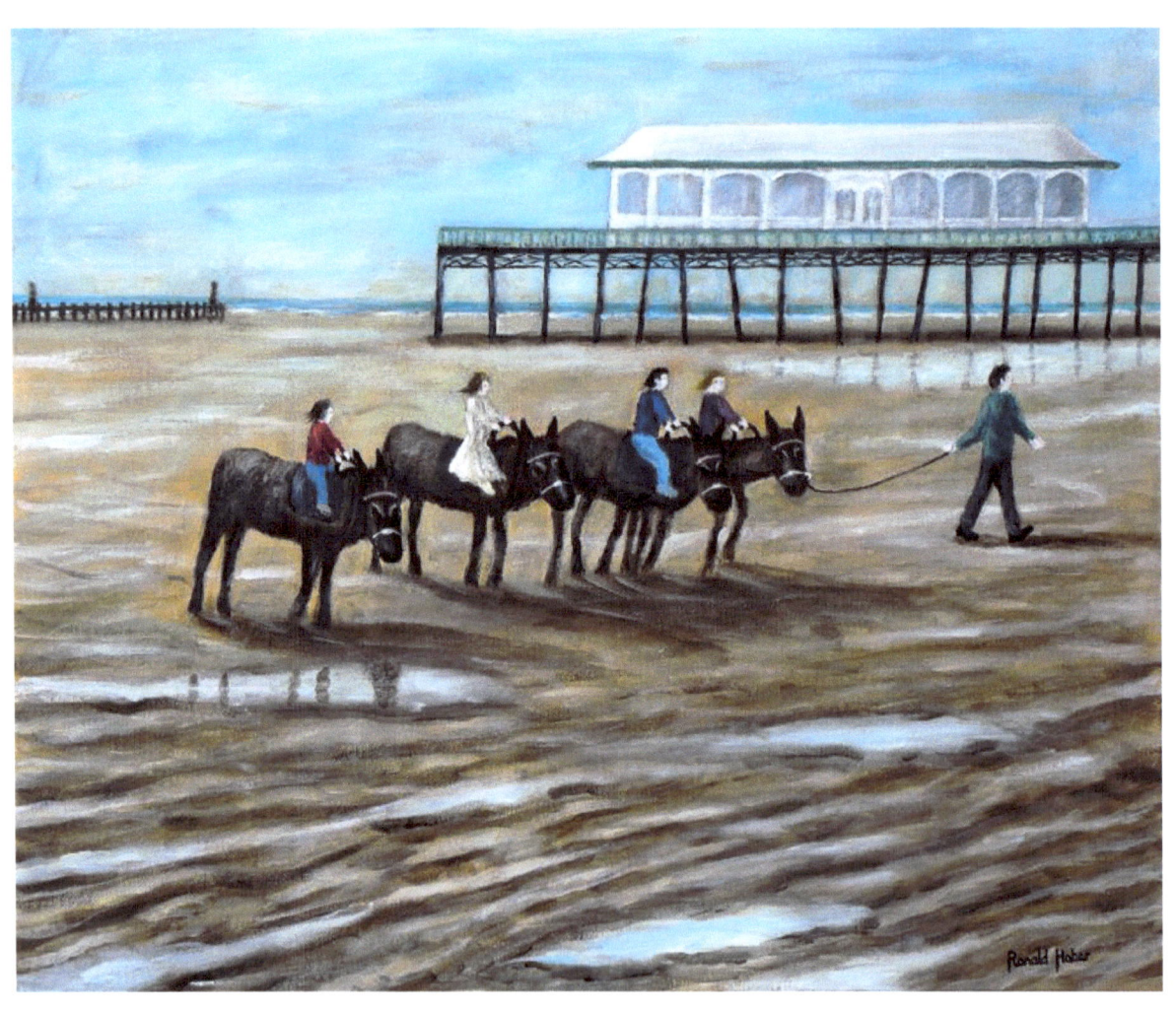

St. Annes on Sea Donkey Rides

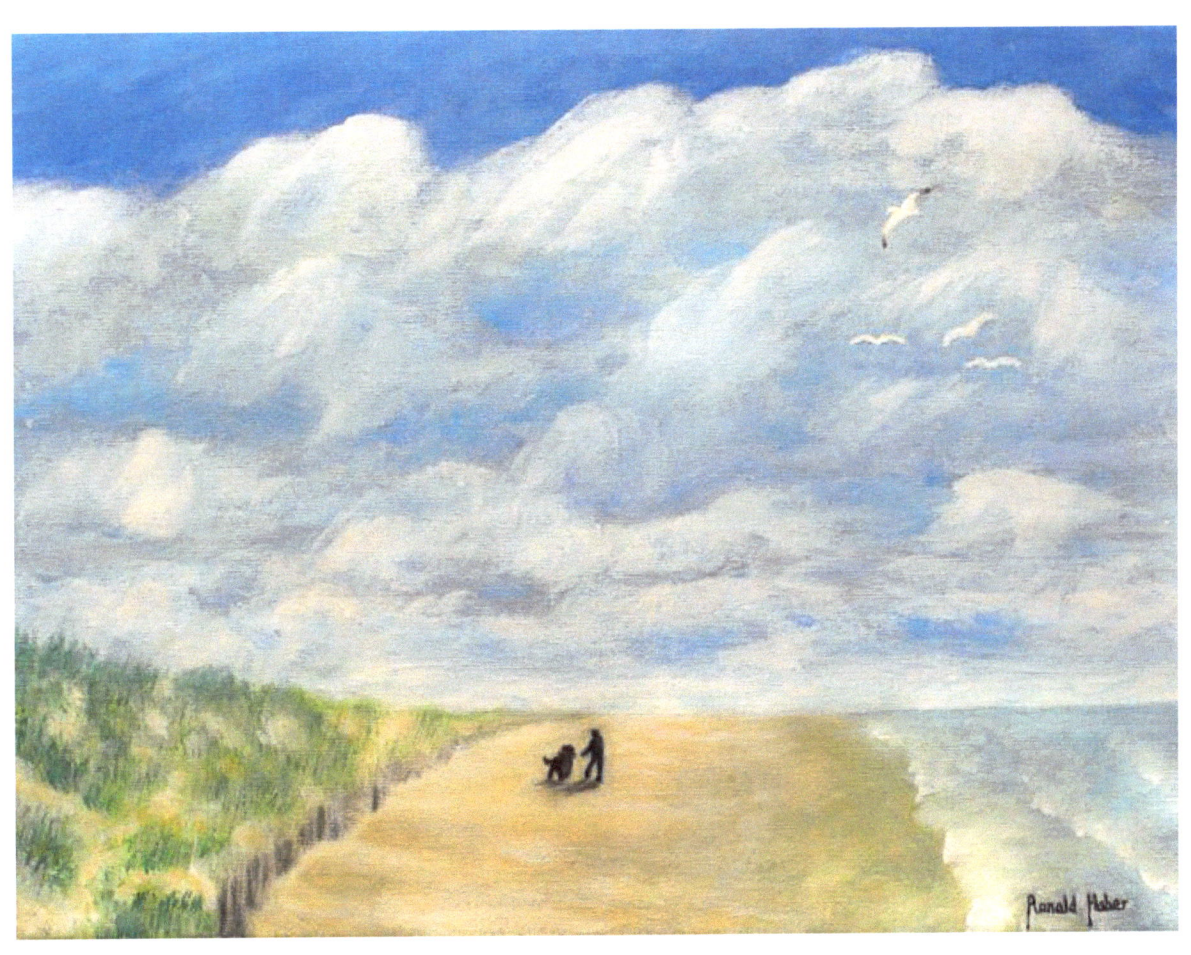

St. Annes on Sea North Beach

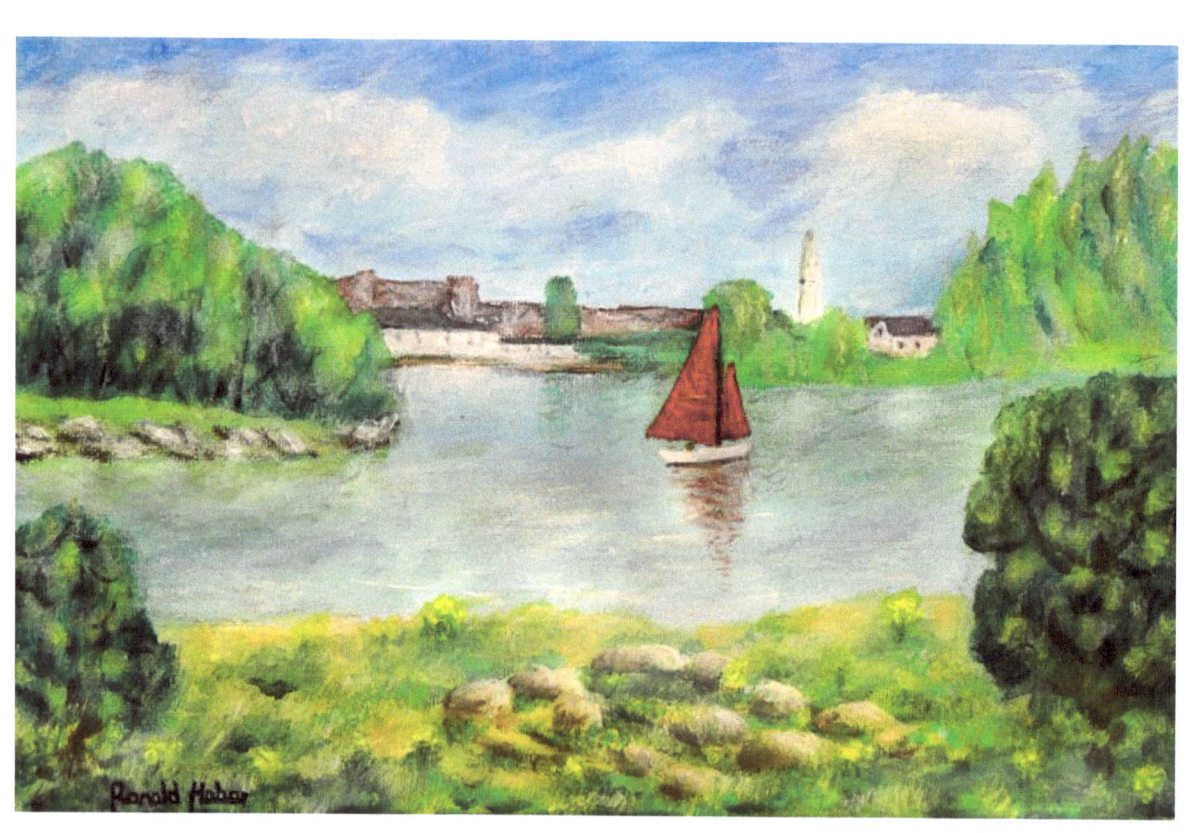

Fairhaven Boating Lake

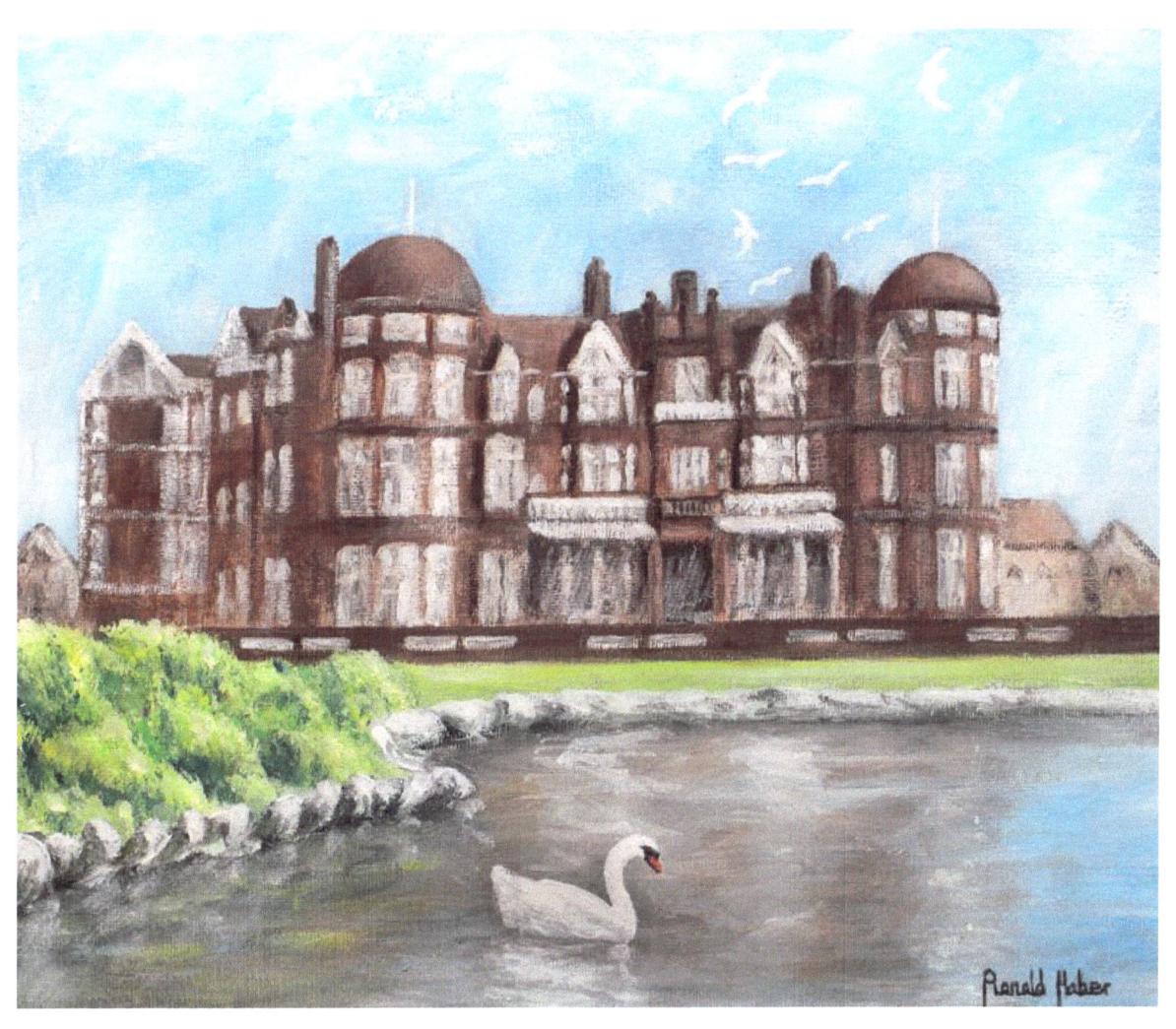

St. Annes on Sea Grand Hotel

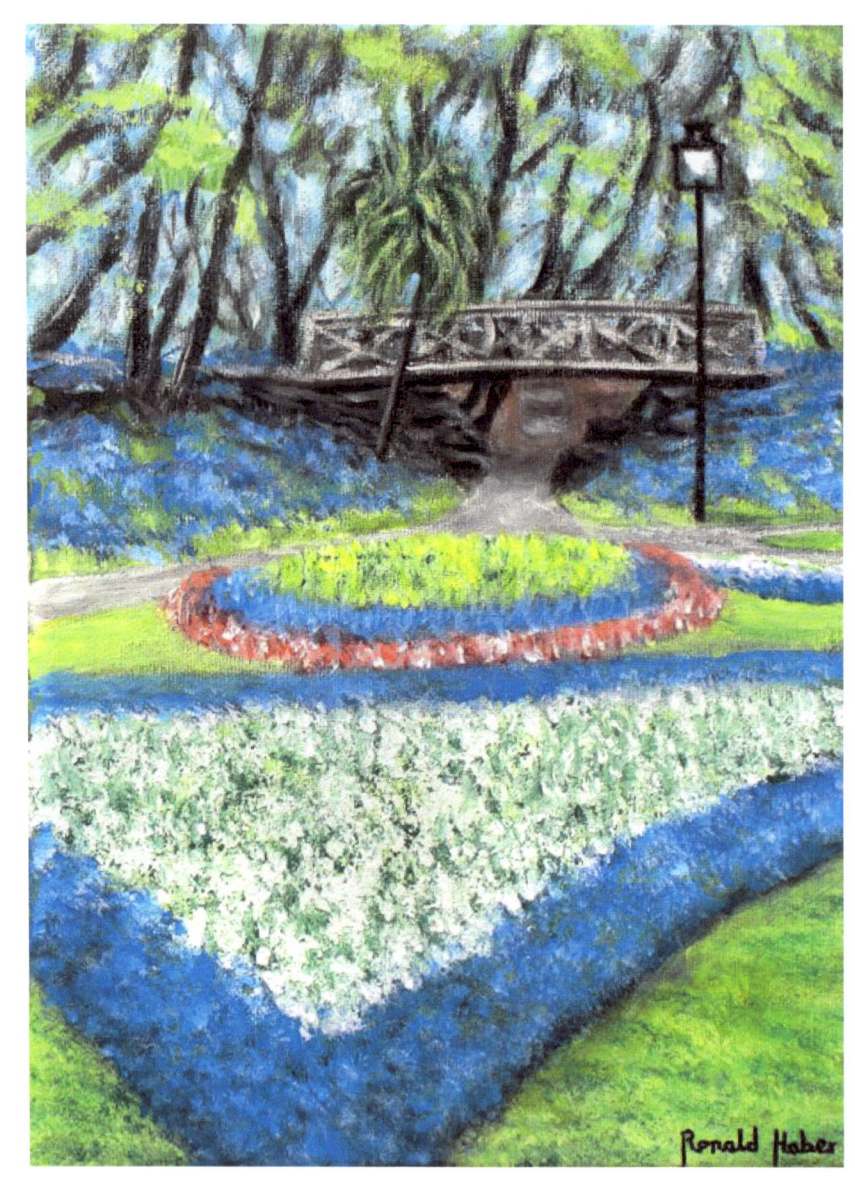

St. Annes on Sea Ashton Gardens Flower Beds

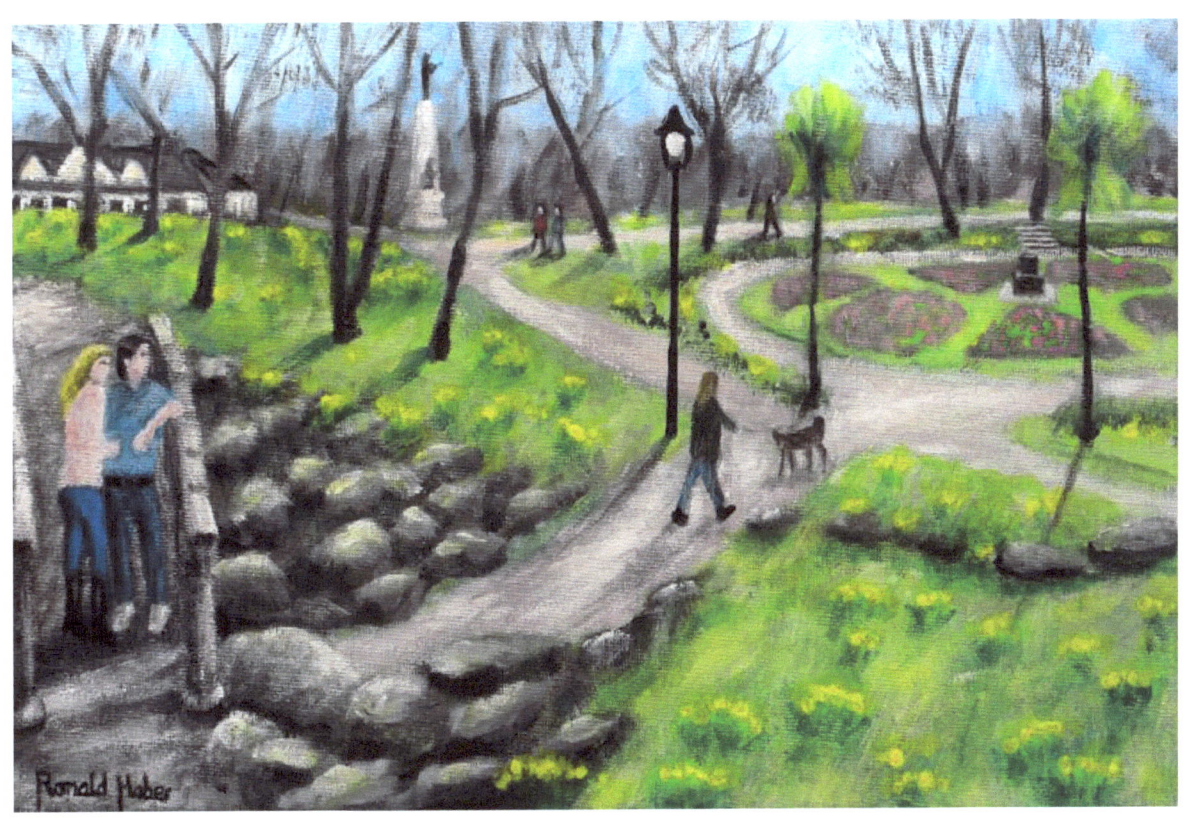

St. Annes on Sea Ashton Gardens in the Spring

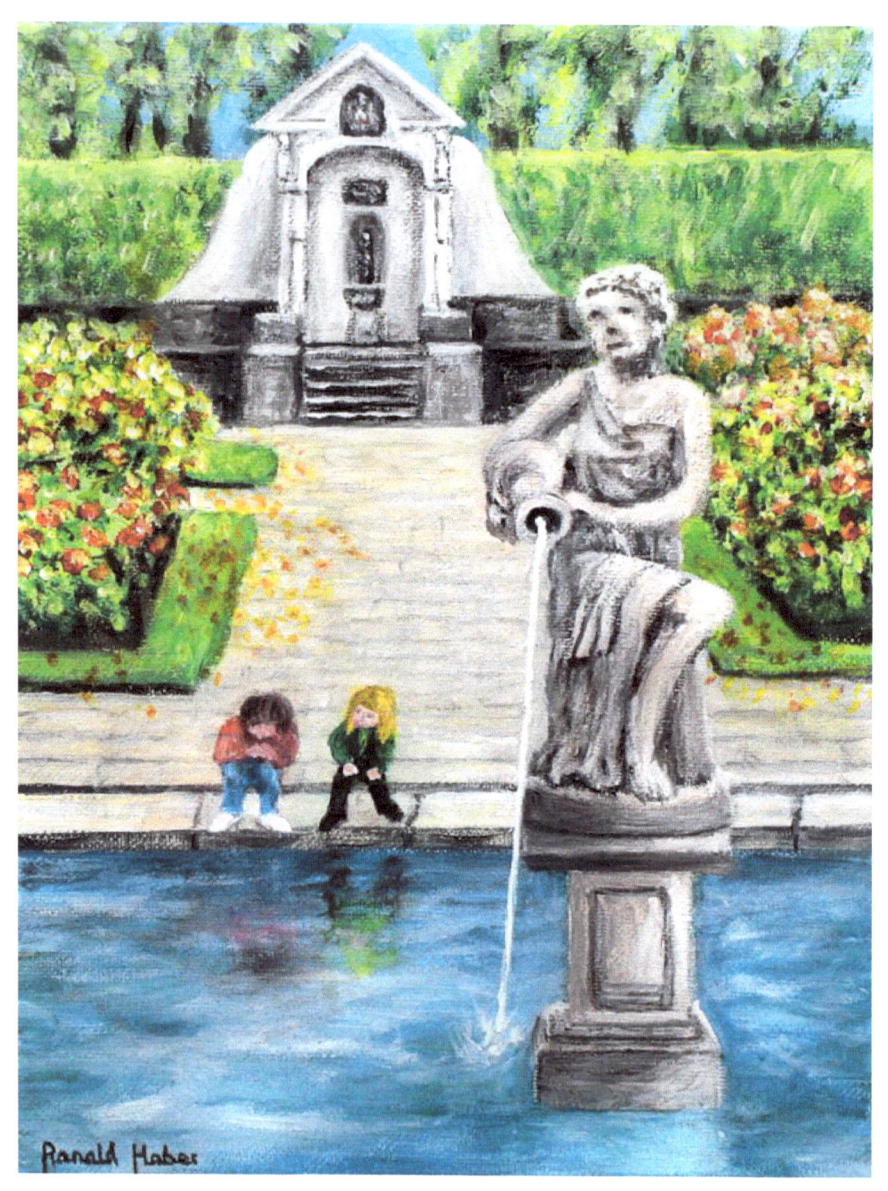

St. Annes on Sea Rose Garden at Ashton Gardens

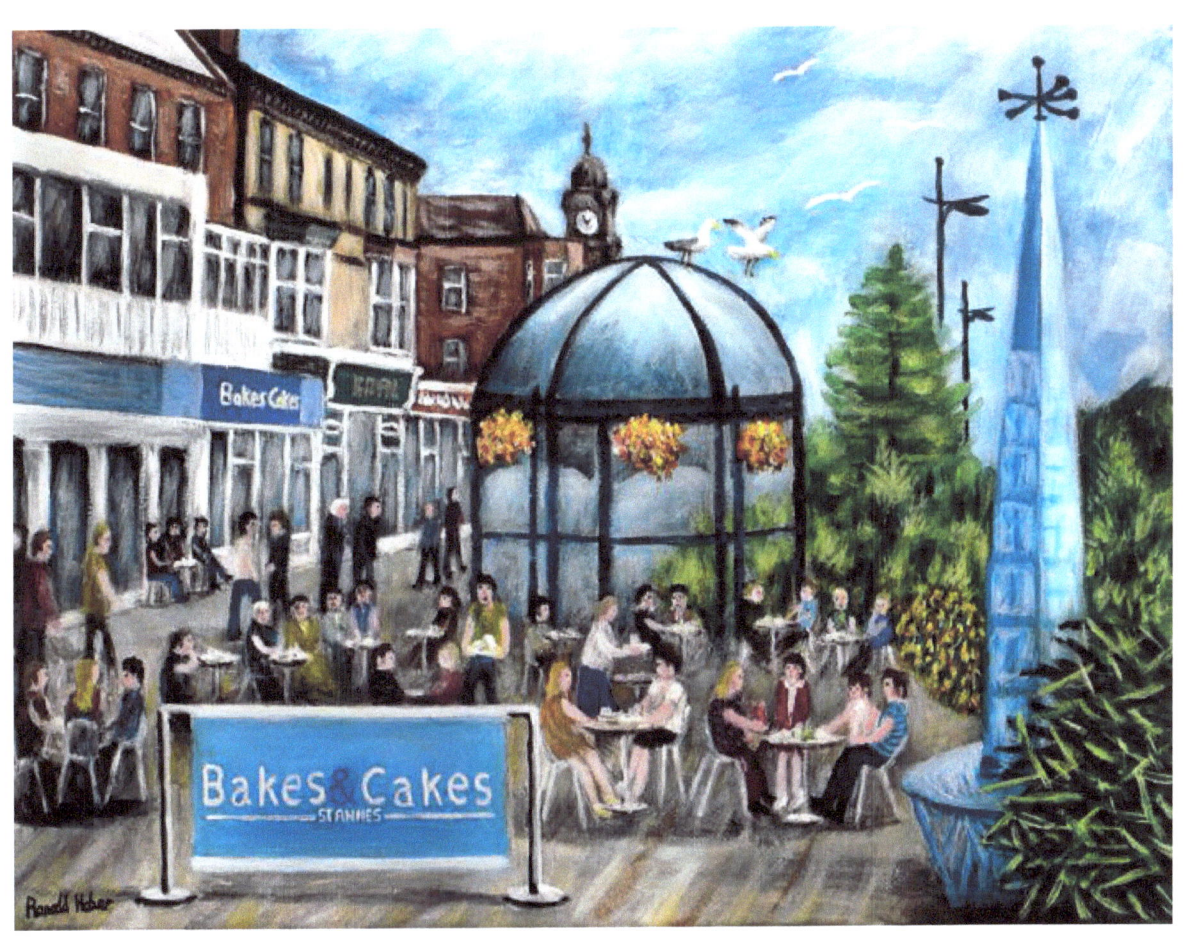

St. Annes on Sea Square

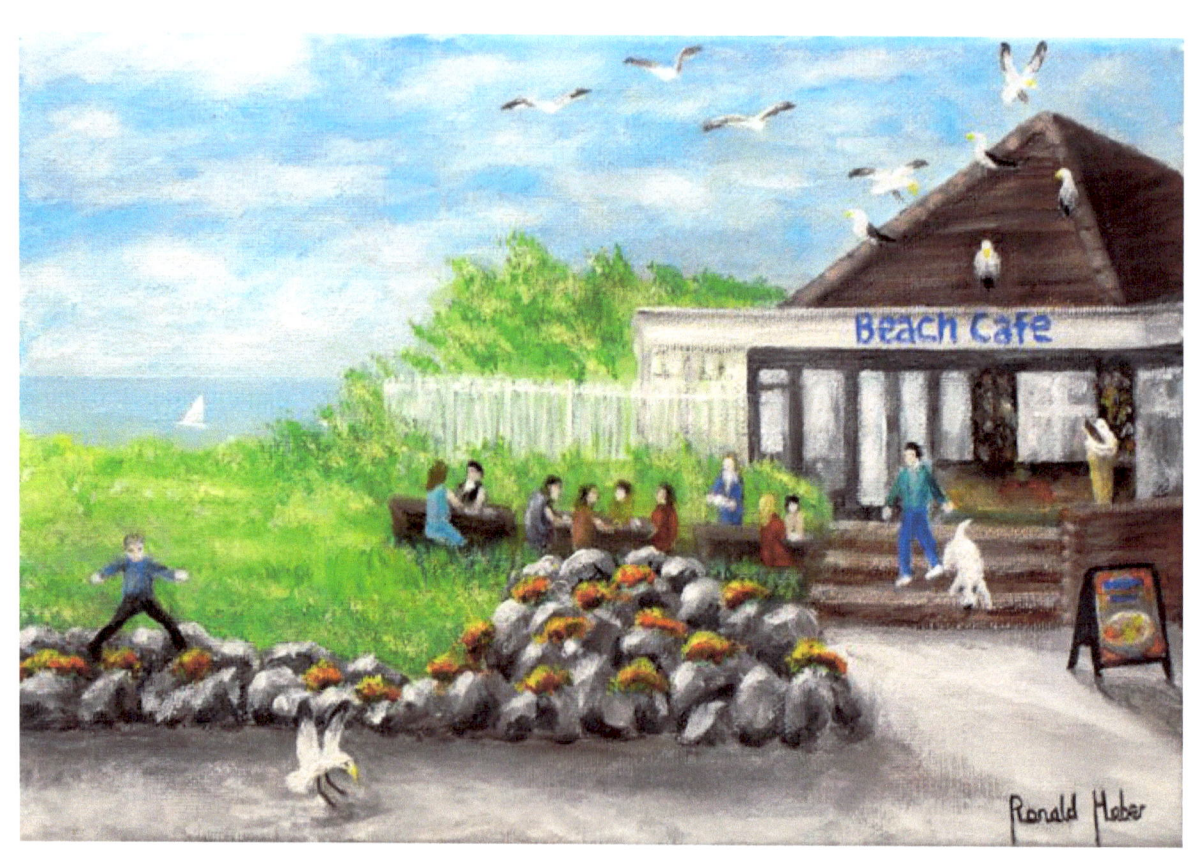

St. Annes on Sea Beach Cafe

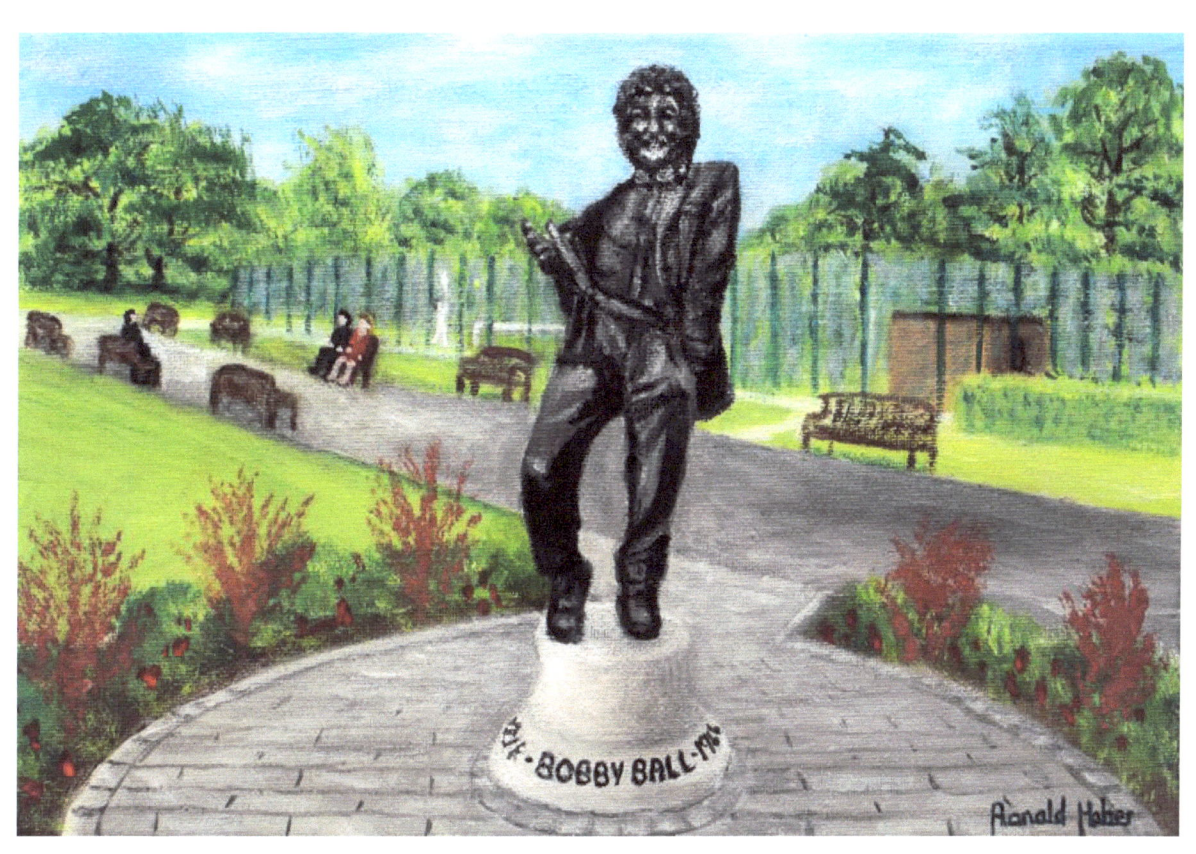

Lytham Lowther Gardens Bobby Ball Statue

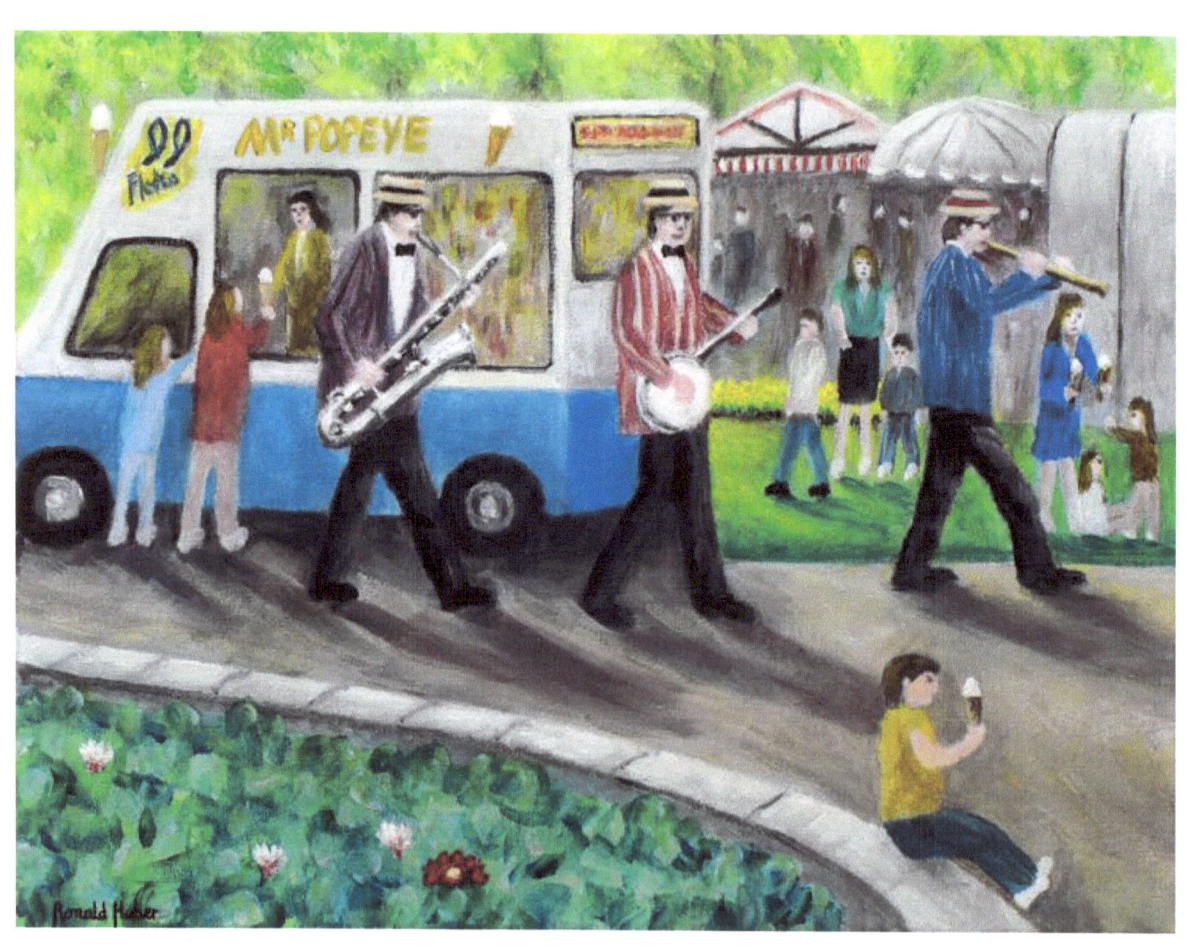

Lytham Lowther Gardens Ice Festival

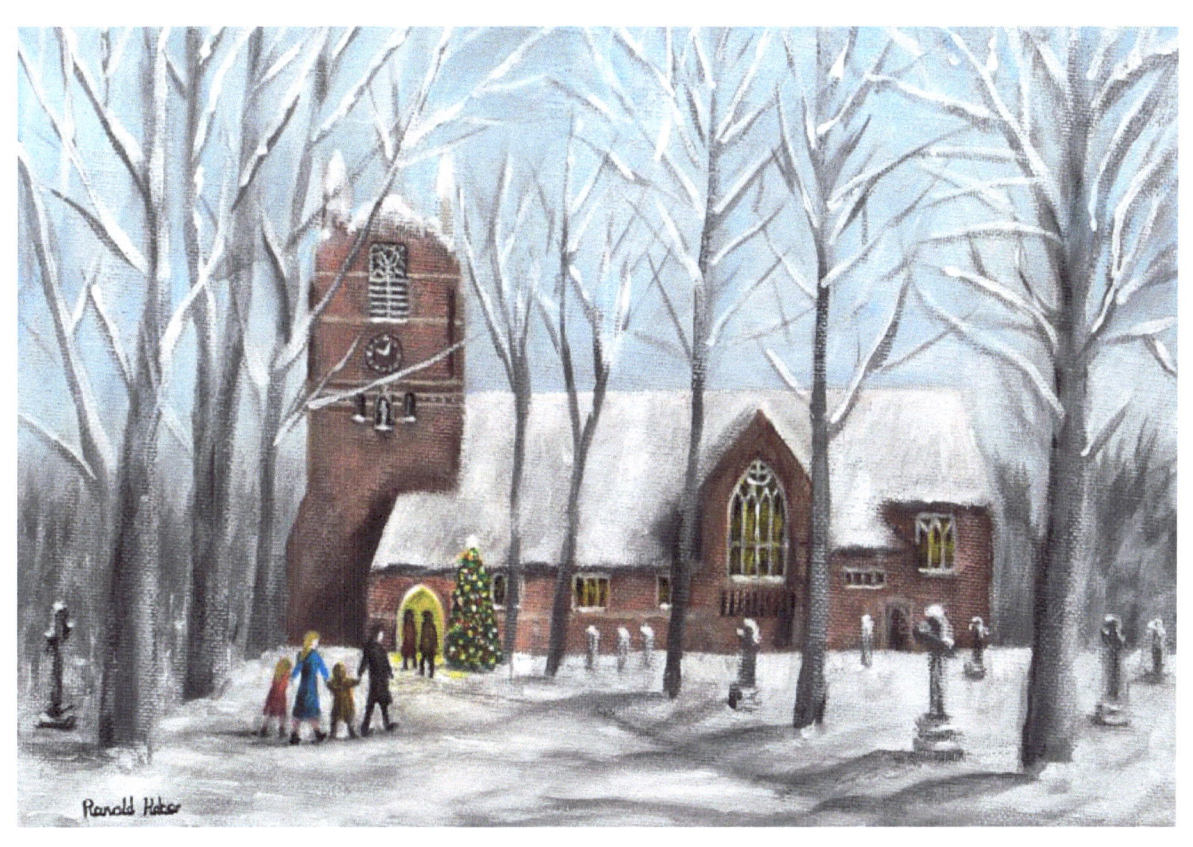

St. Annes Church at Christmas

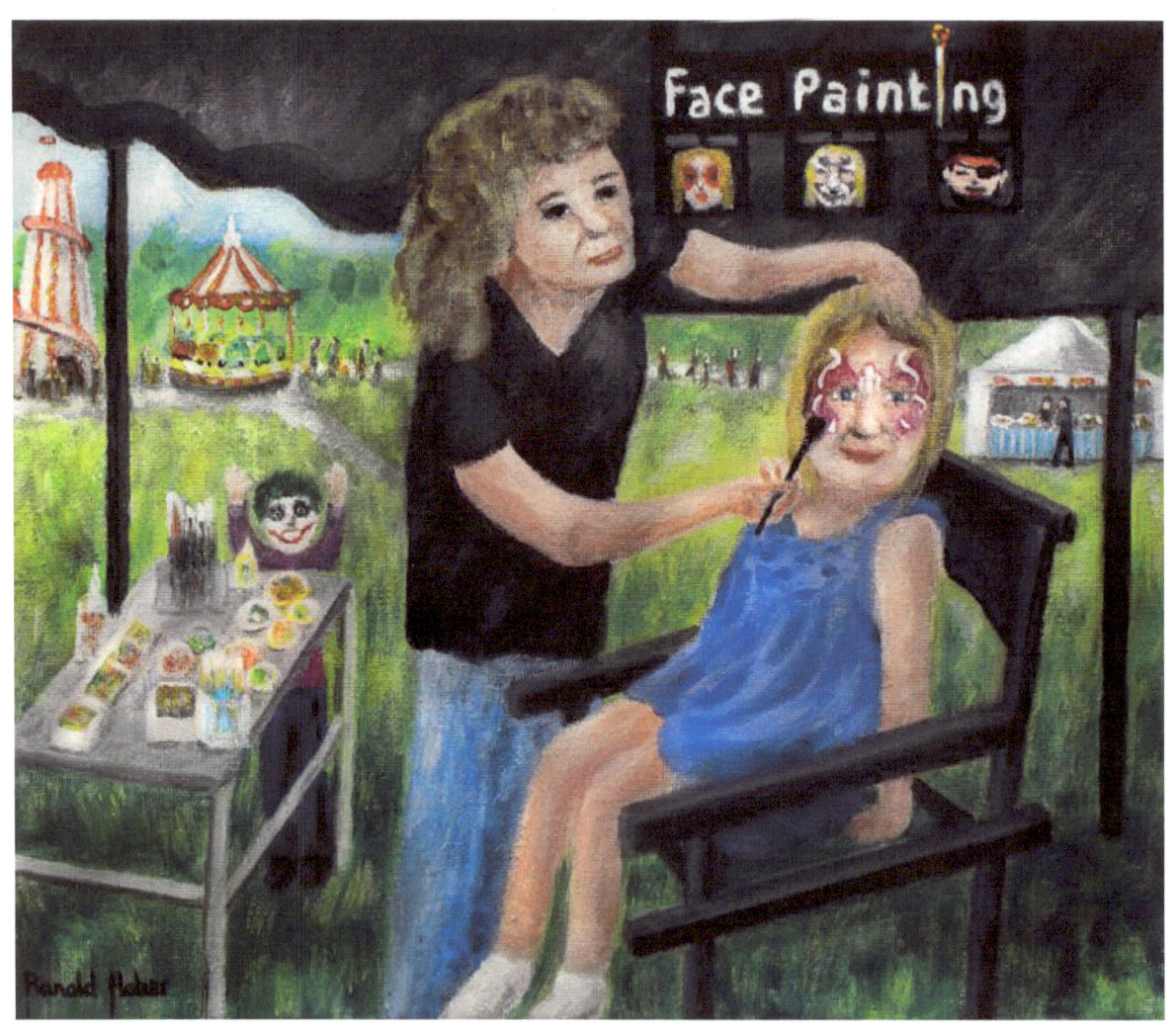

Lowther Gardens Face Painting

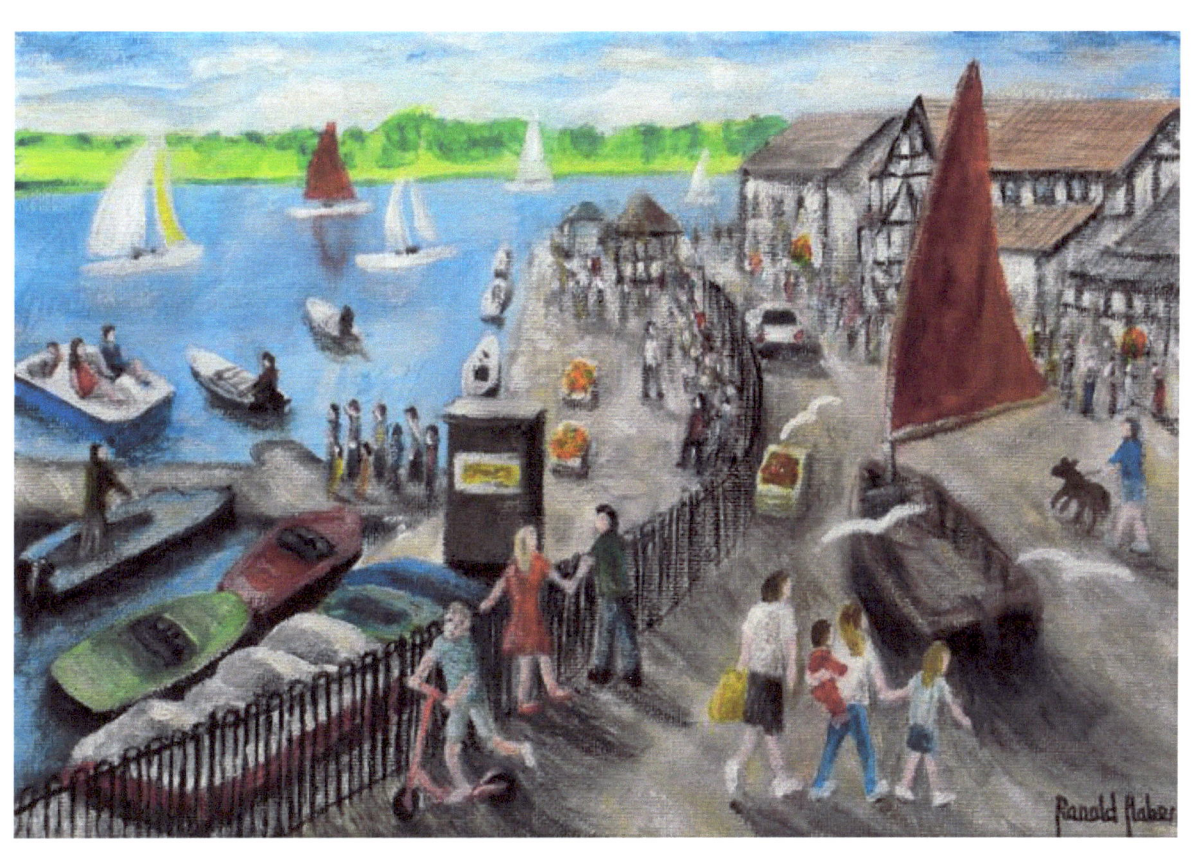

Fairhaven Lake on a Summer's Day

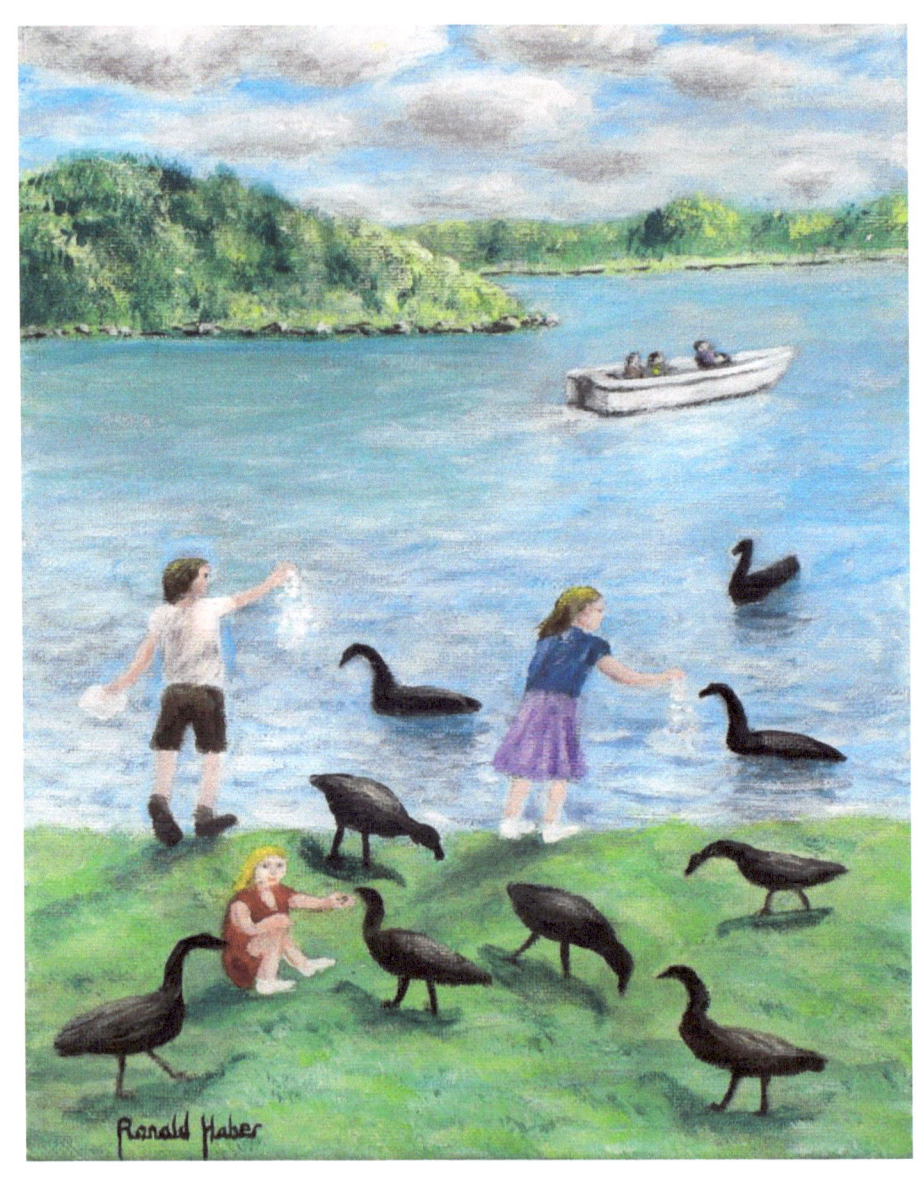

Fairhaven Lake Feeding the Ducks

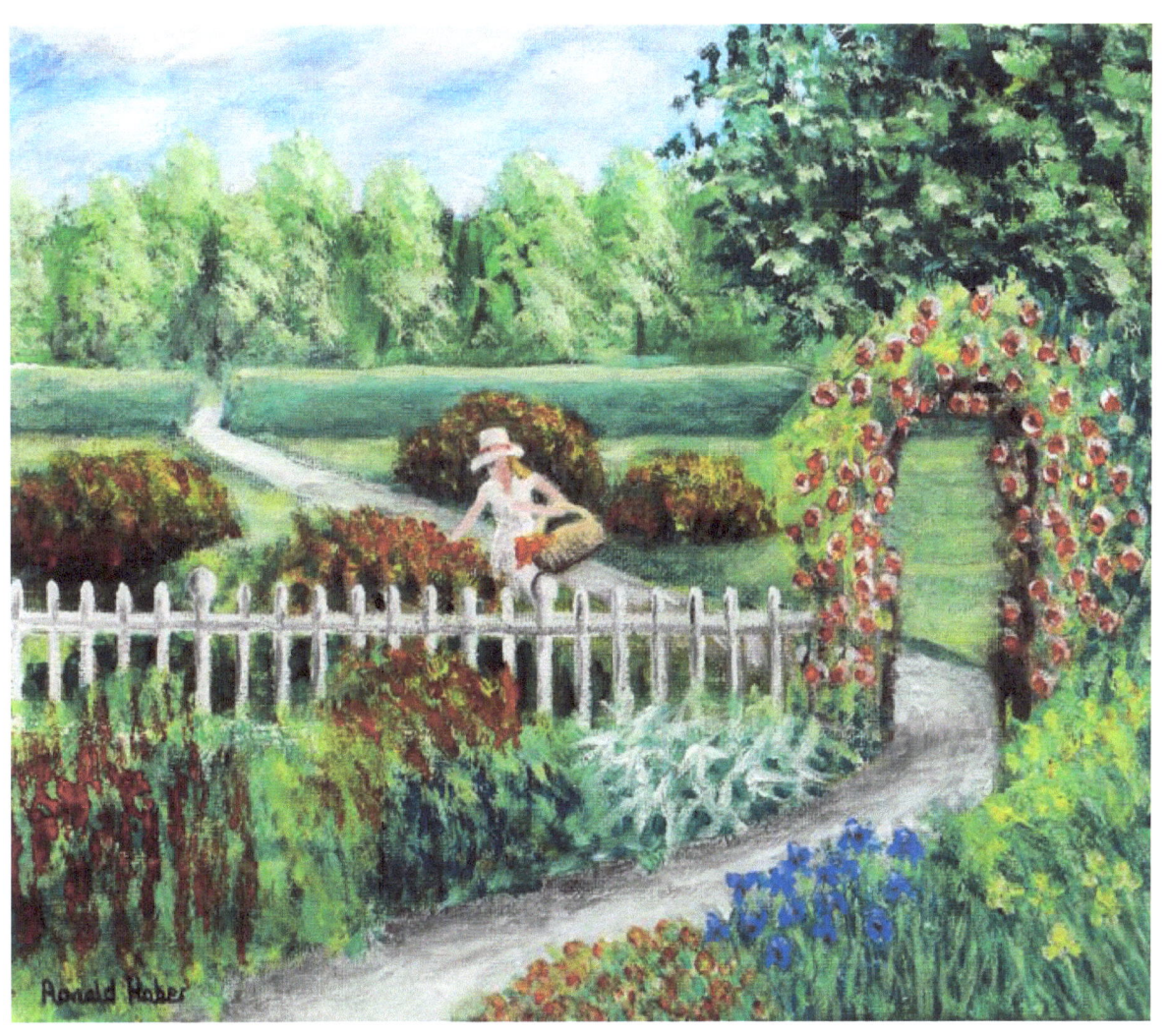

Lowther Gardens Lytham

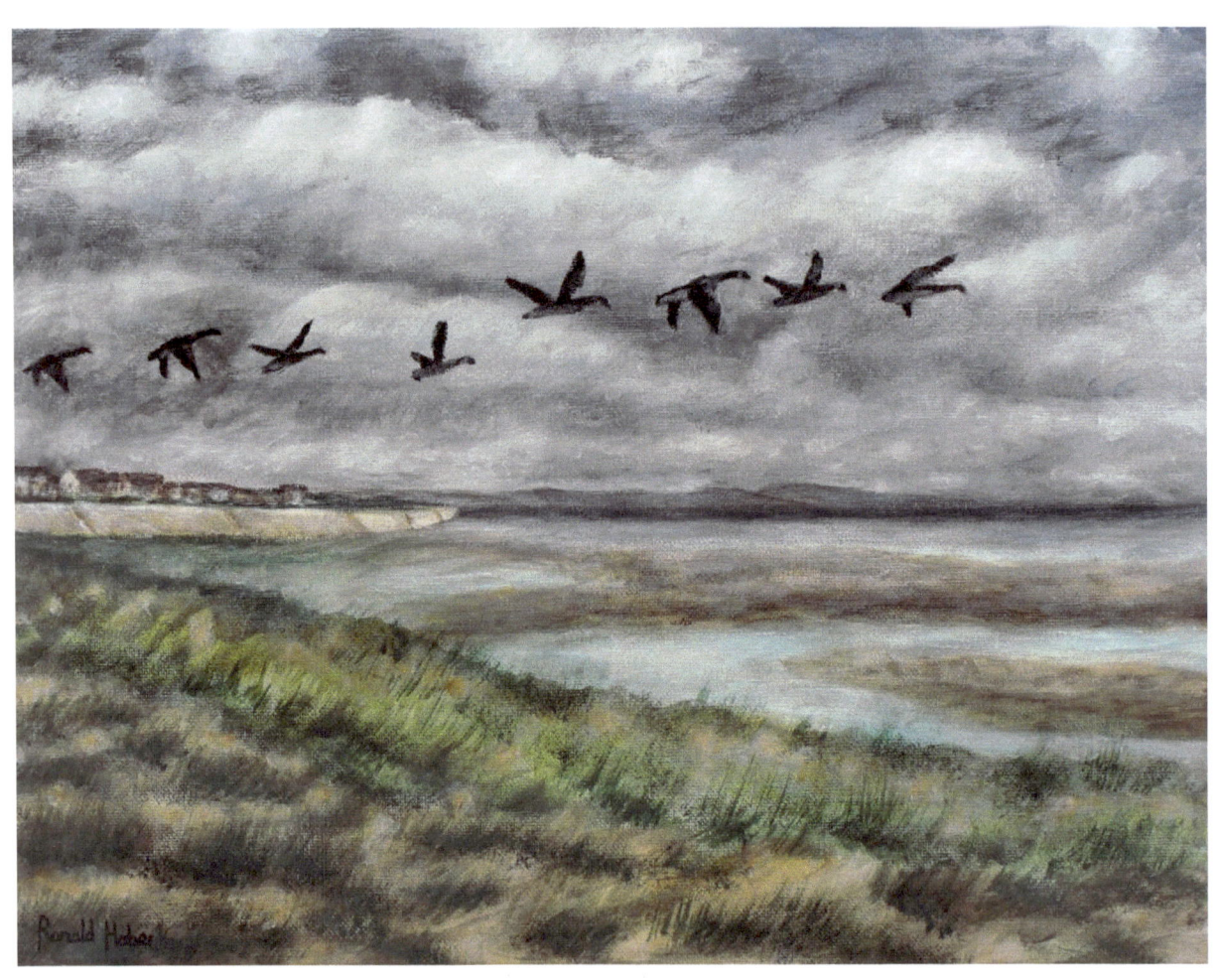

Geese over Lytham

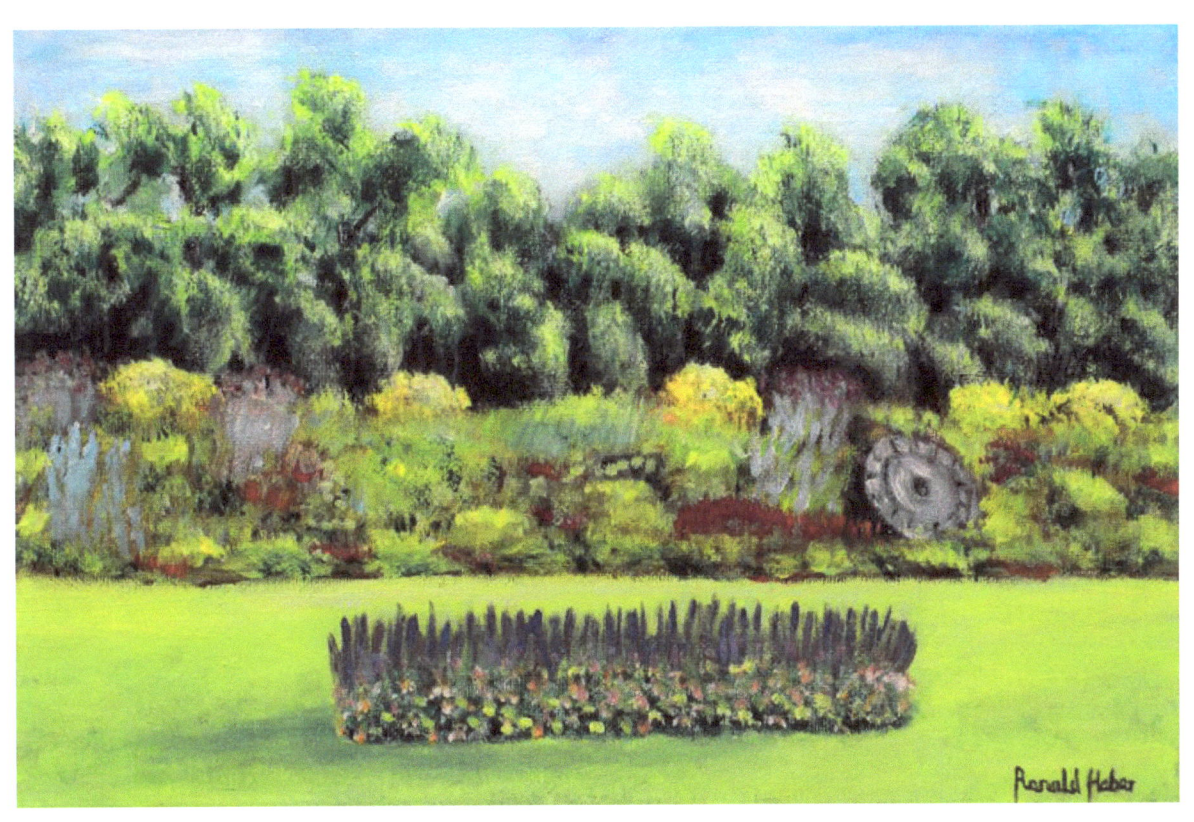

Herbaceous Border Lowther Gardens

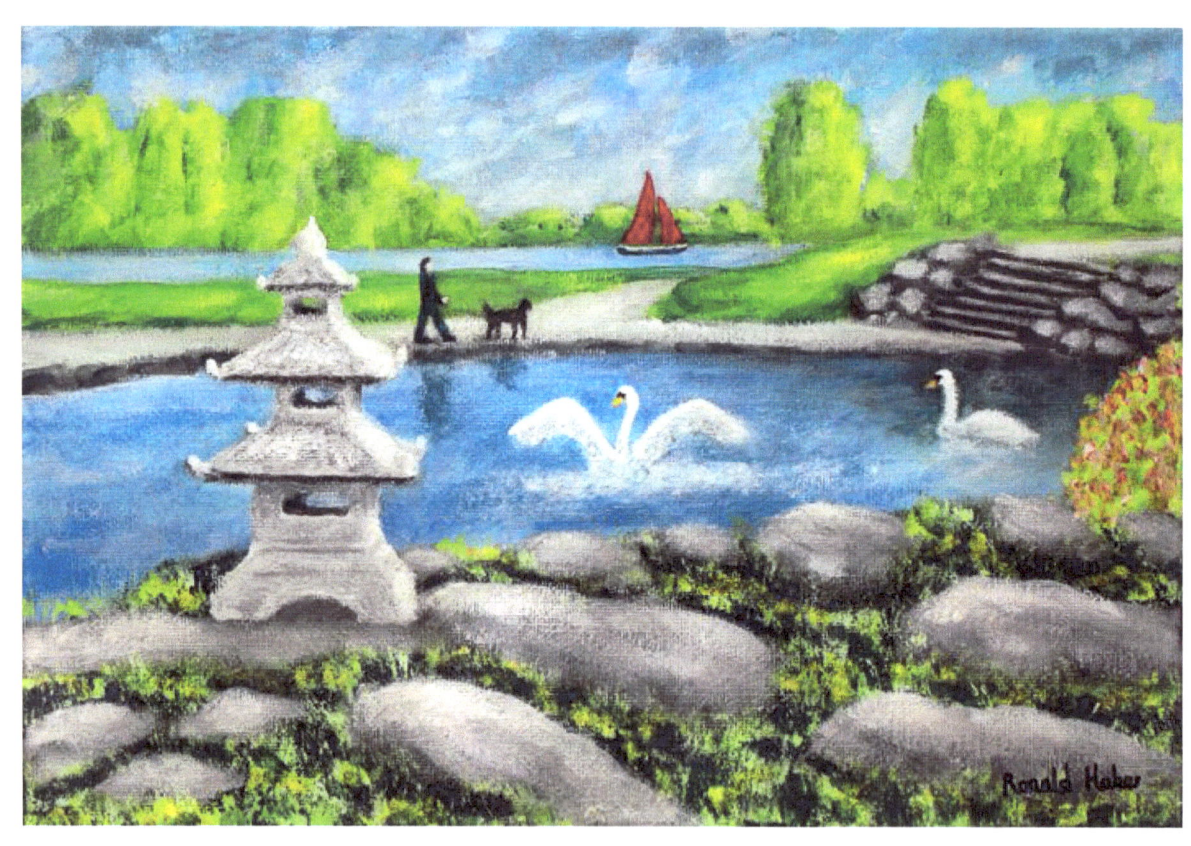

Japanese Gardens Fairhaven Lake

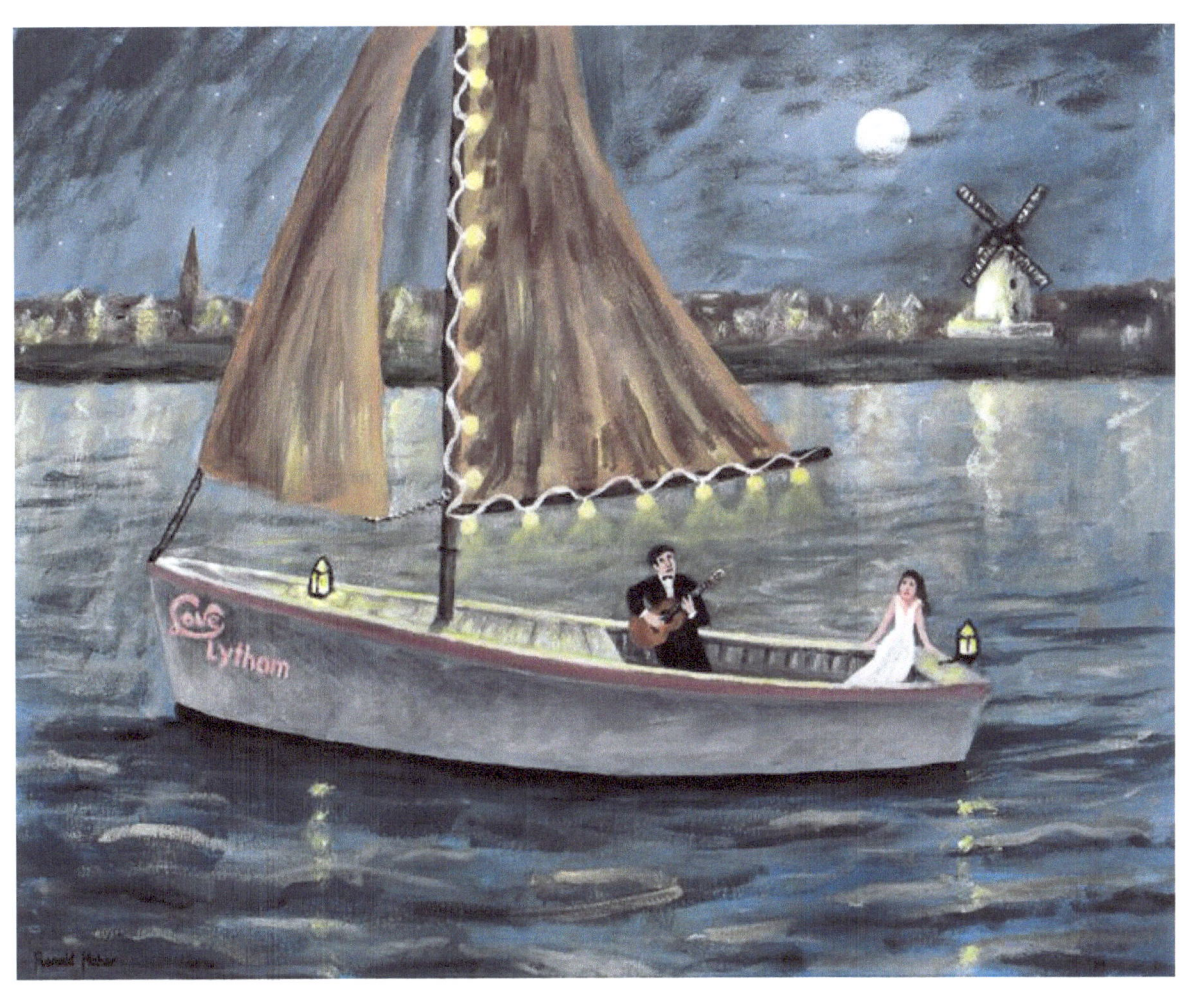

Lytham By Night

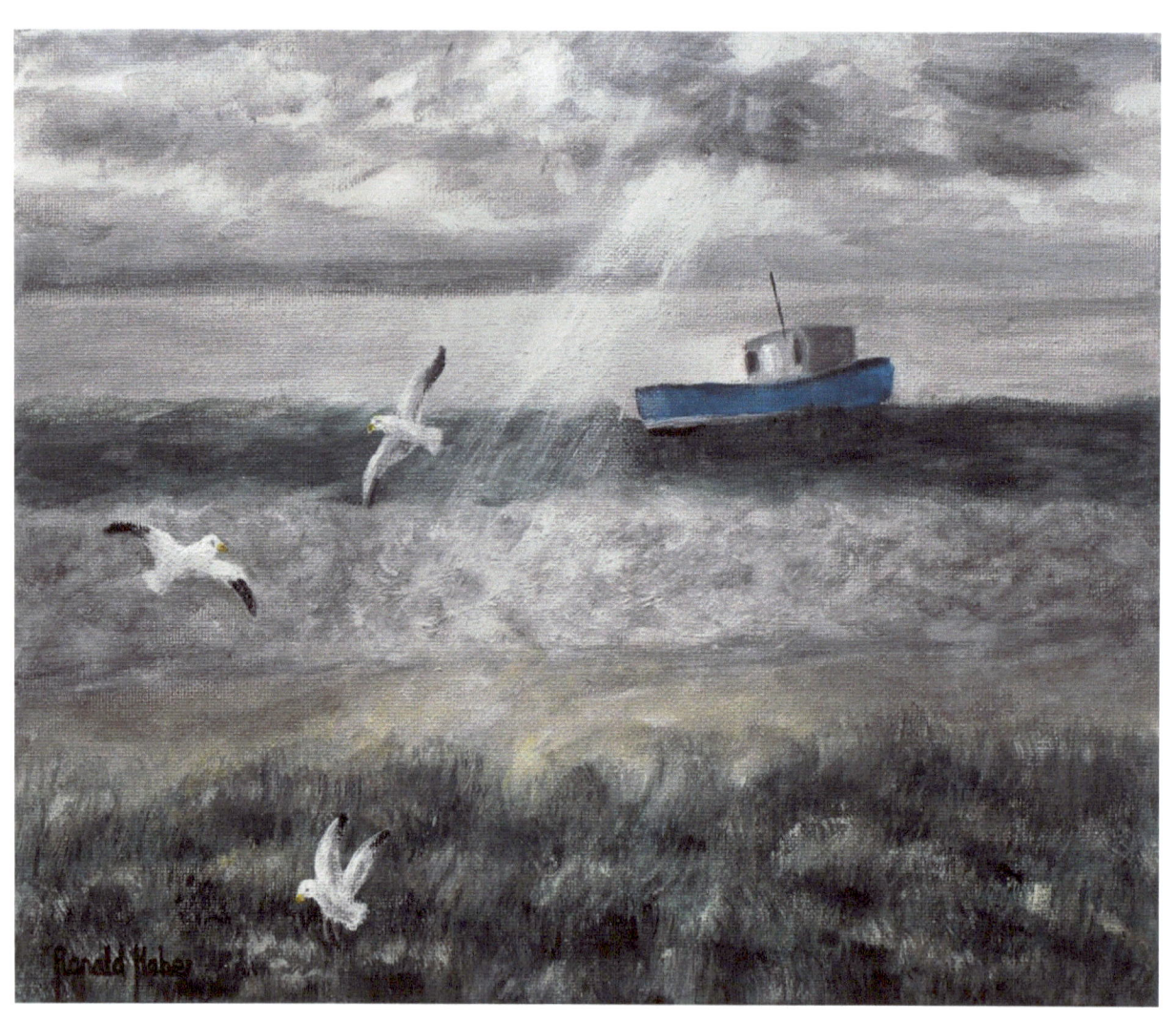

Sunbeams over Lytham

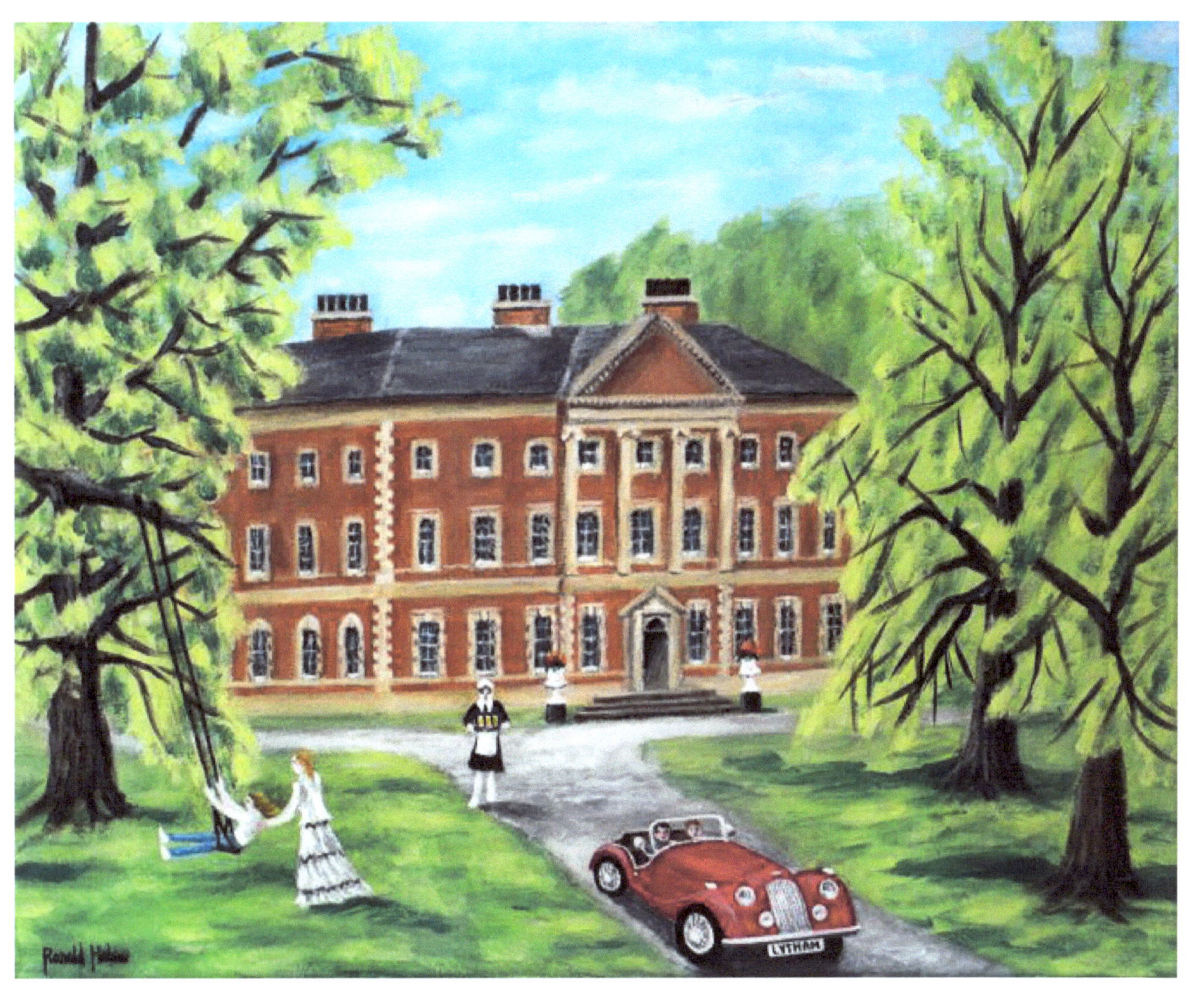

Lytham Hall in Days Gone By

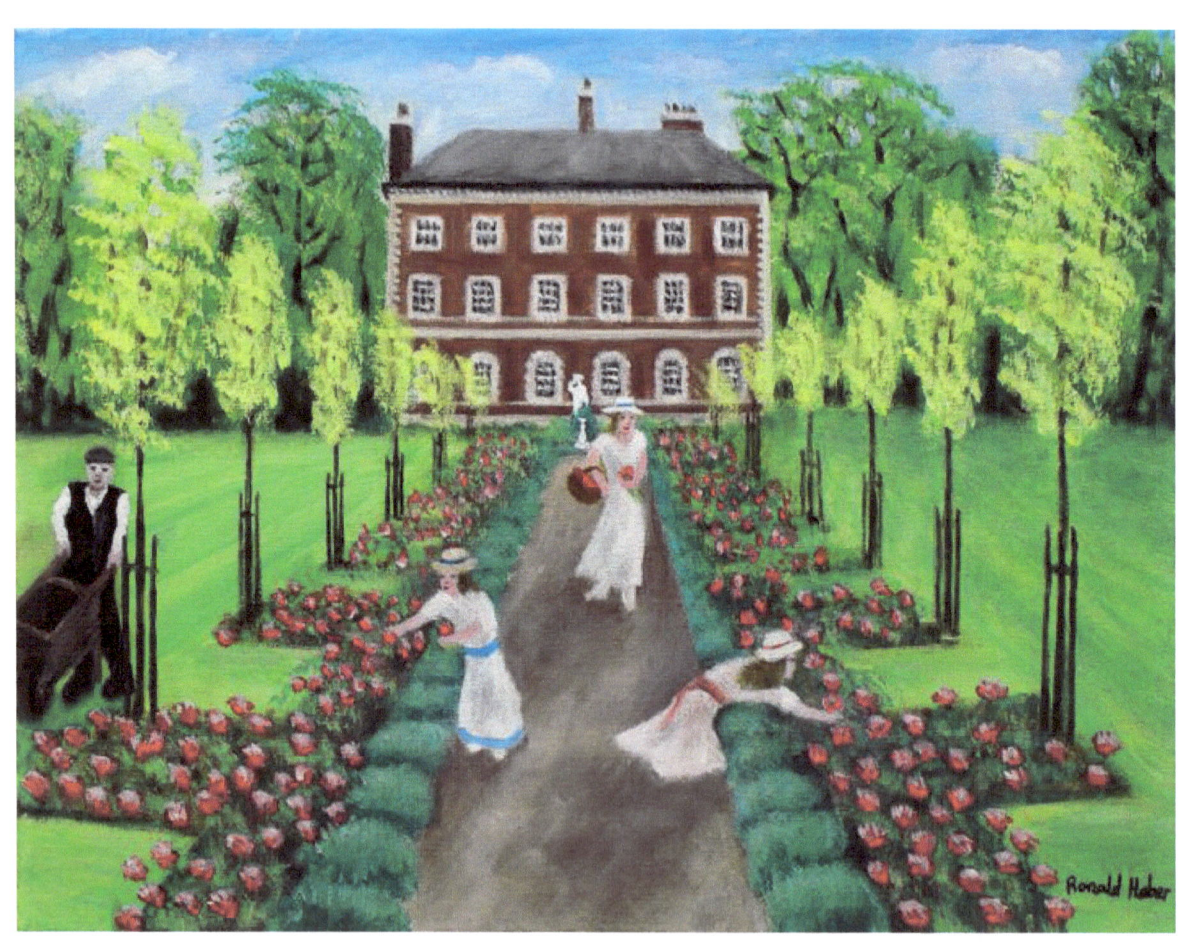

Lytham Hall in Edwardian Times

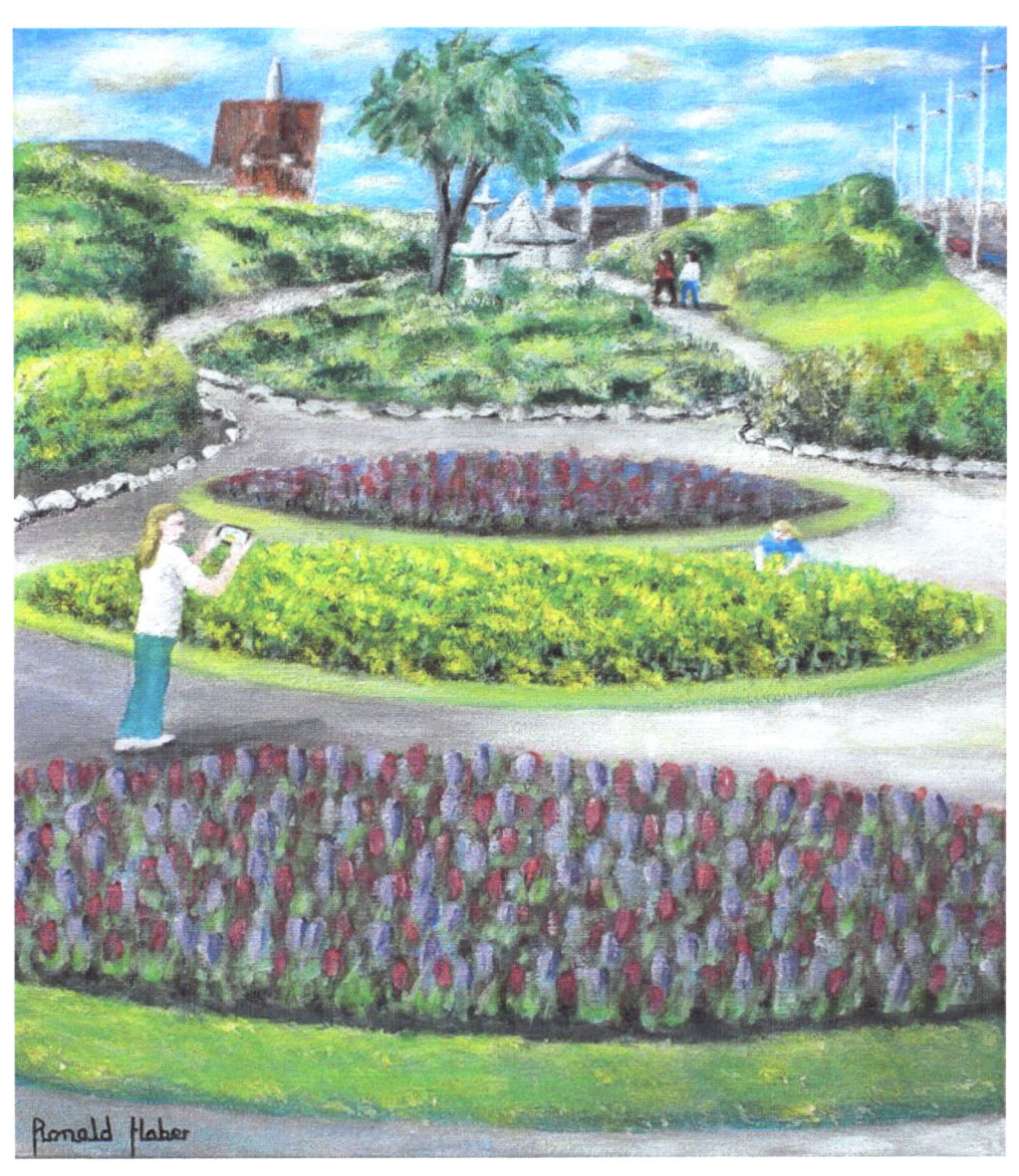

St. Annes on Sea Promenade Walk

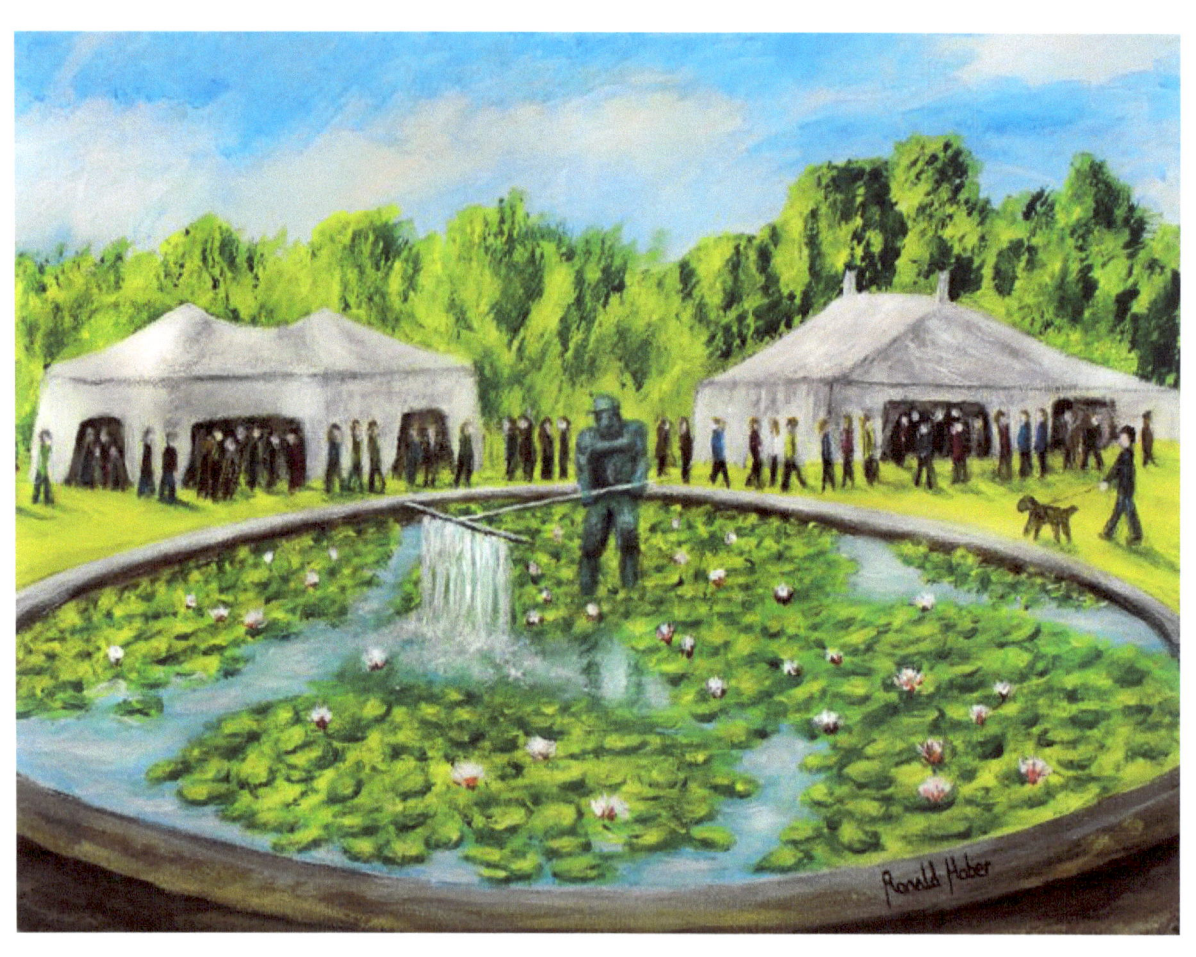

Lytham Lowther Gardens Food Festival

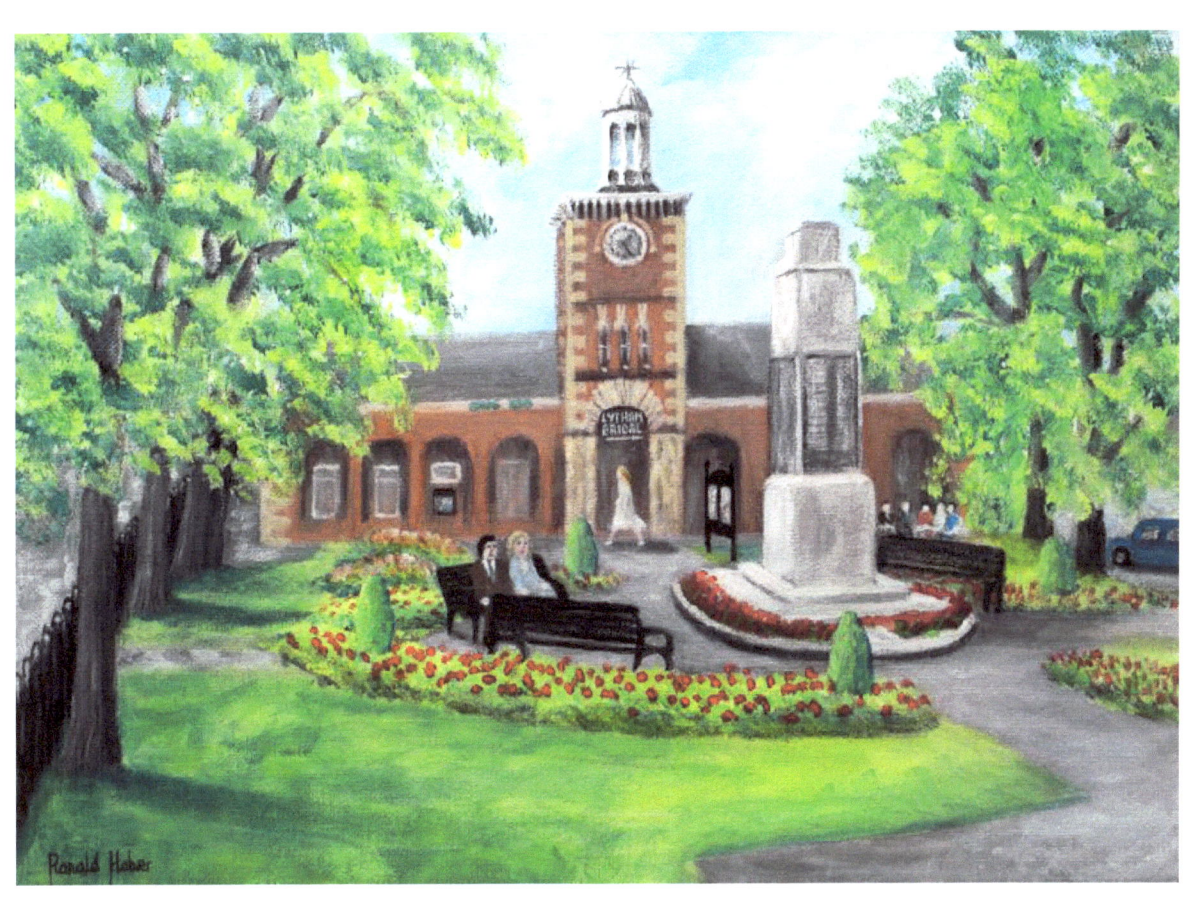

Lytham Memorial Garden

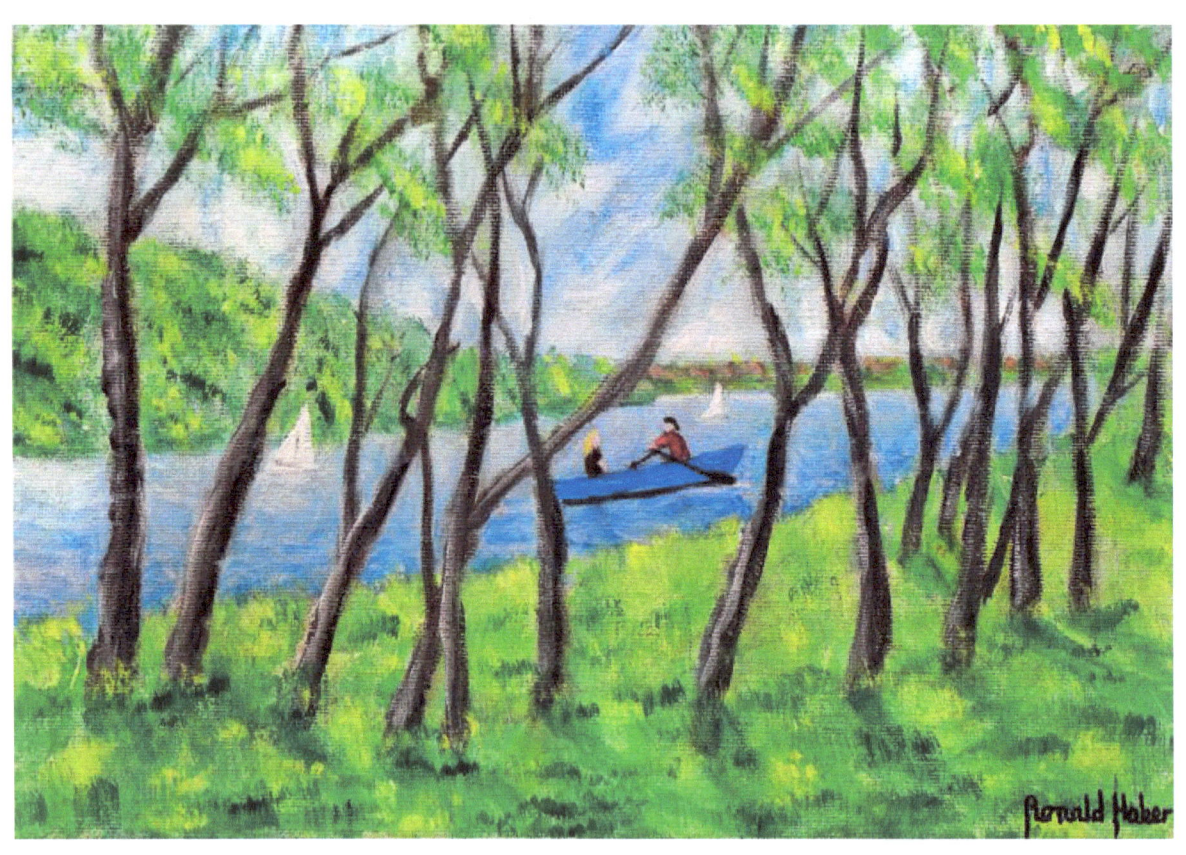

Fairhaven Lake View Through the Woods

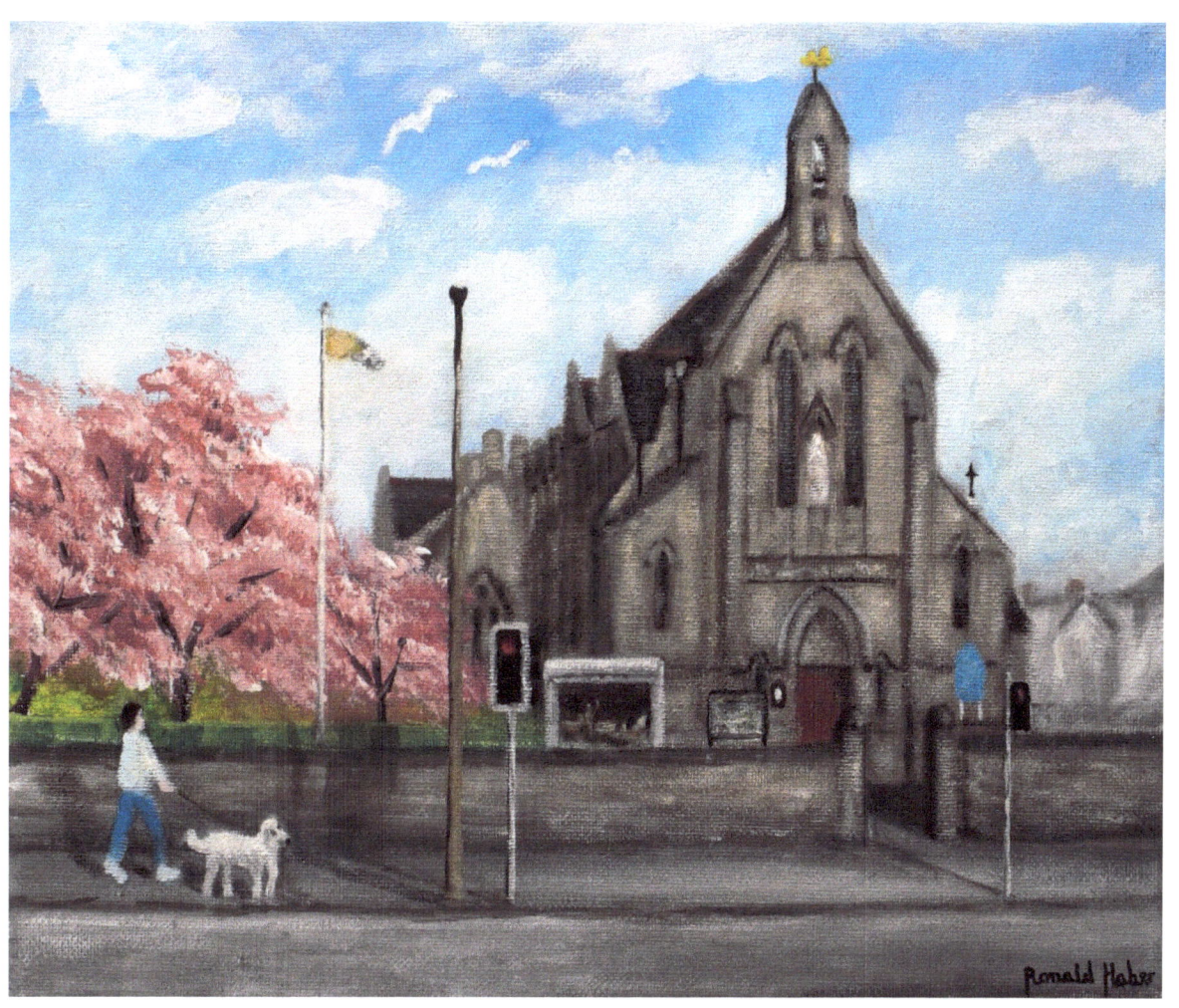

St. Annes on Sea Our Lady Star of the Sea Church

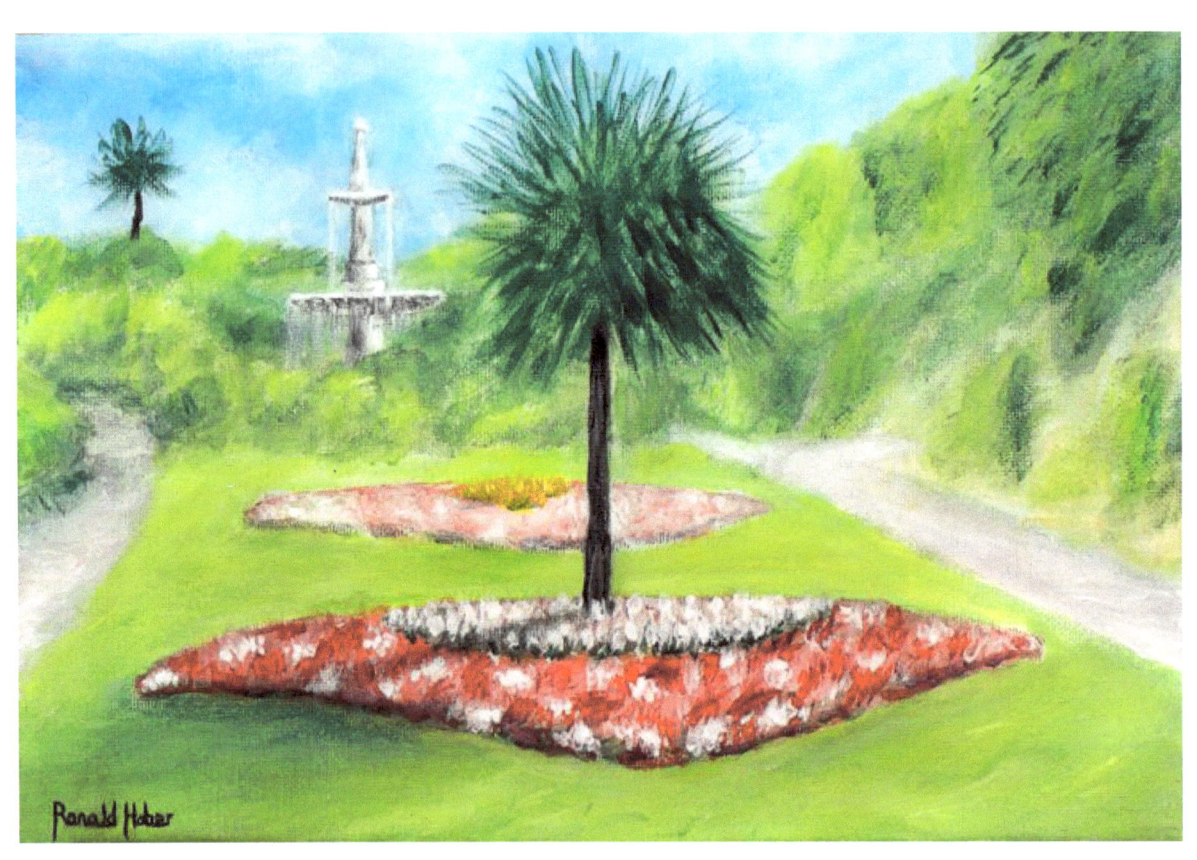

St. Annes on Sea Promenade Fountain and Flower Beds

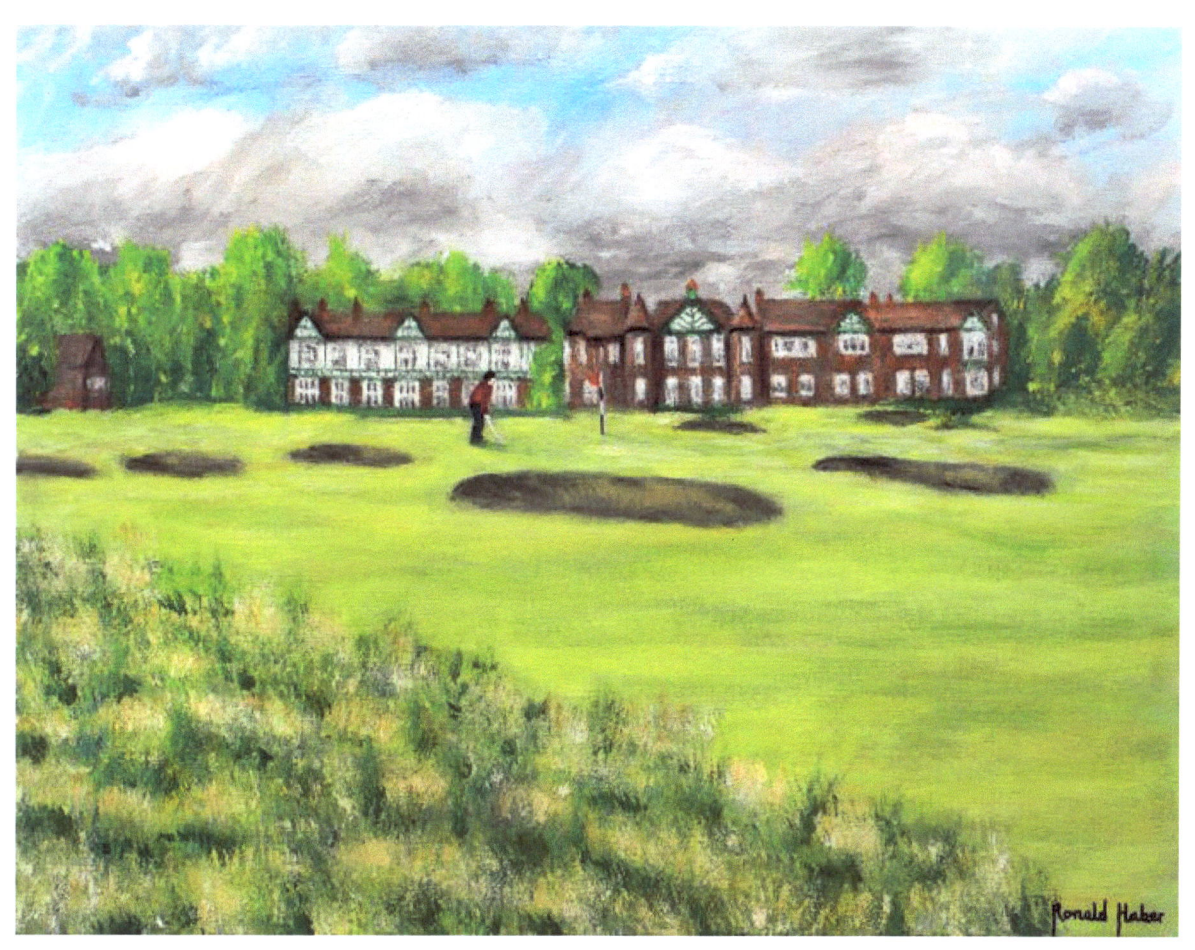

St. Annes on Sea Golf Course

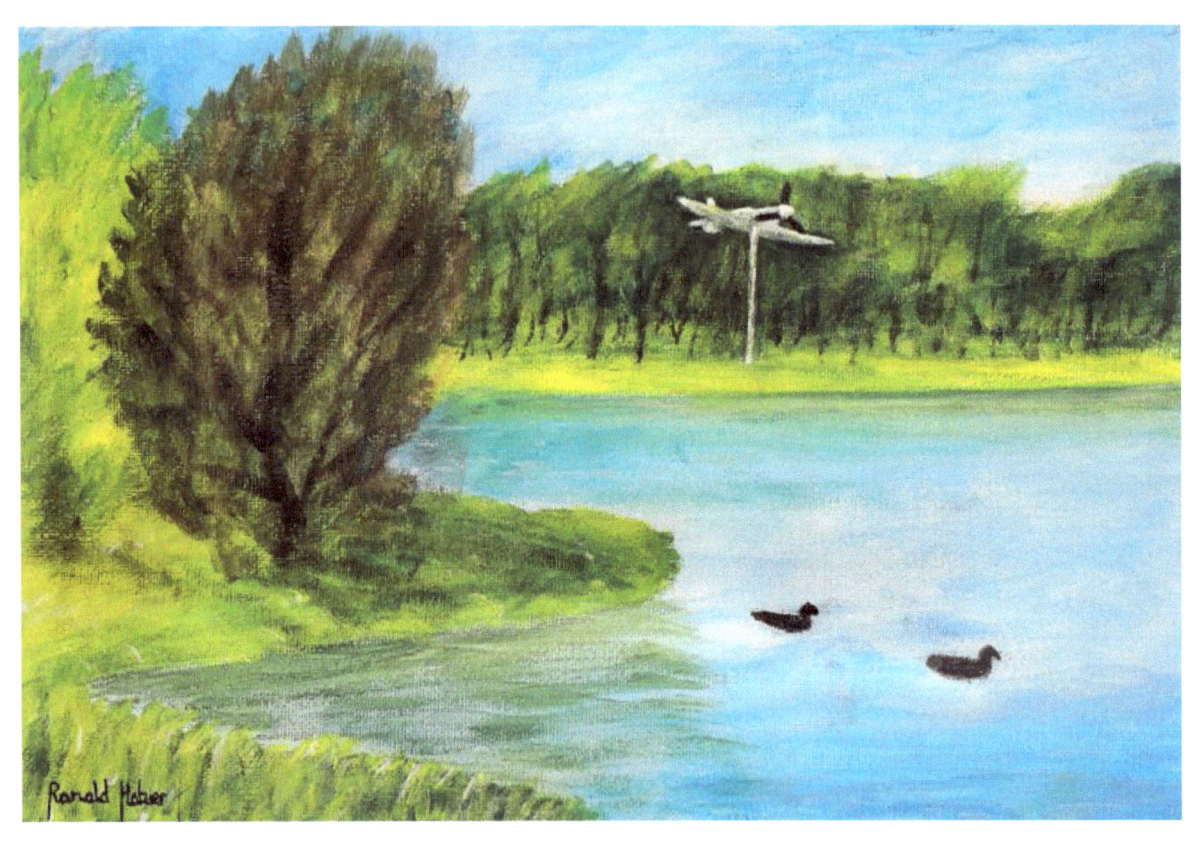

Fairhaven Lake and Spitfire Monument

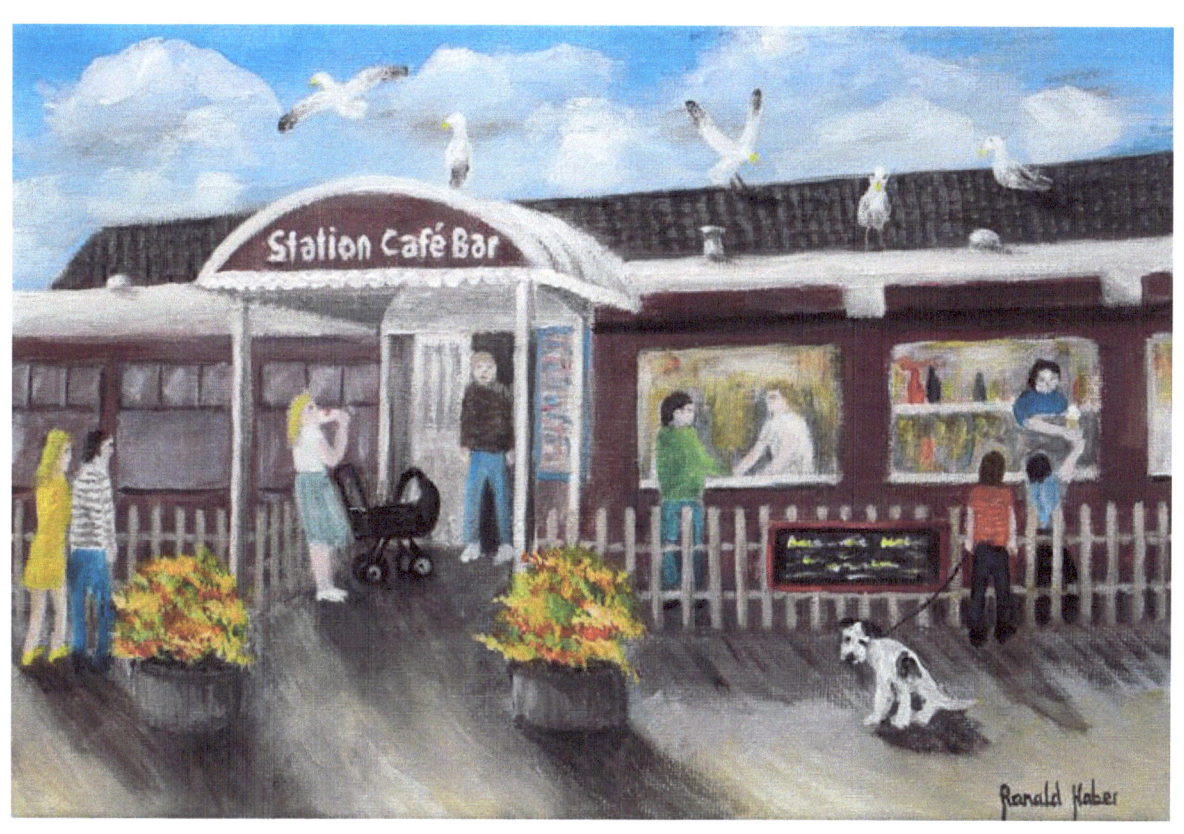

St. Annes on Sea Station Café Bar

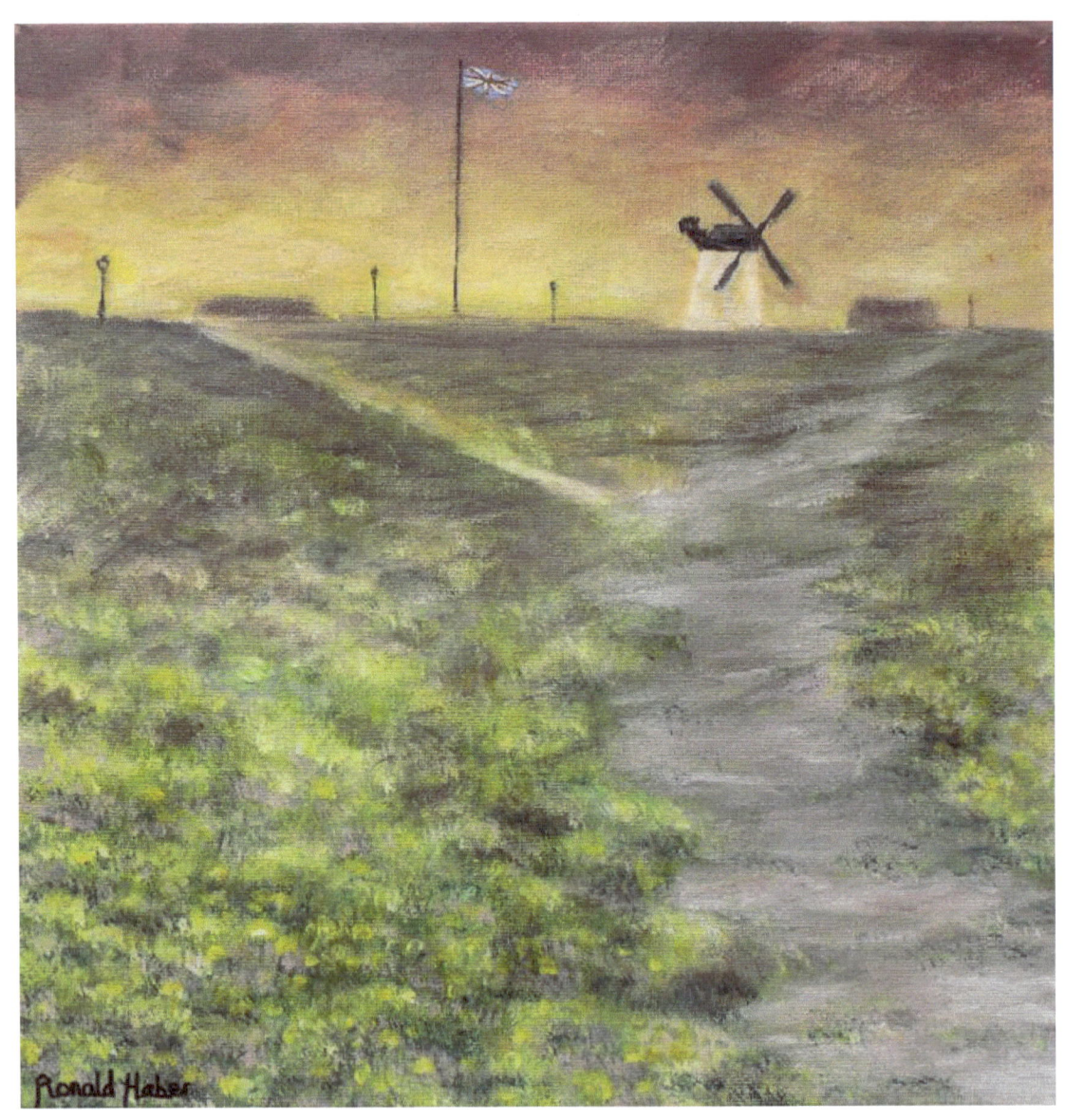

Sunset over Lytham

56

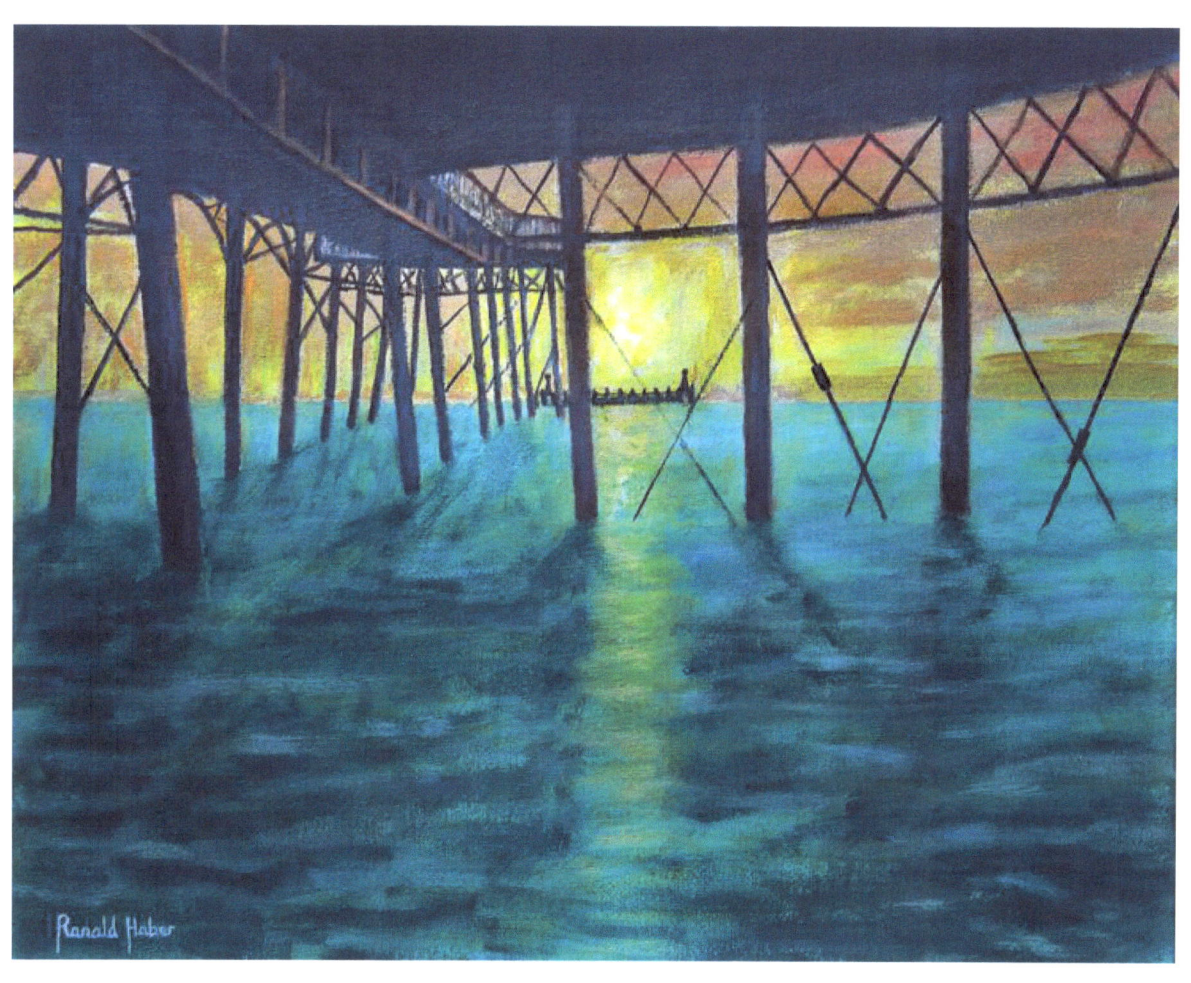

St. Annes on Sea Sunset under the Pier

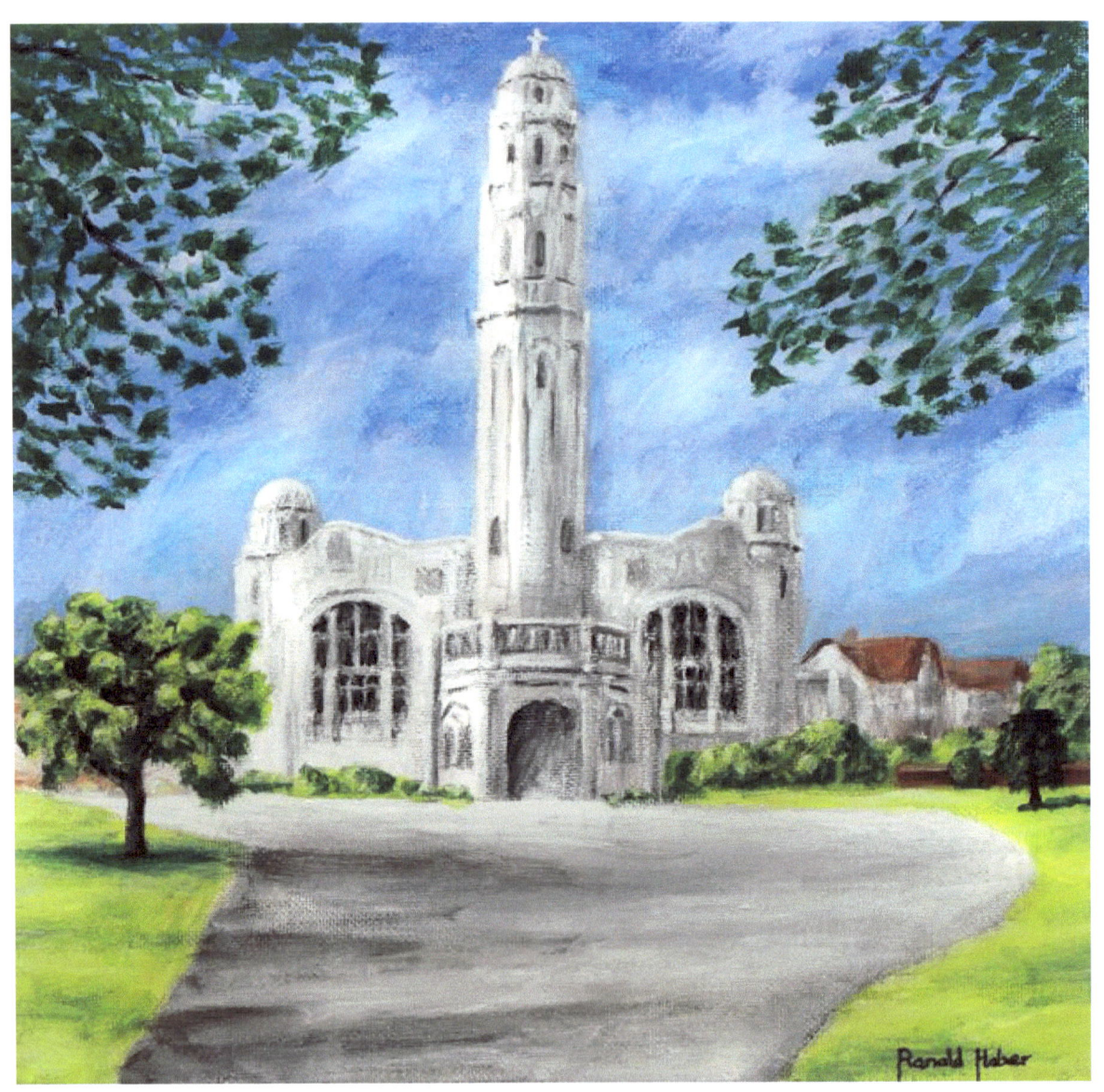

St. Annes on Sea White Church

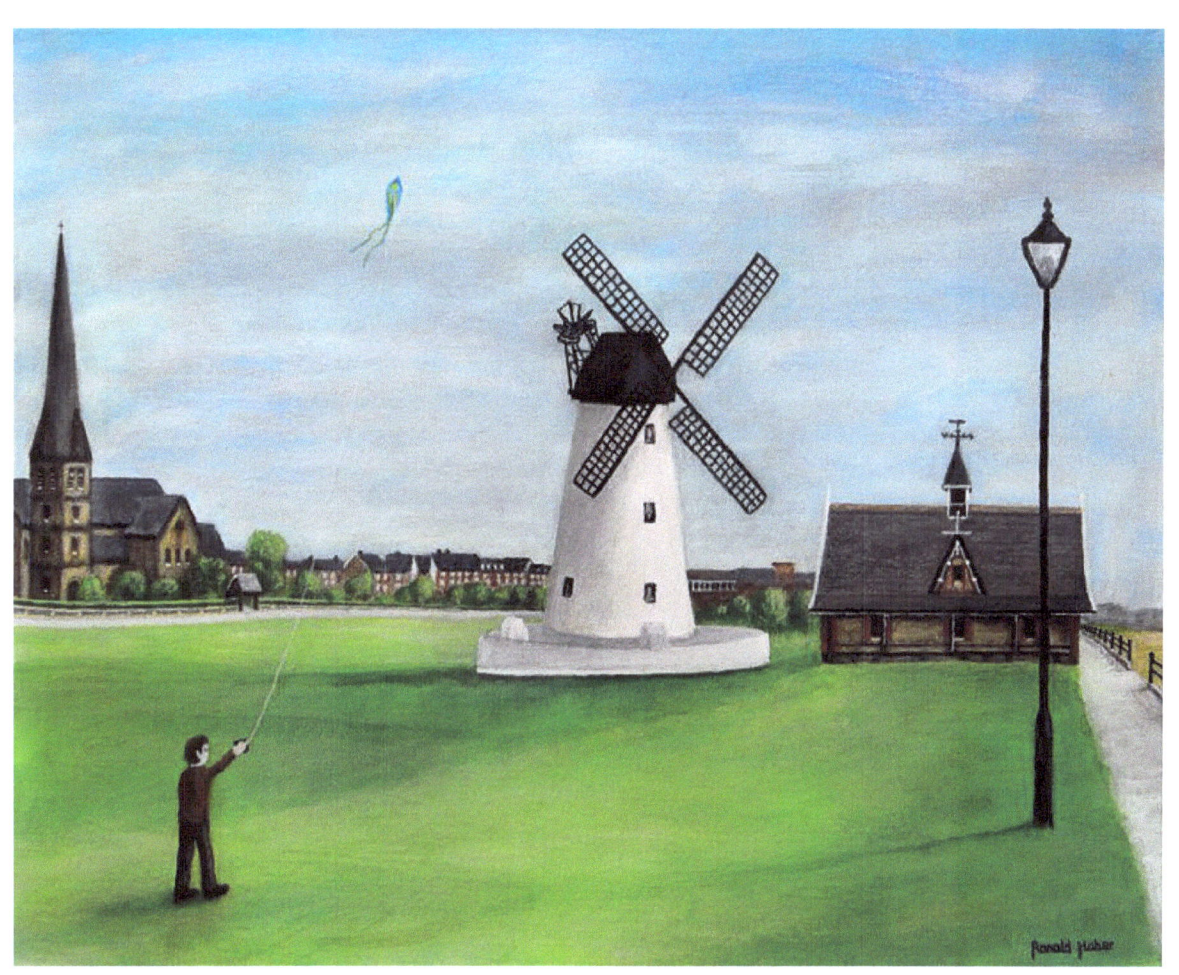

Lytham Windmill

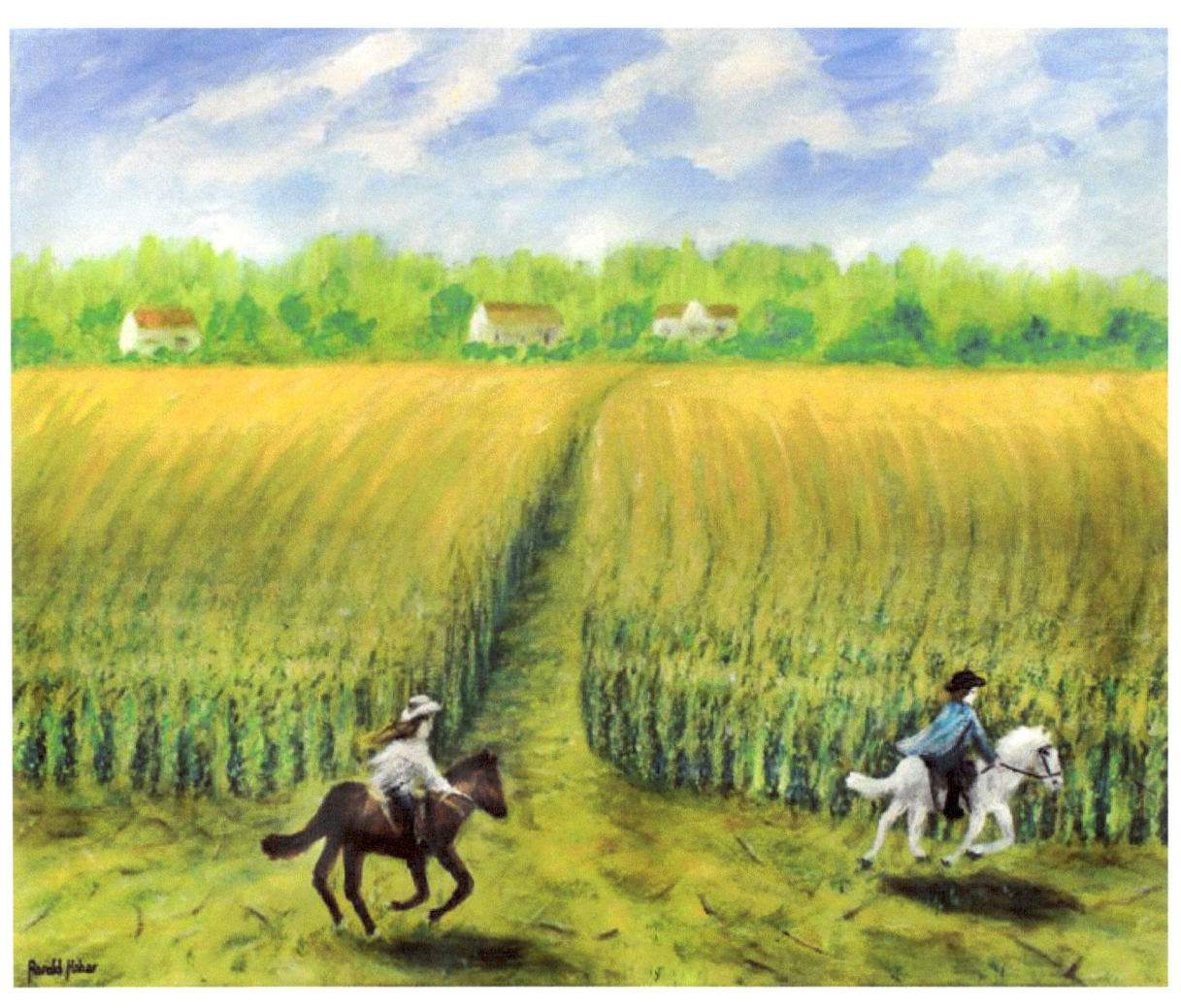

St. Annes on Sea Riders through the Cornfield

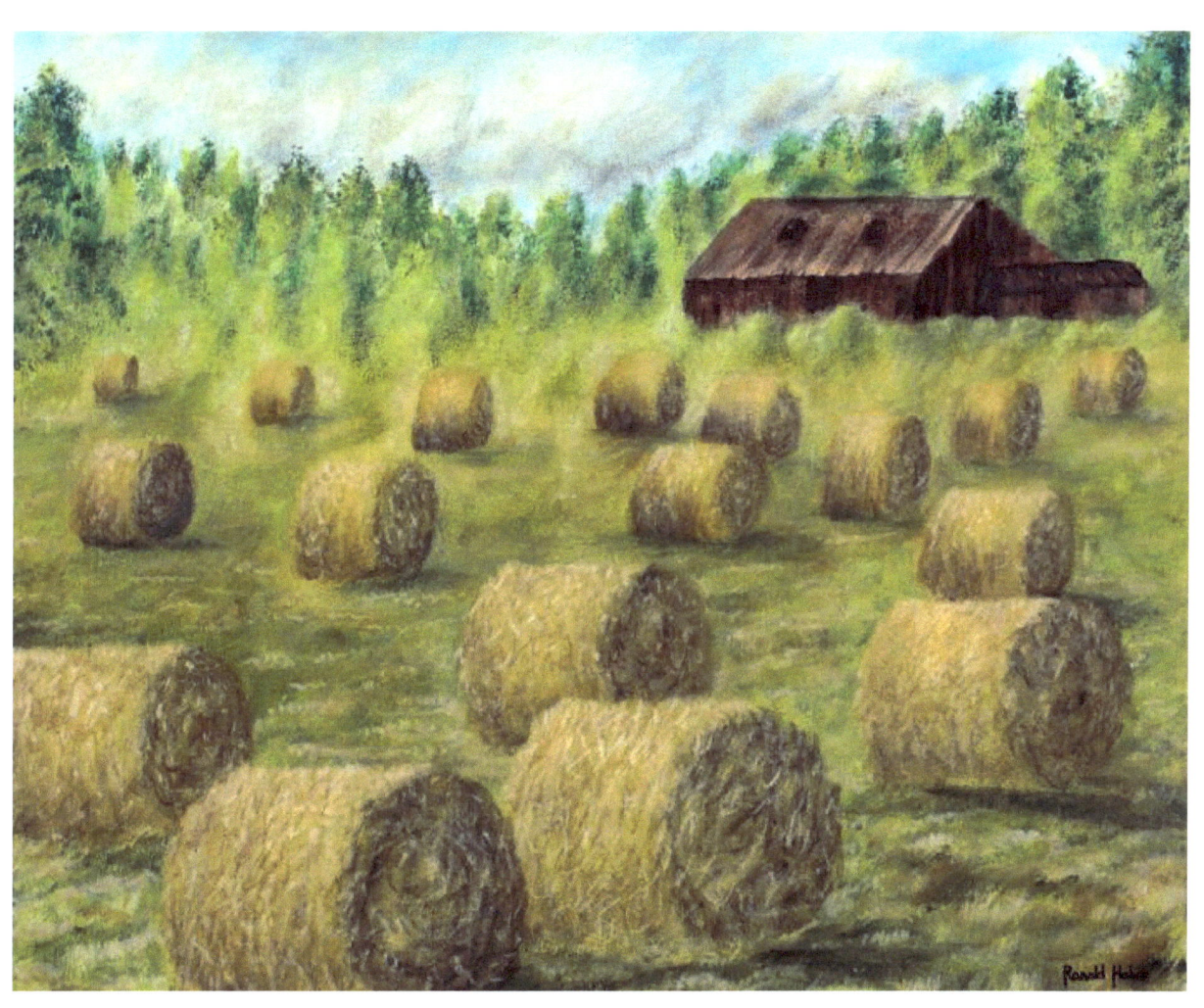

St. Annes on Sea Haystacks

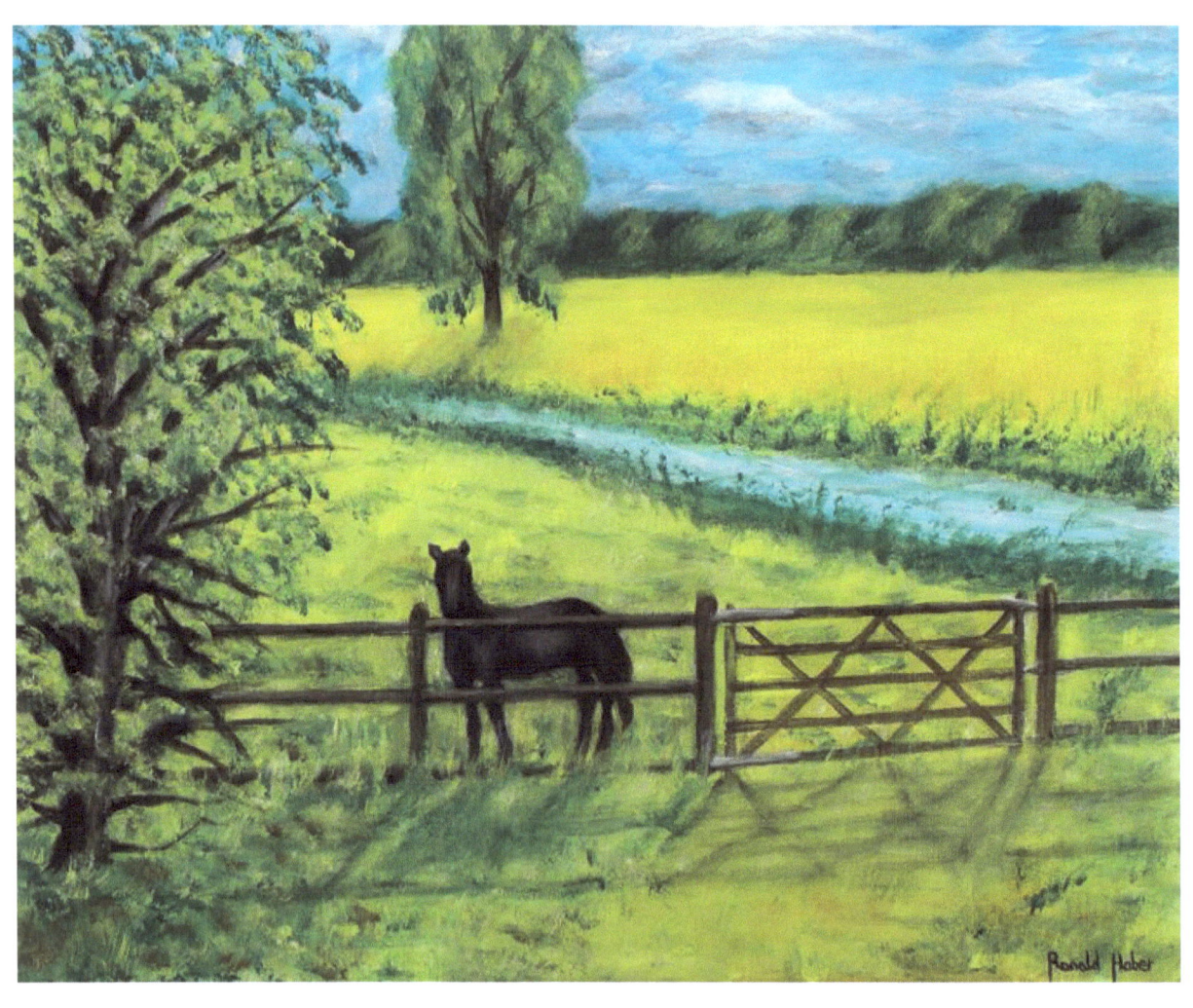

St. Annes on Sea Farm and Cornfield

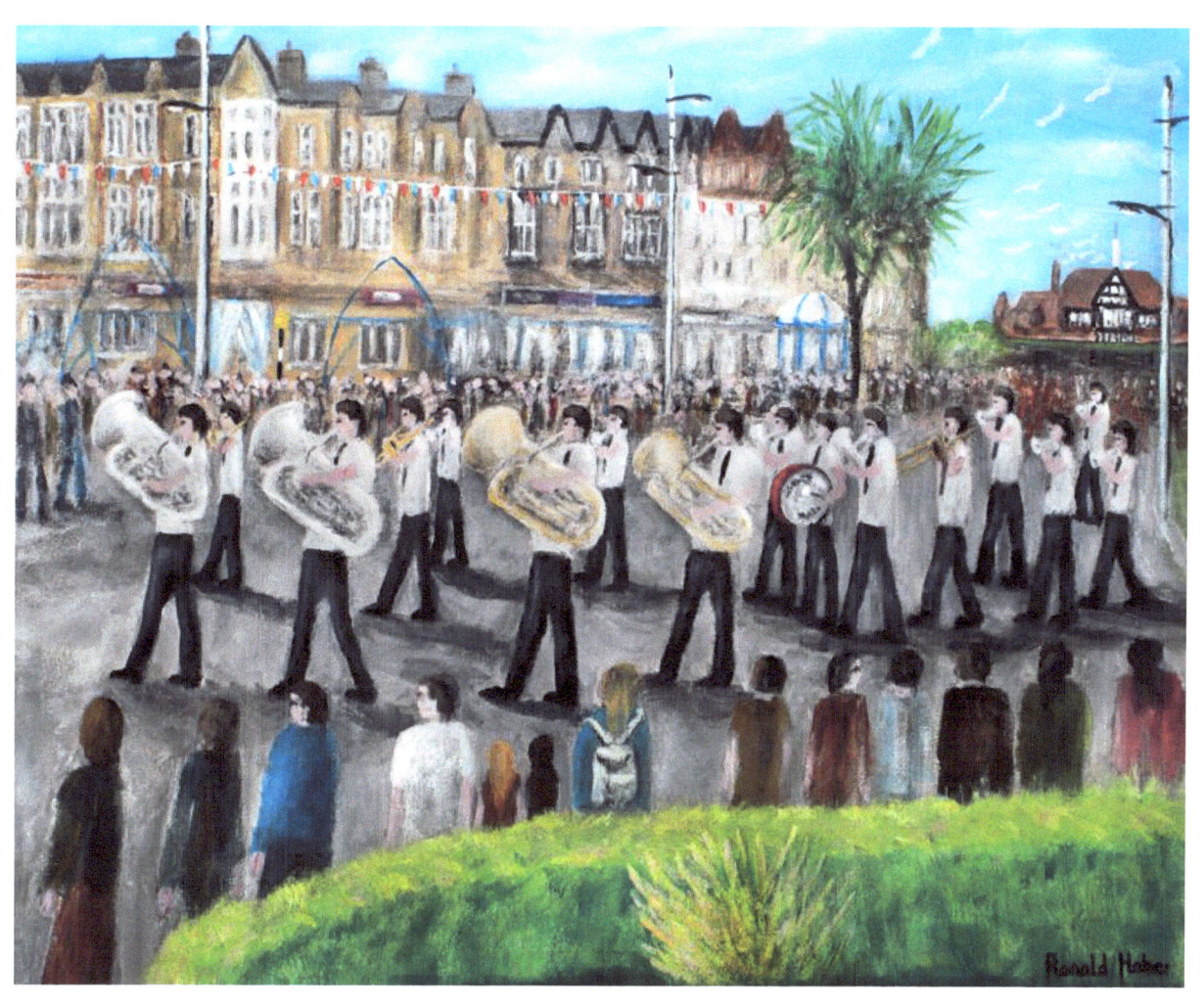

St. Annes on Sea Carnival

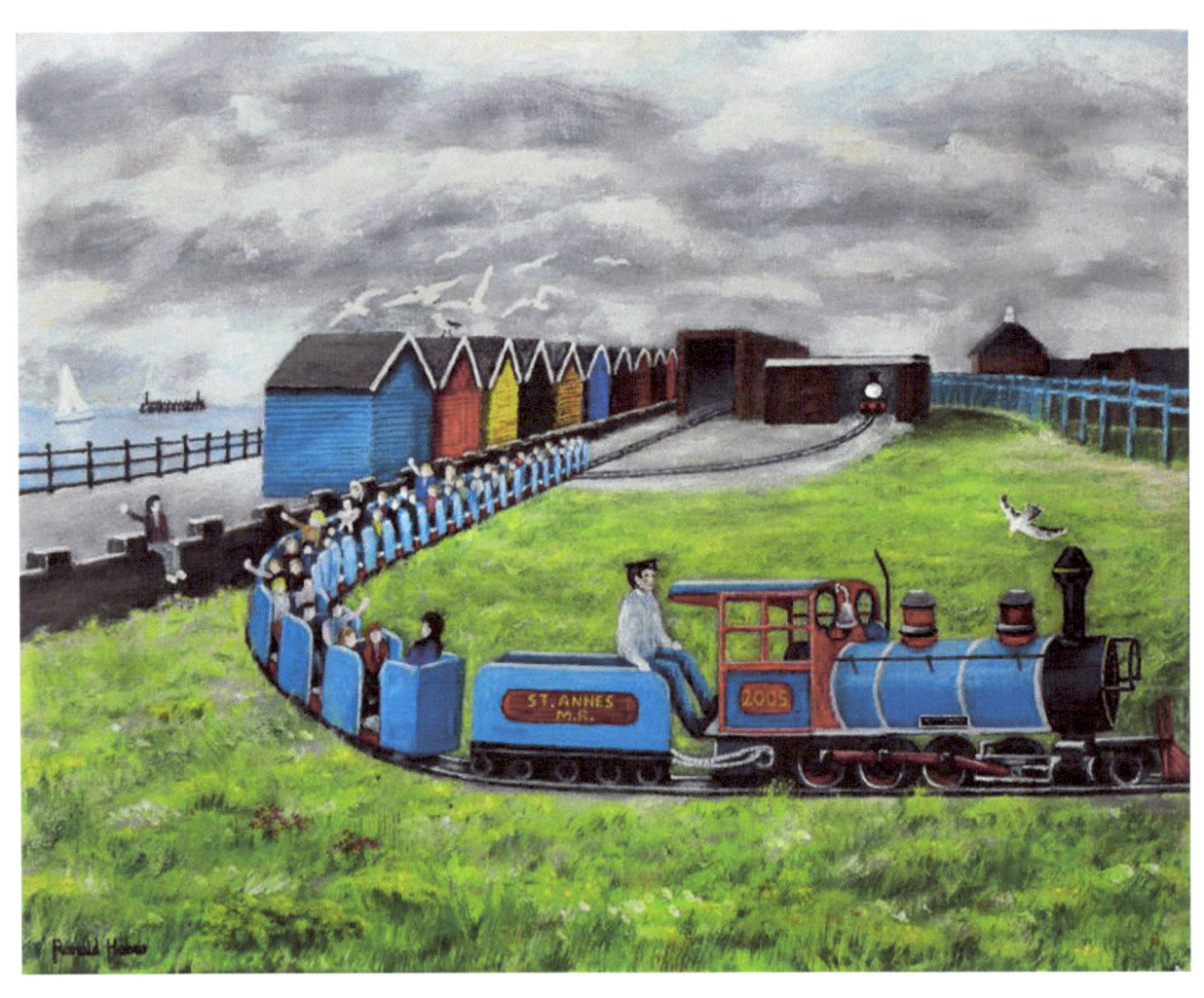

St. Annes on Sea Miniature Railway

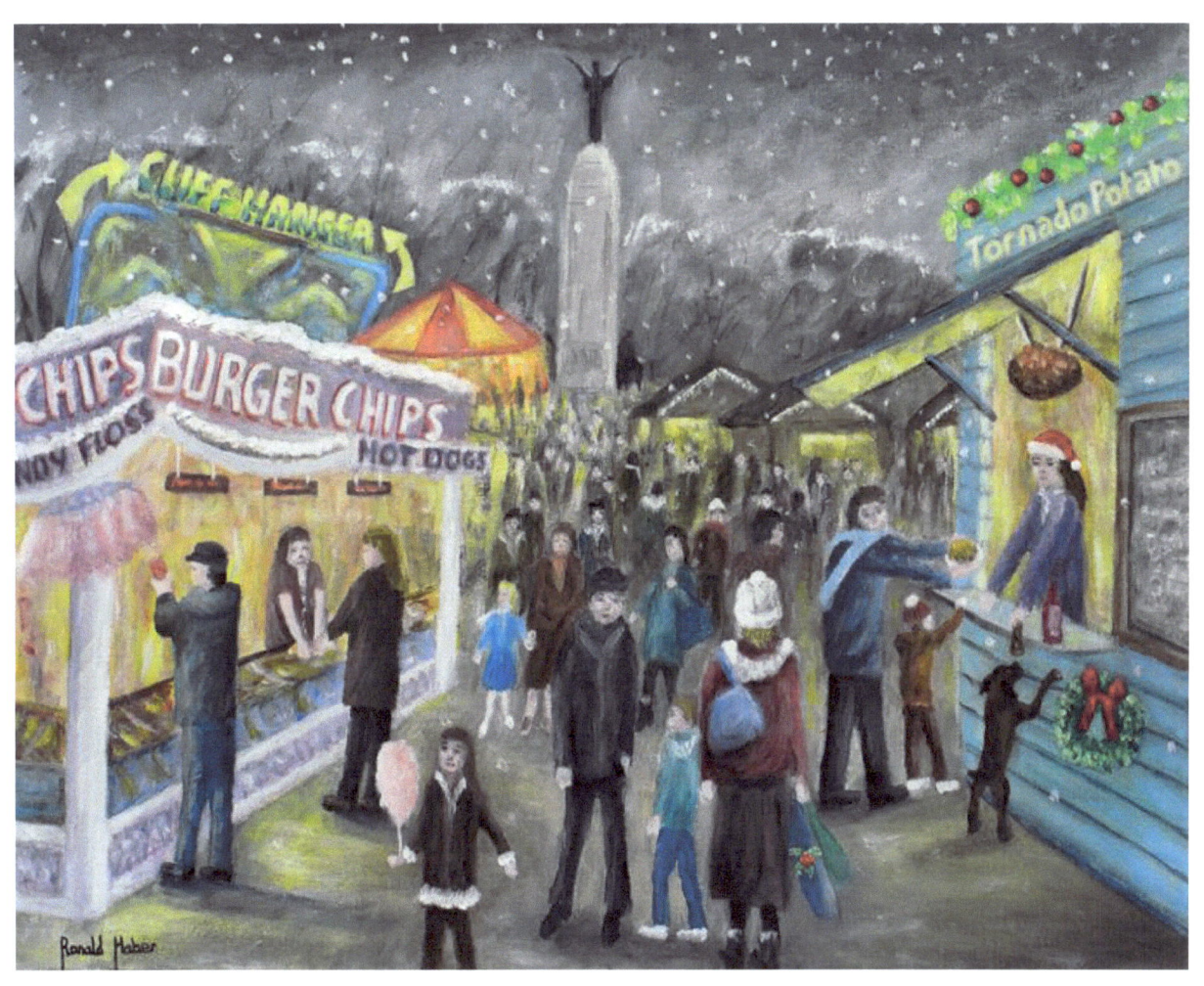

St. Annes on Sea Ashton Gardens Christmas Markets

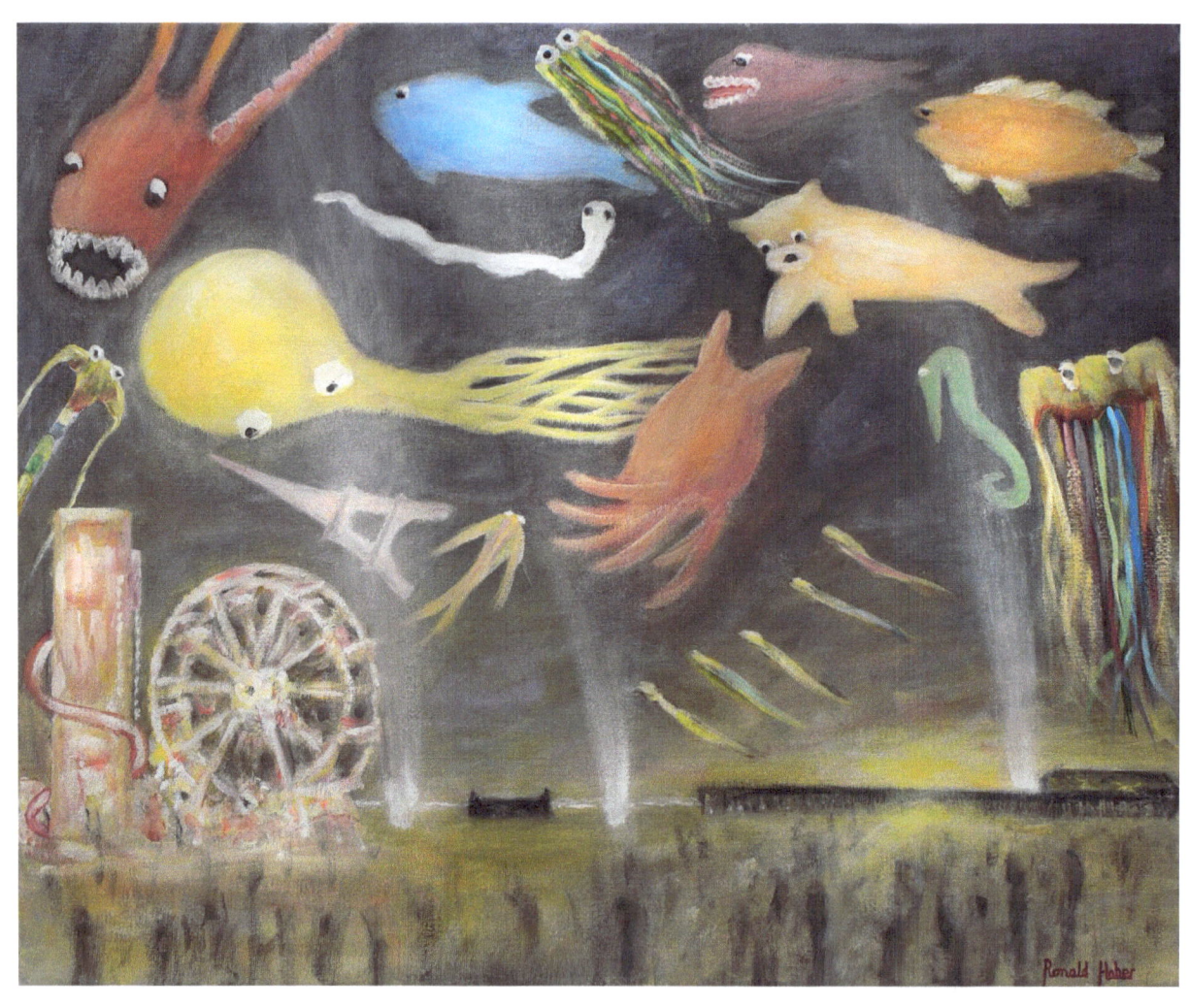

St. Annes on Sea International Kite Festival at Night

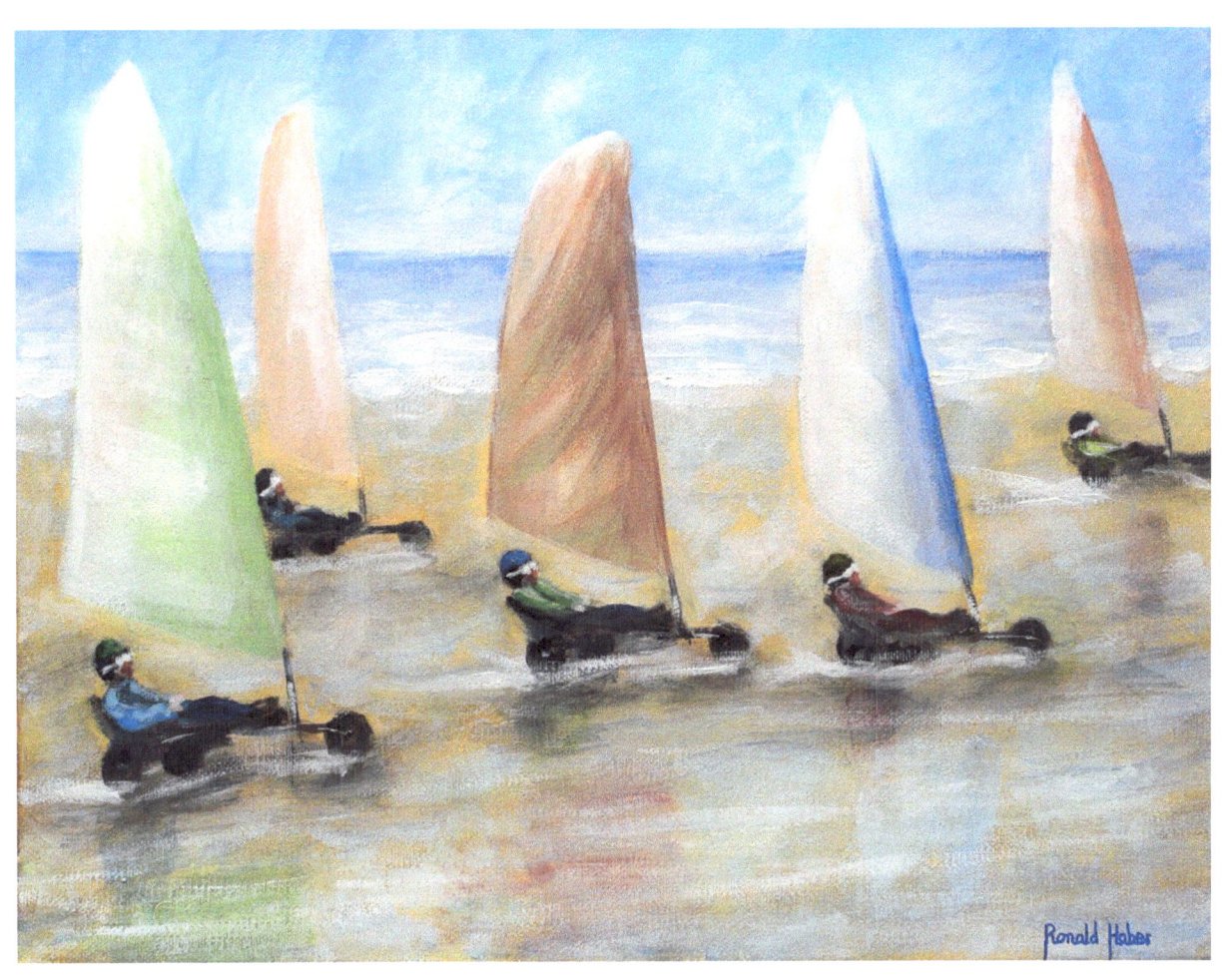

St. Annes on Sea Sand Yachting

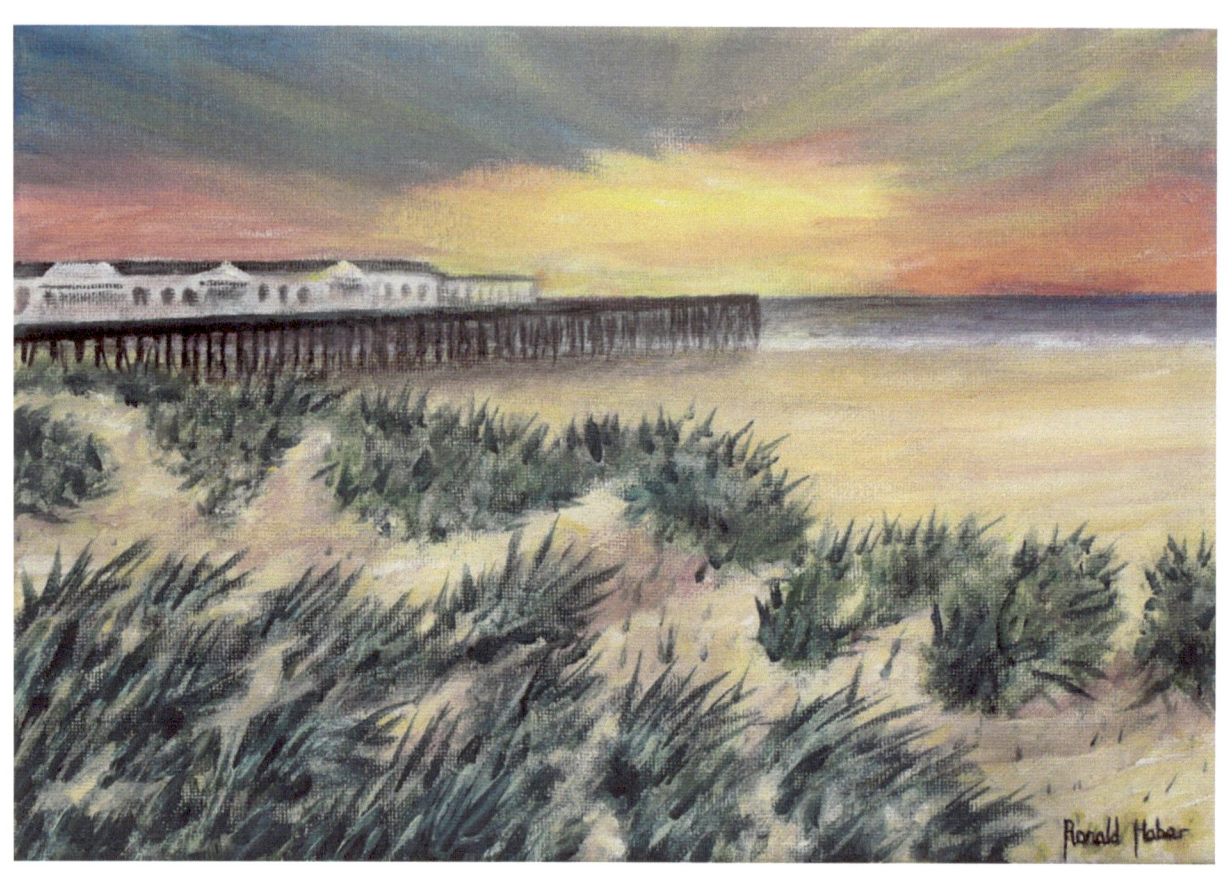

St. Annes on Sea Sunset over the Sand Dunes and Pier

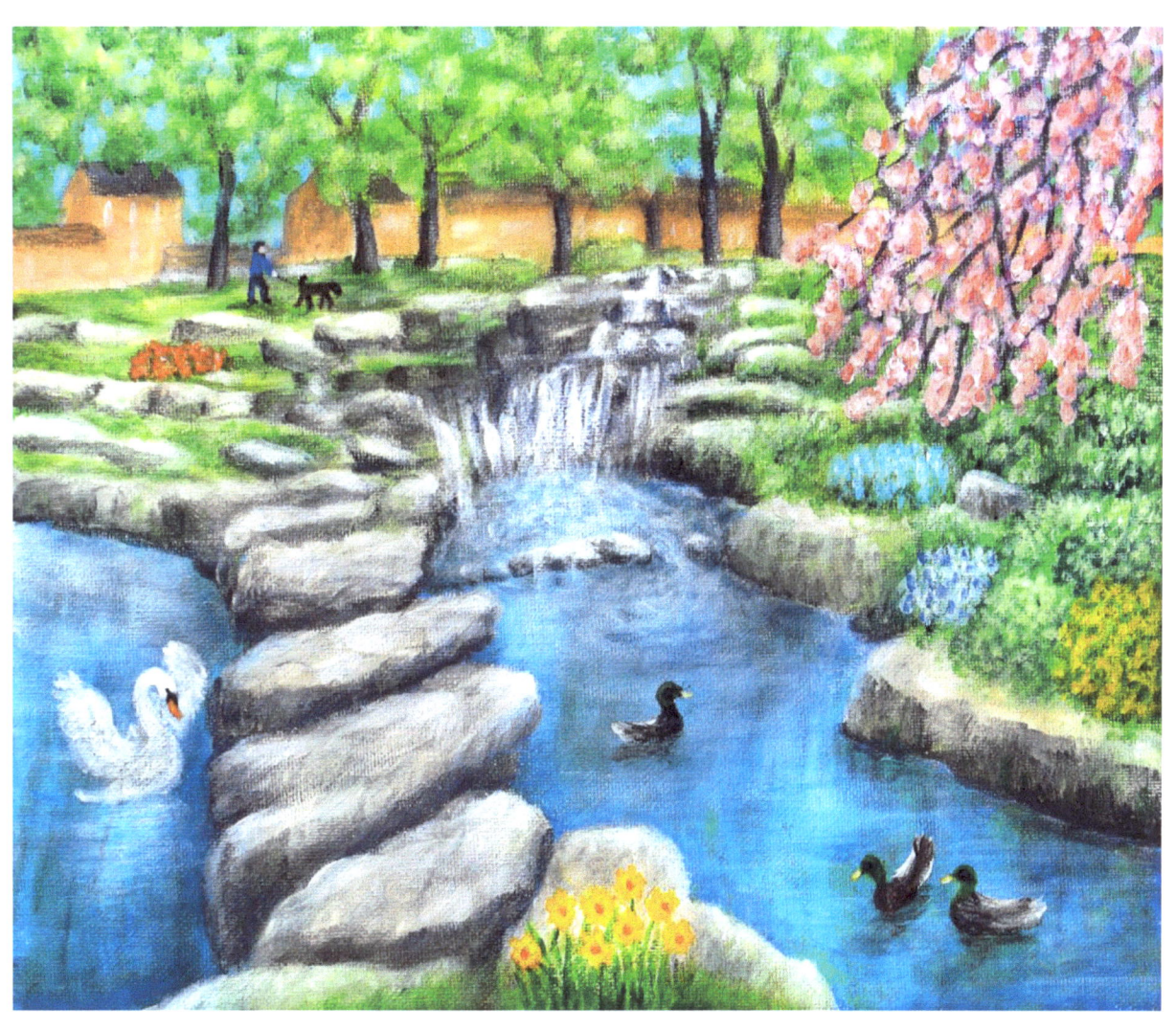

St. Annes on Sea Ashton Gardens Lake, Cherry Tree and Waterfall

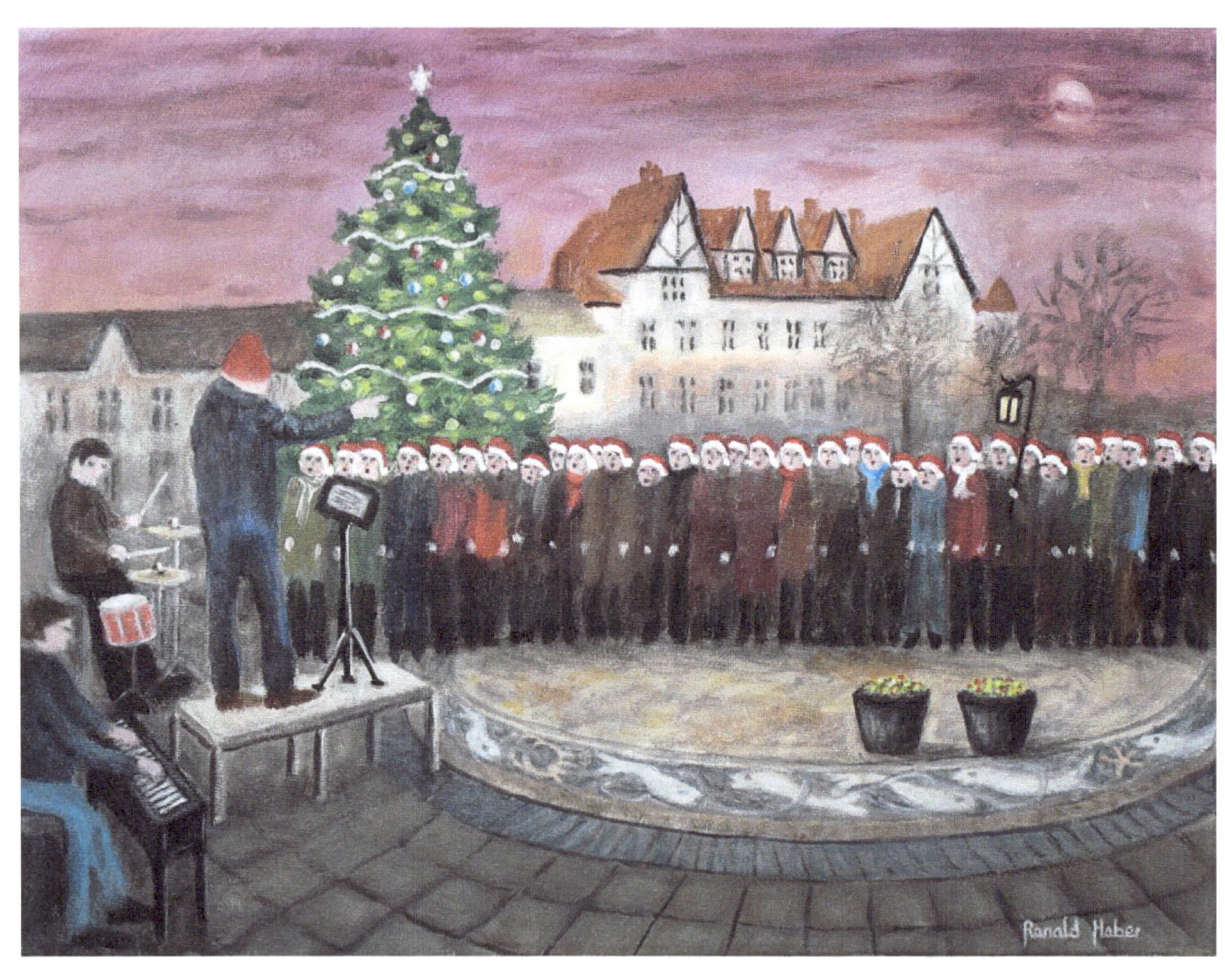

Lytham Carol Singers at Christmas

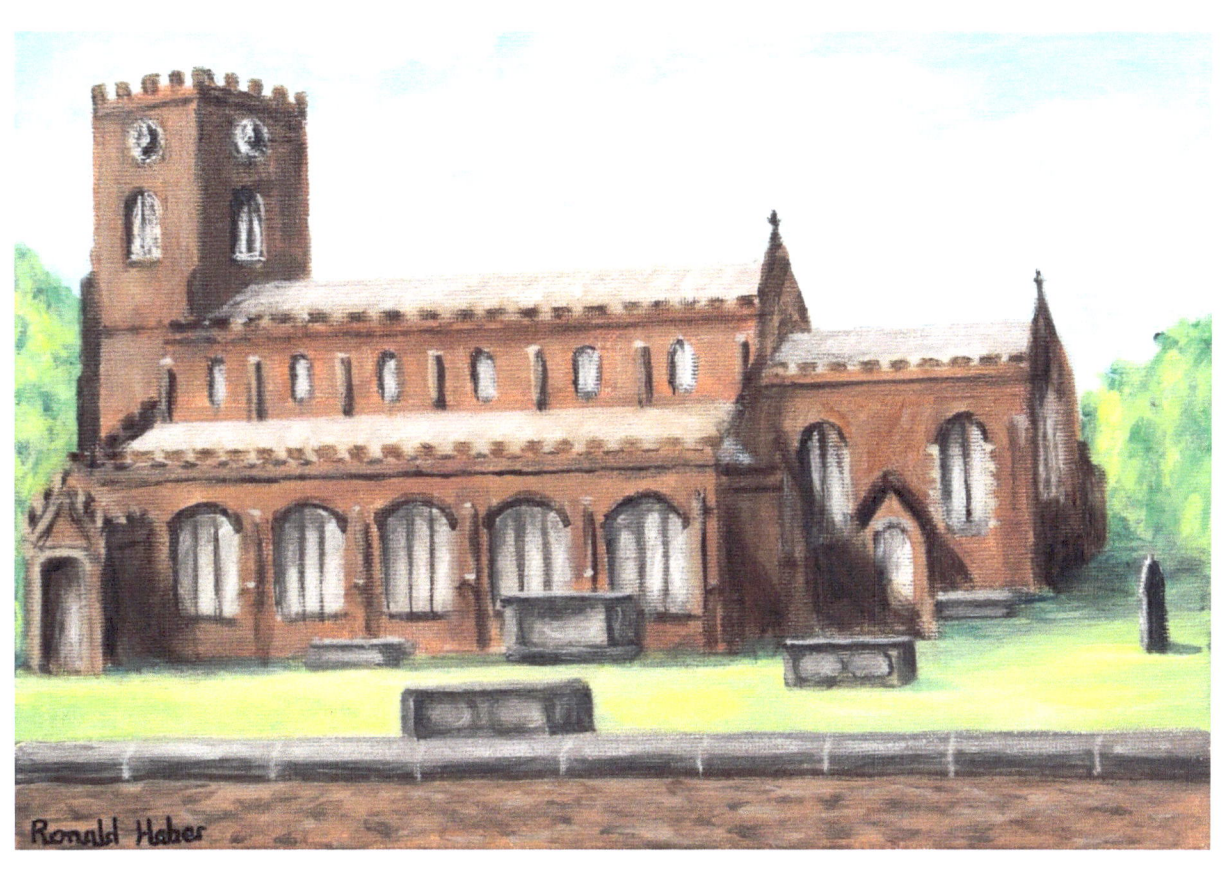

St. Cuthbert's Church Lytham

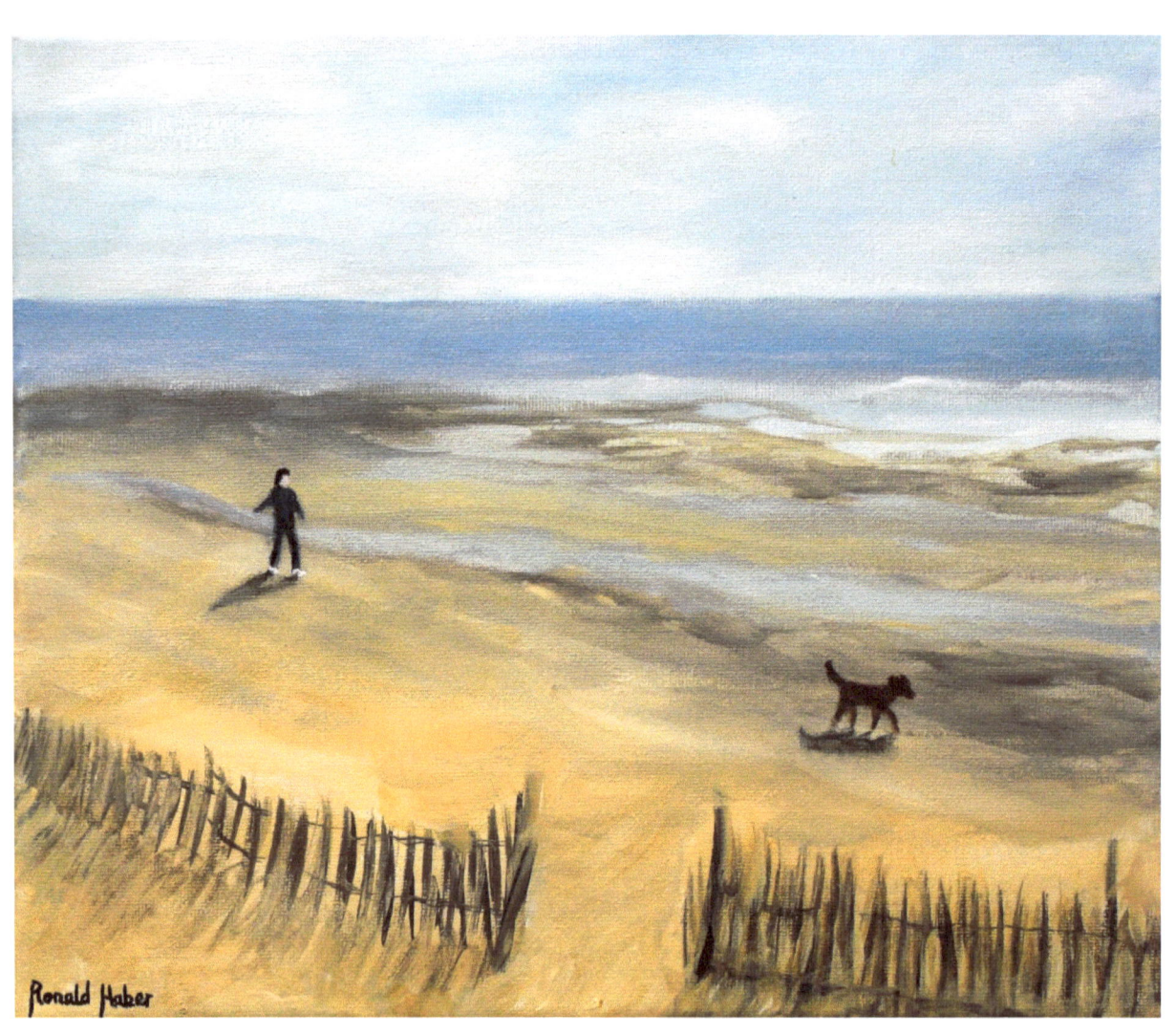

St. Annes on Sea Dog Walker on North Beach

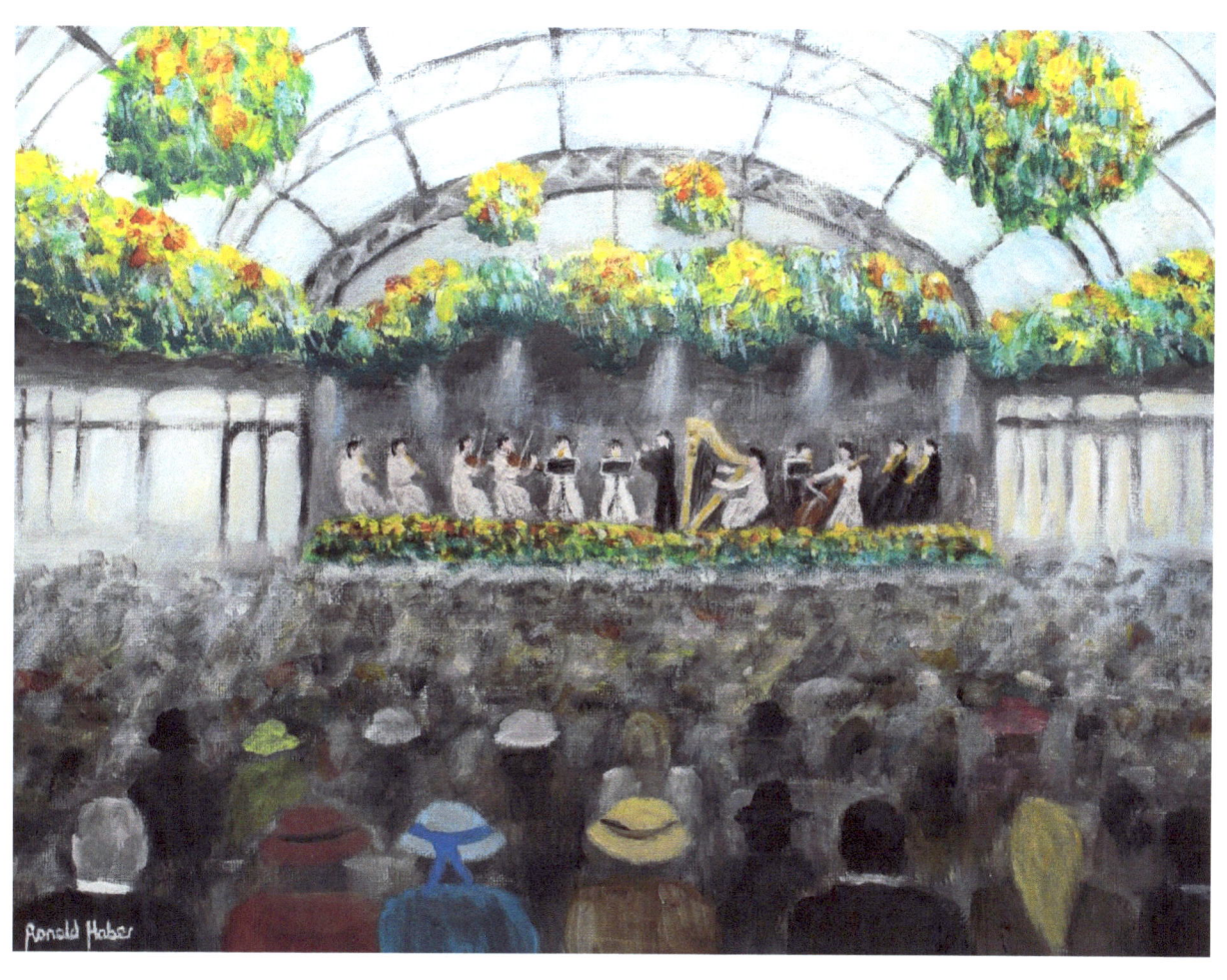

St. Annes on Sea The Floral Hall and Orchestra in the 1930's

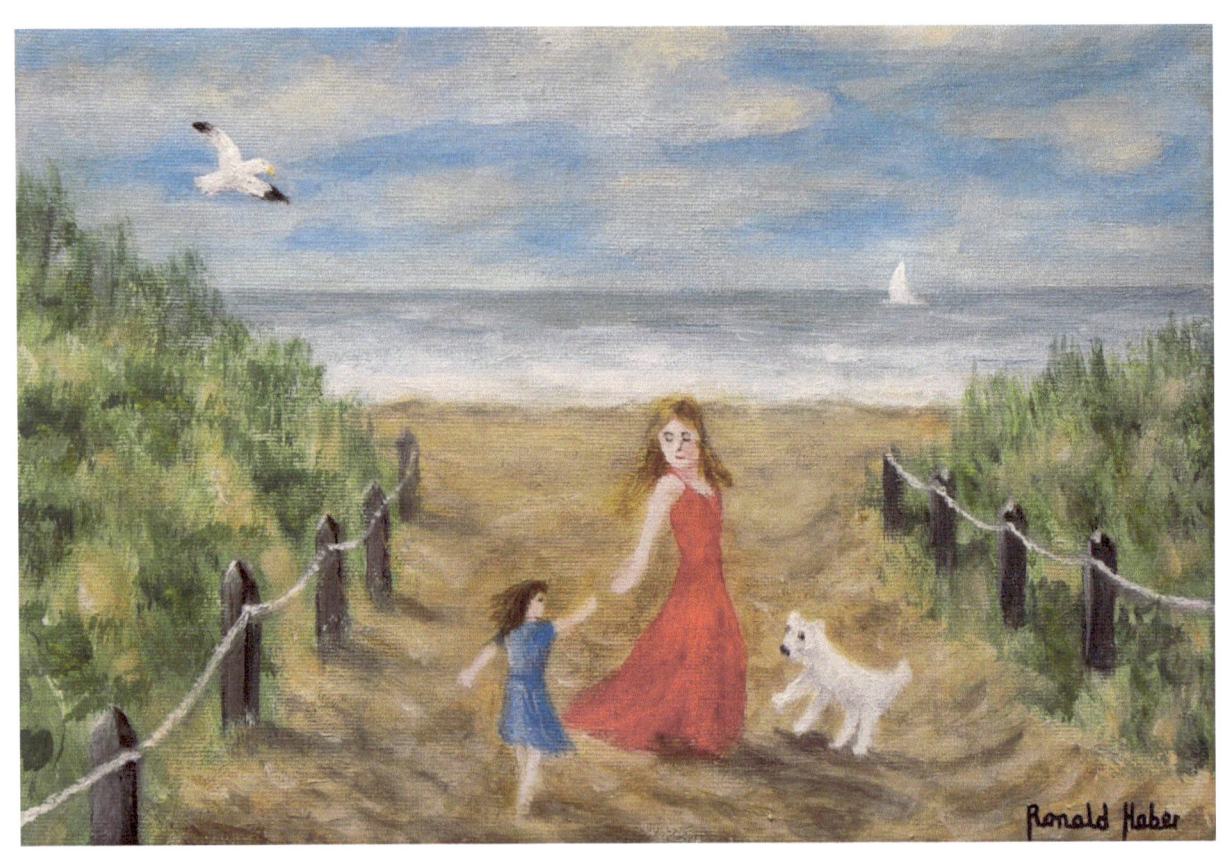

St. Annes on Sea Going to the Beach

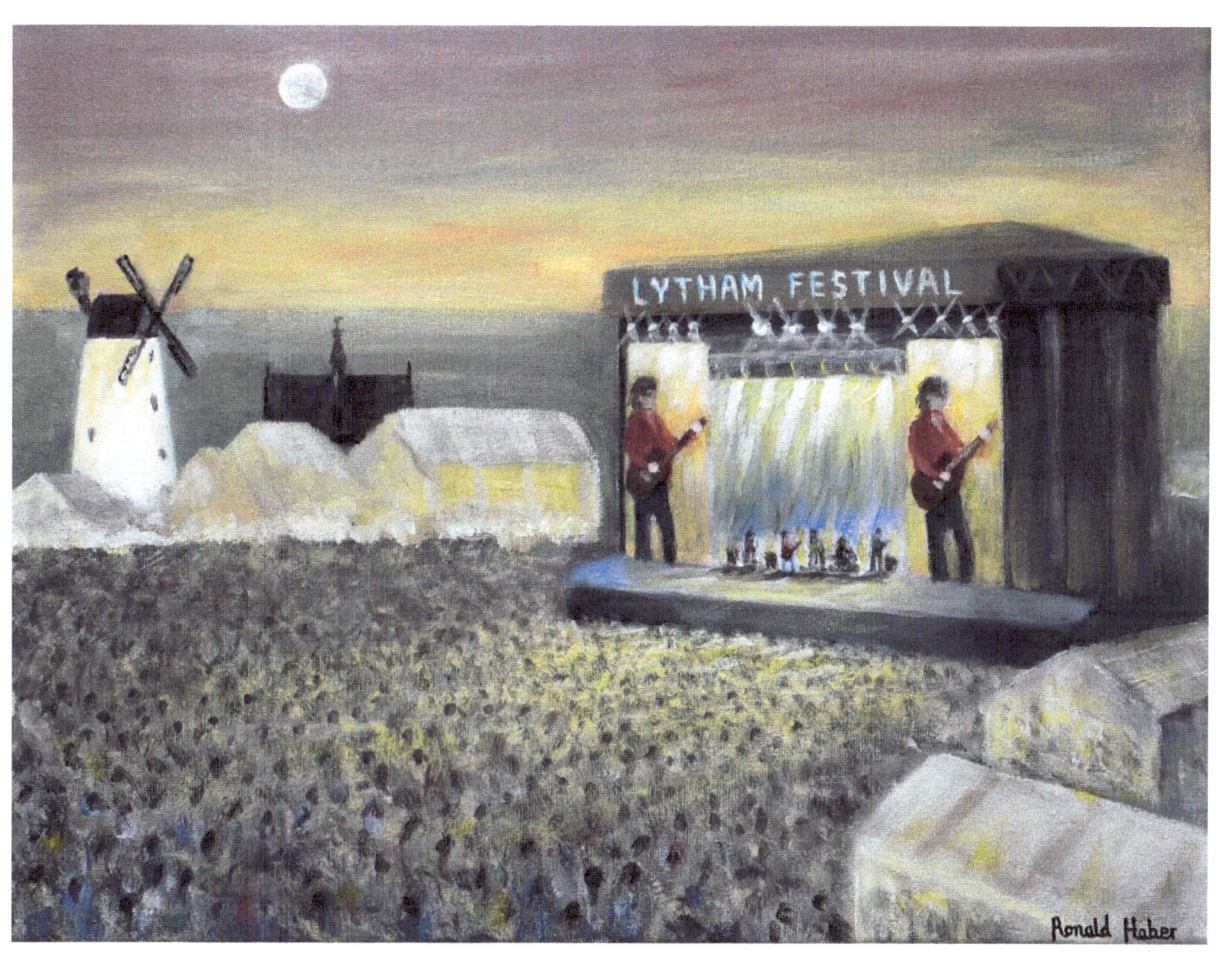

Lytham Festival

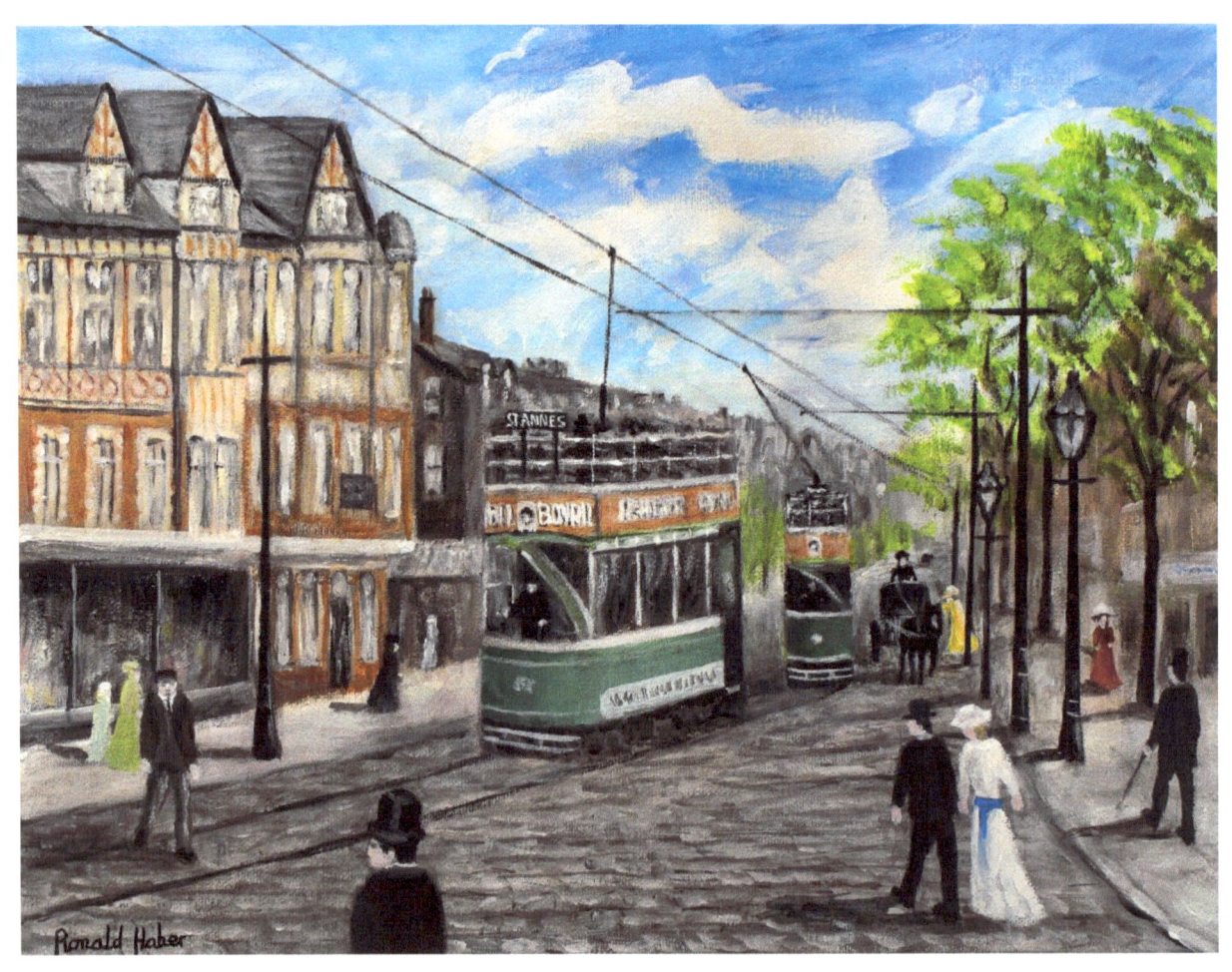

Lytham 1905

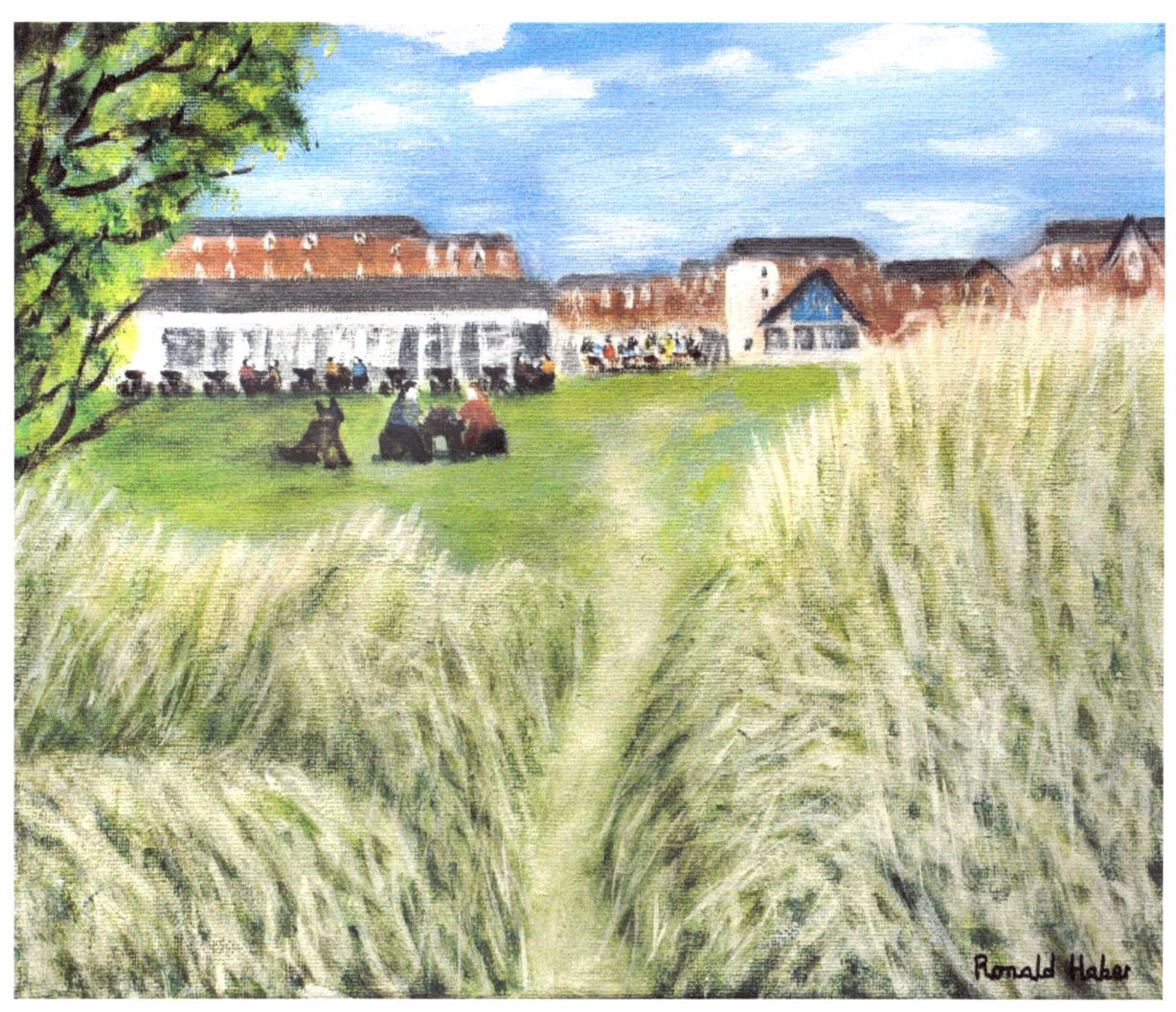

St. Annes on Sea Beach Café View from Sand Dunes

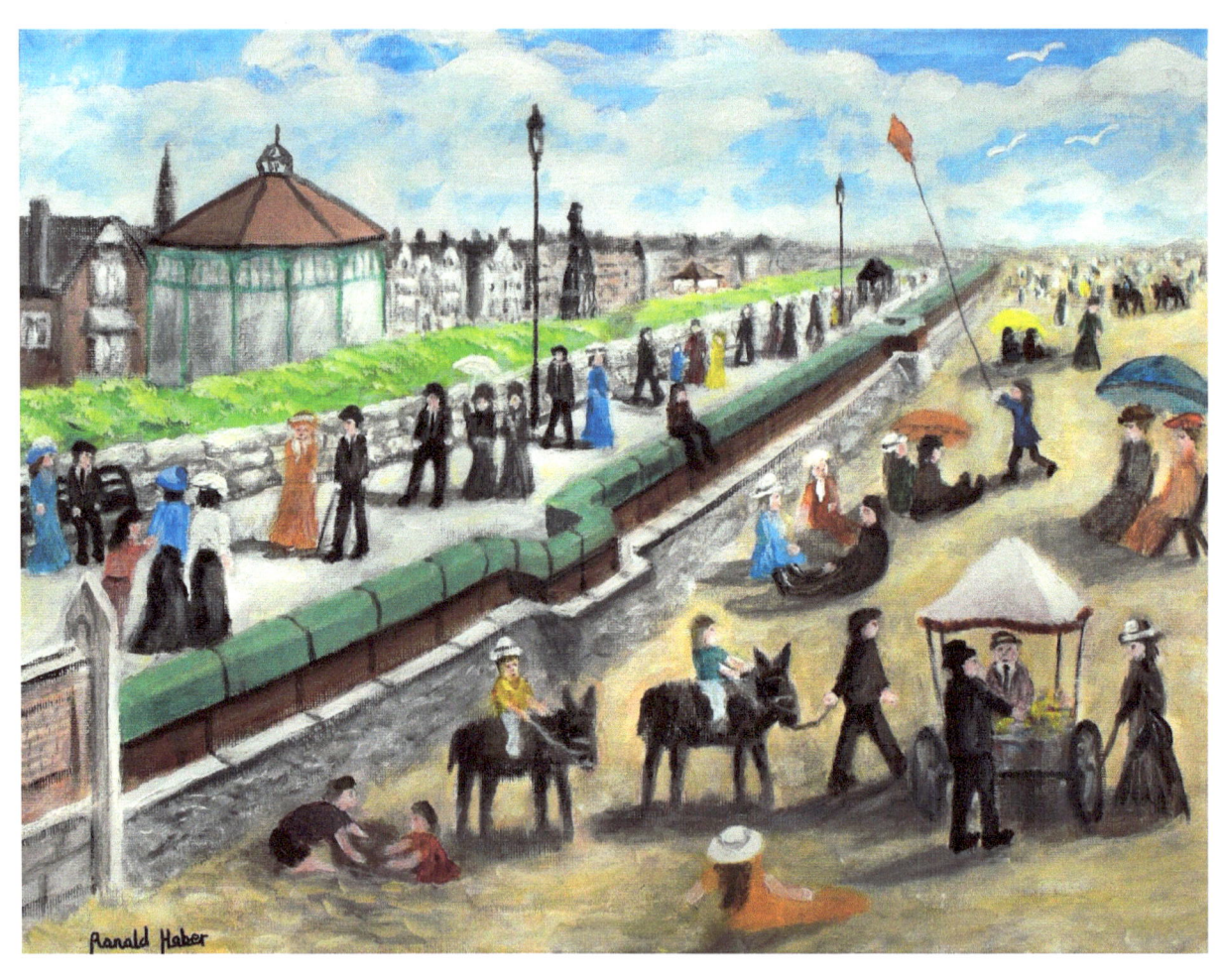

St. Annes on Sea Victorian Promenade 1905

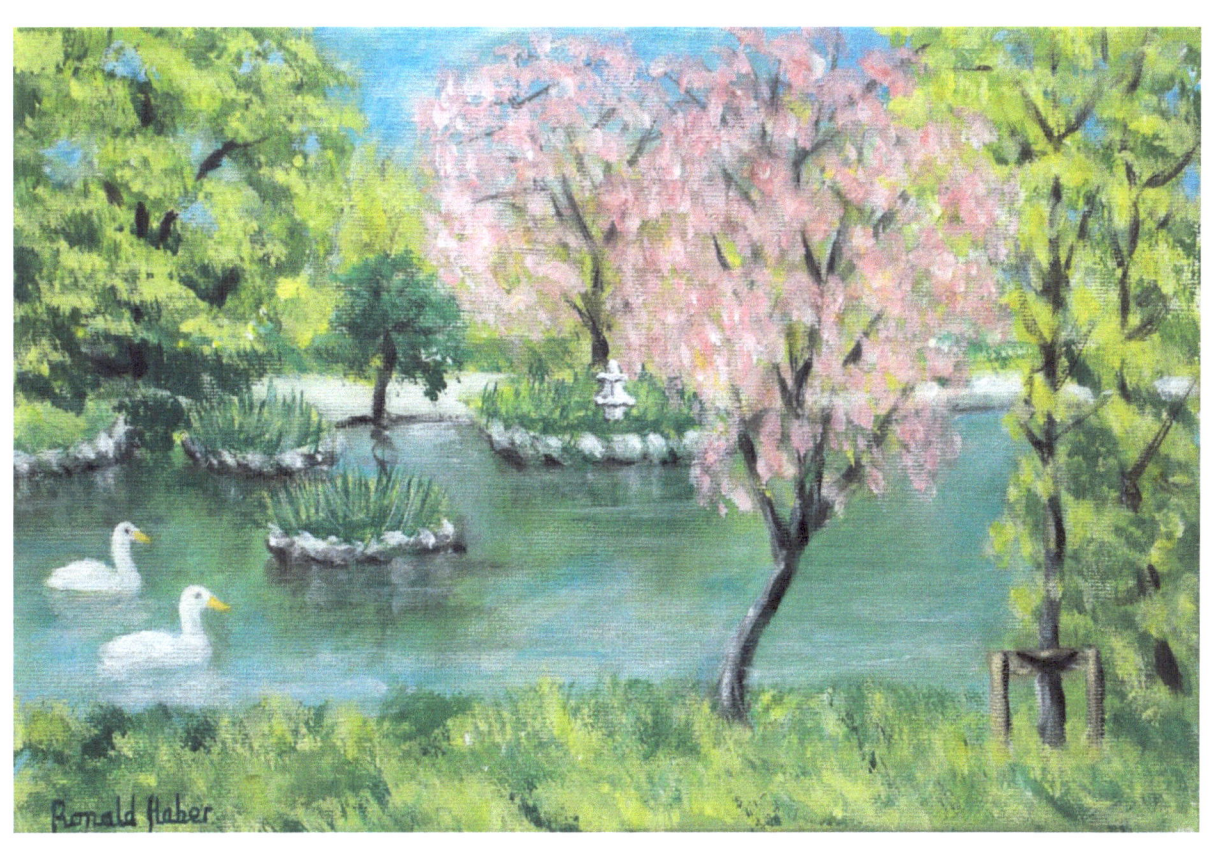

St. Annes on Sea Ashton Gardens Cherry Trees

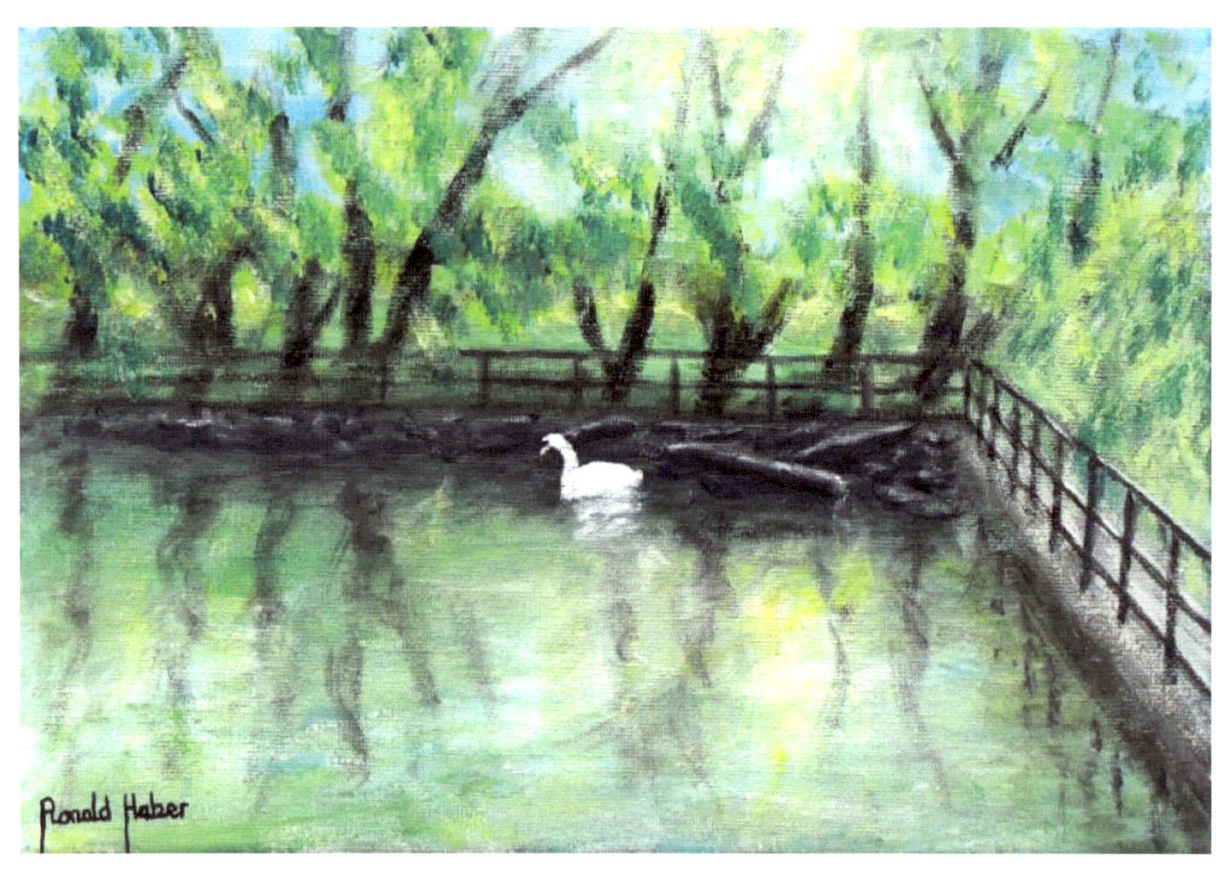

Lytham Fairhaven Lake

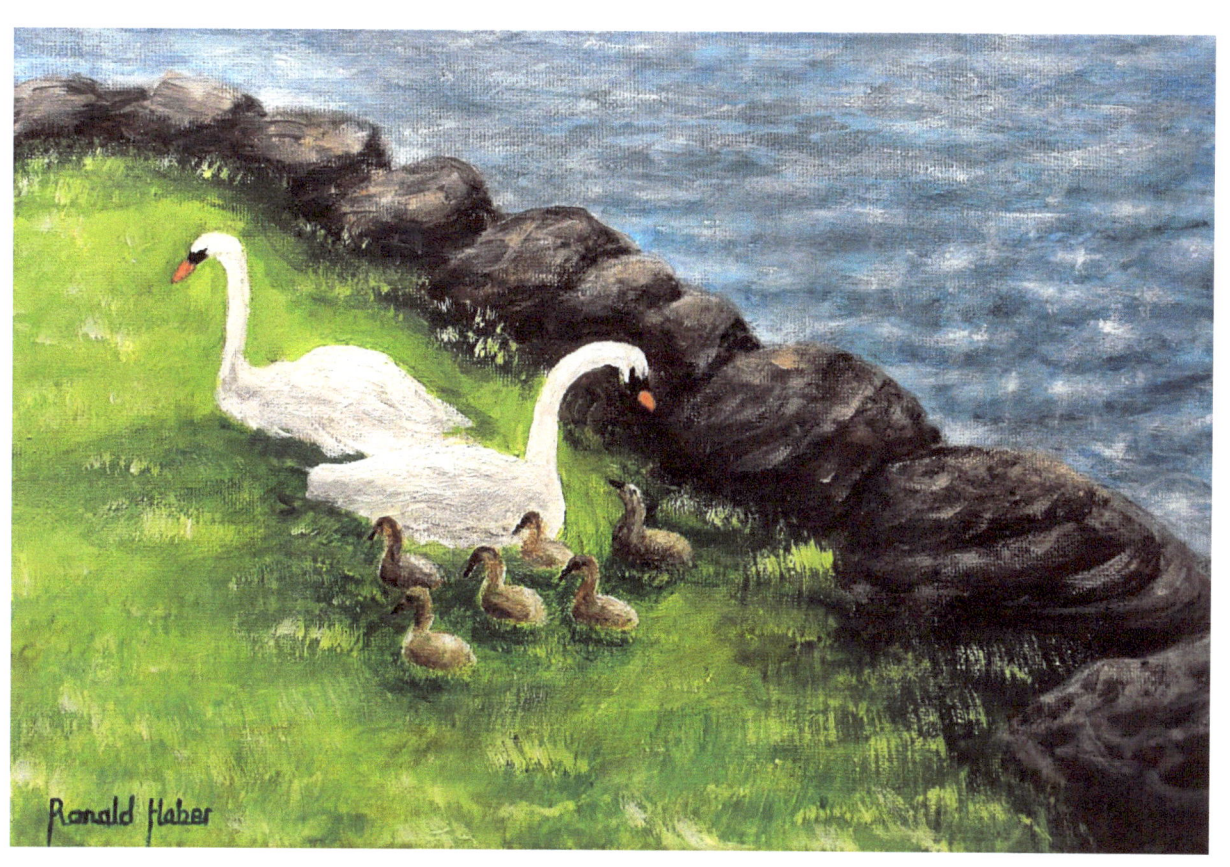

St. Annes on Sea Promenade Swans

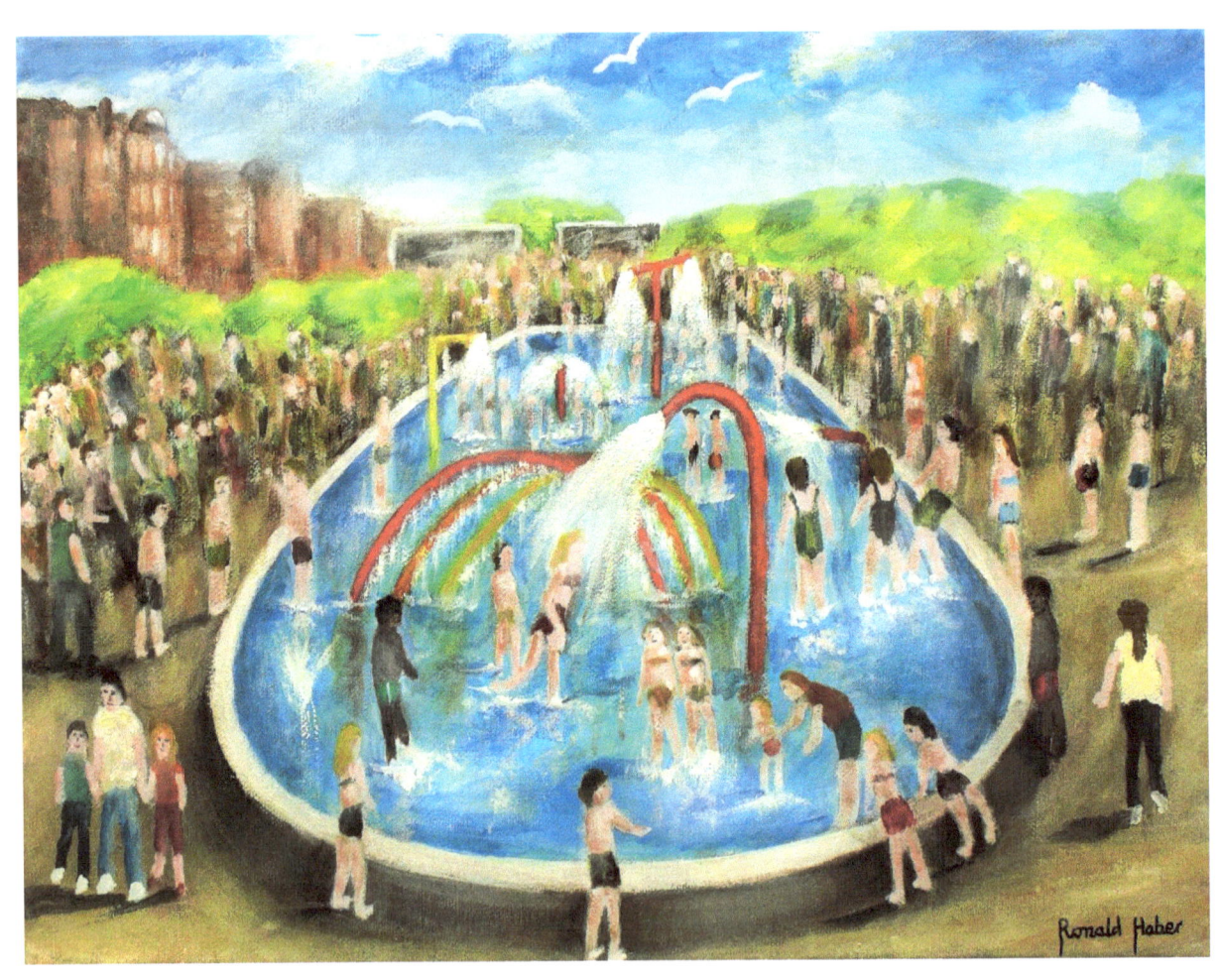

St. Annes on Sea Splash Park

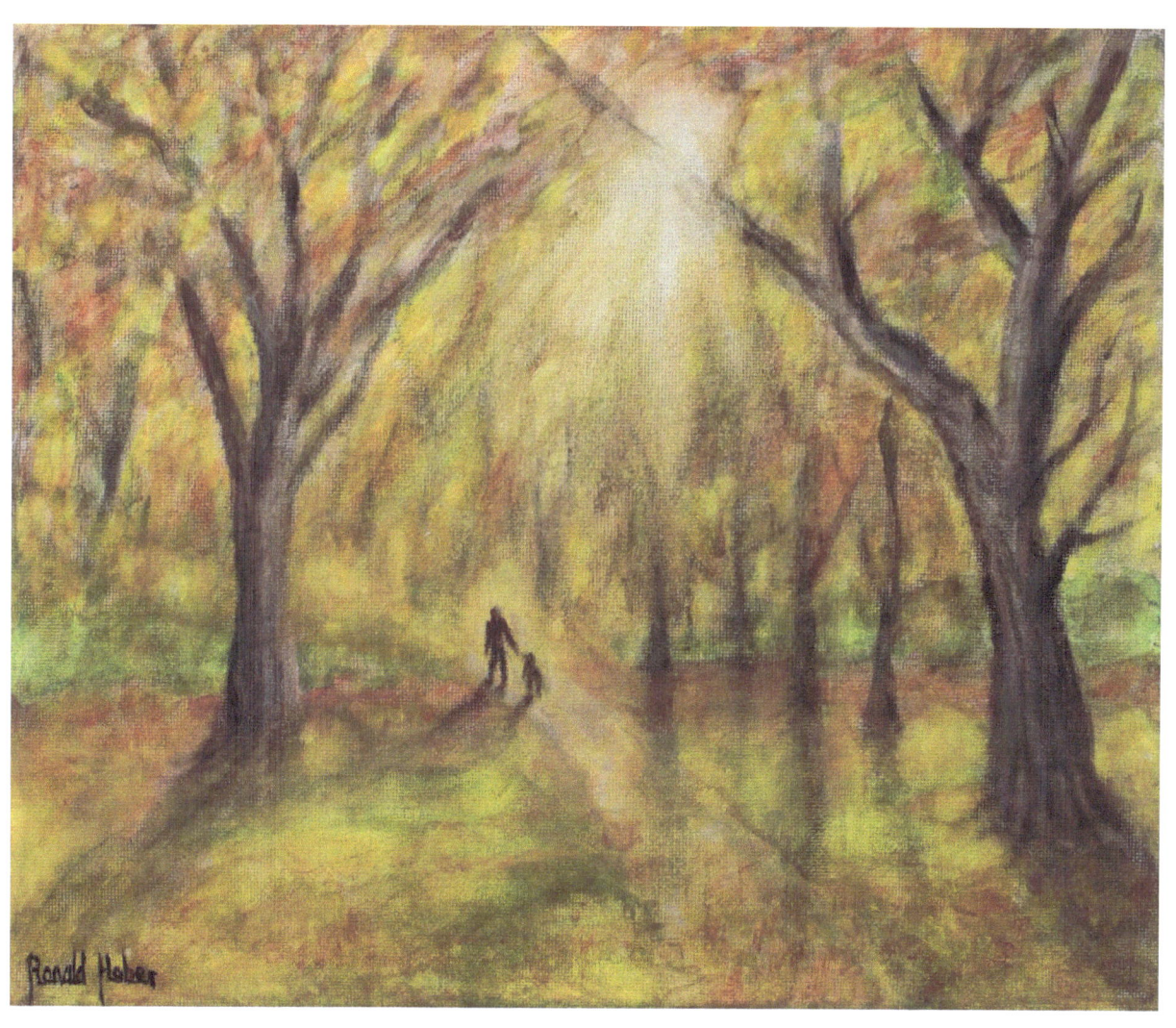

Lytham Lowther Gardens in the Autumn

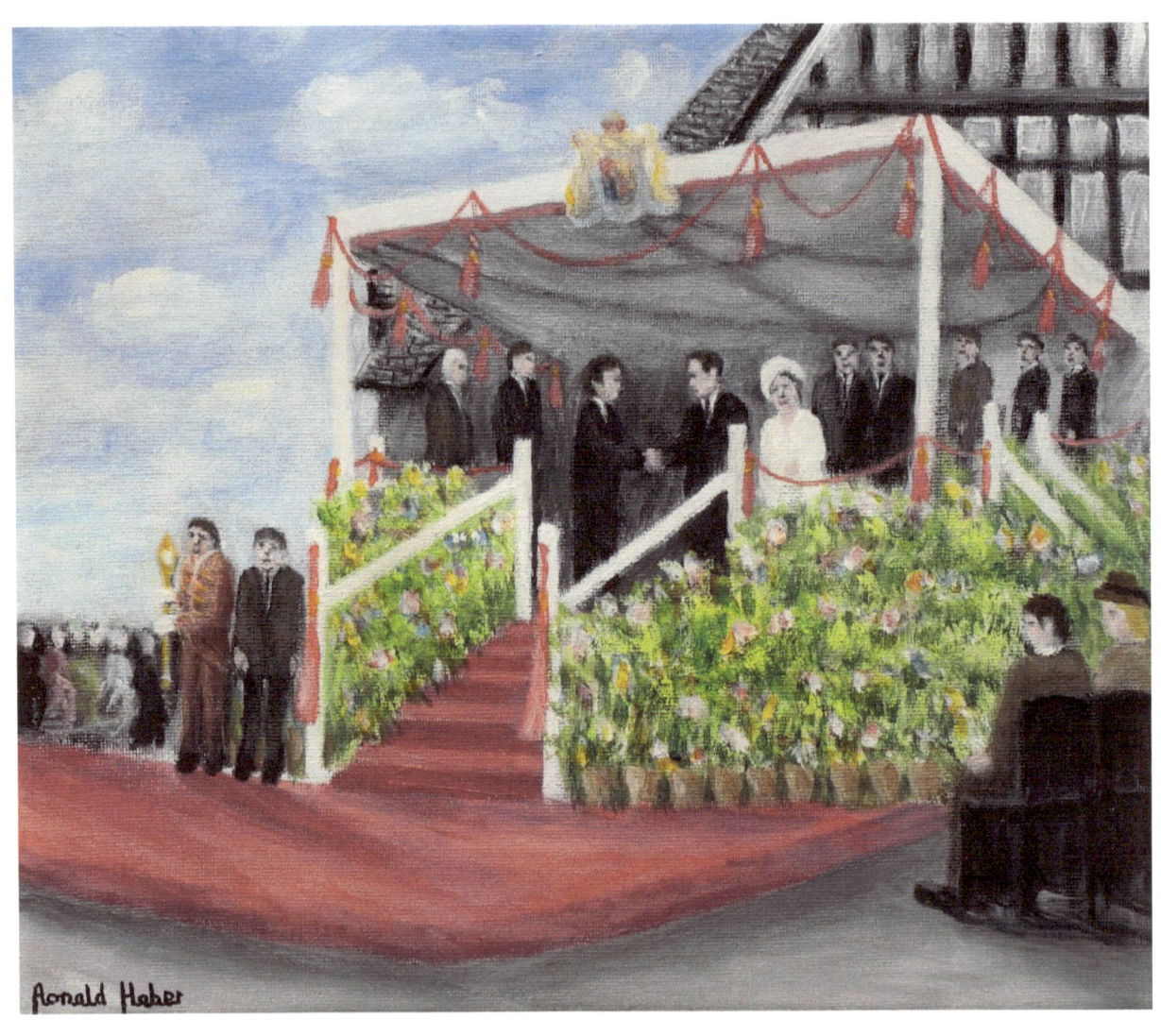

King George VI and Queen Elizabeth Visit to St. Annes on Sea 1938

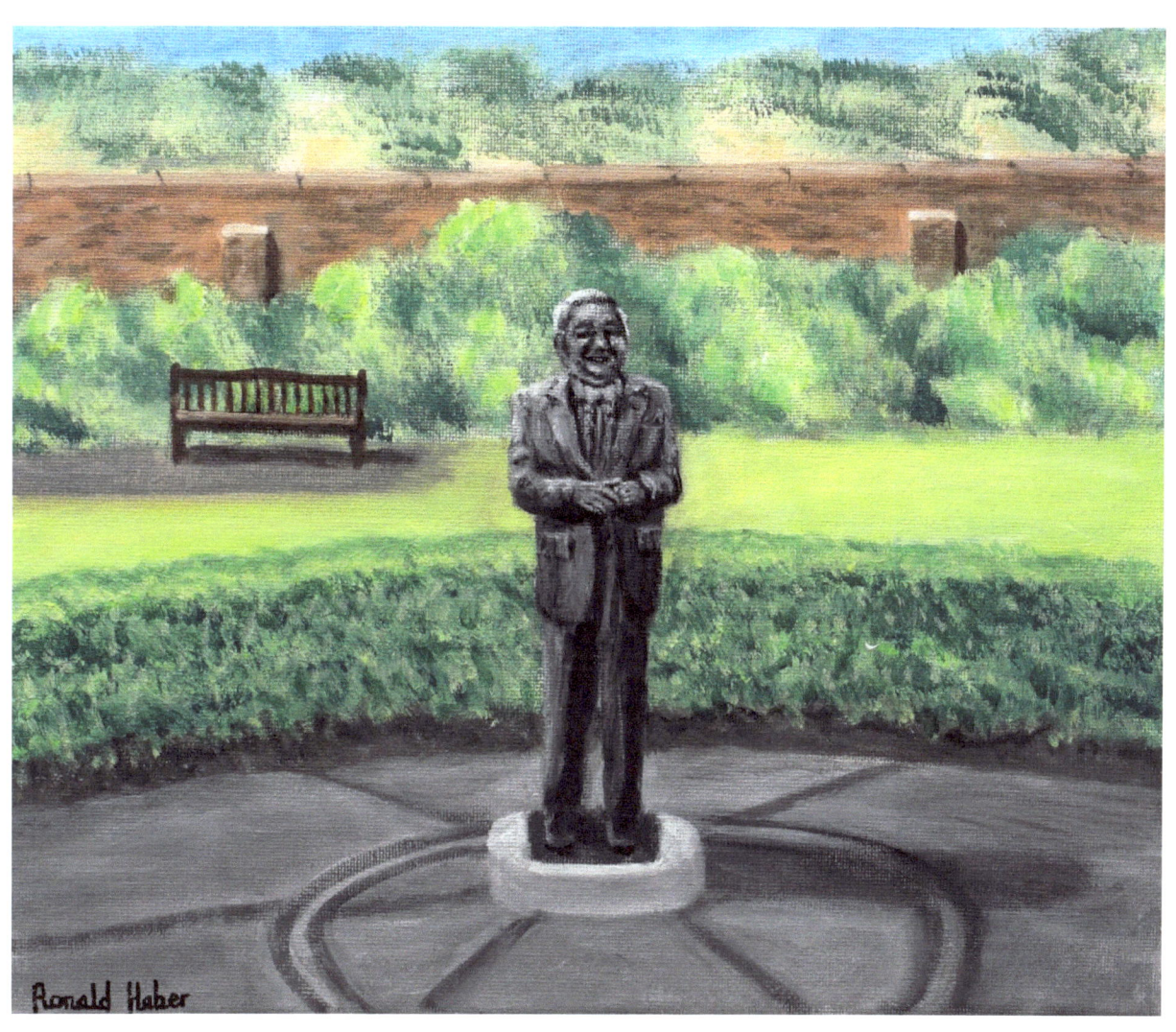

St. Annes on Sea Les Dawson Statue

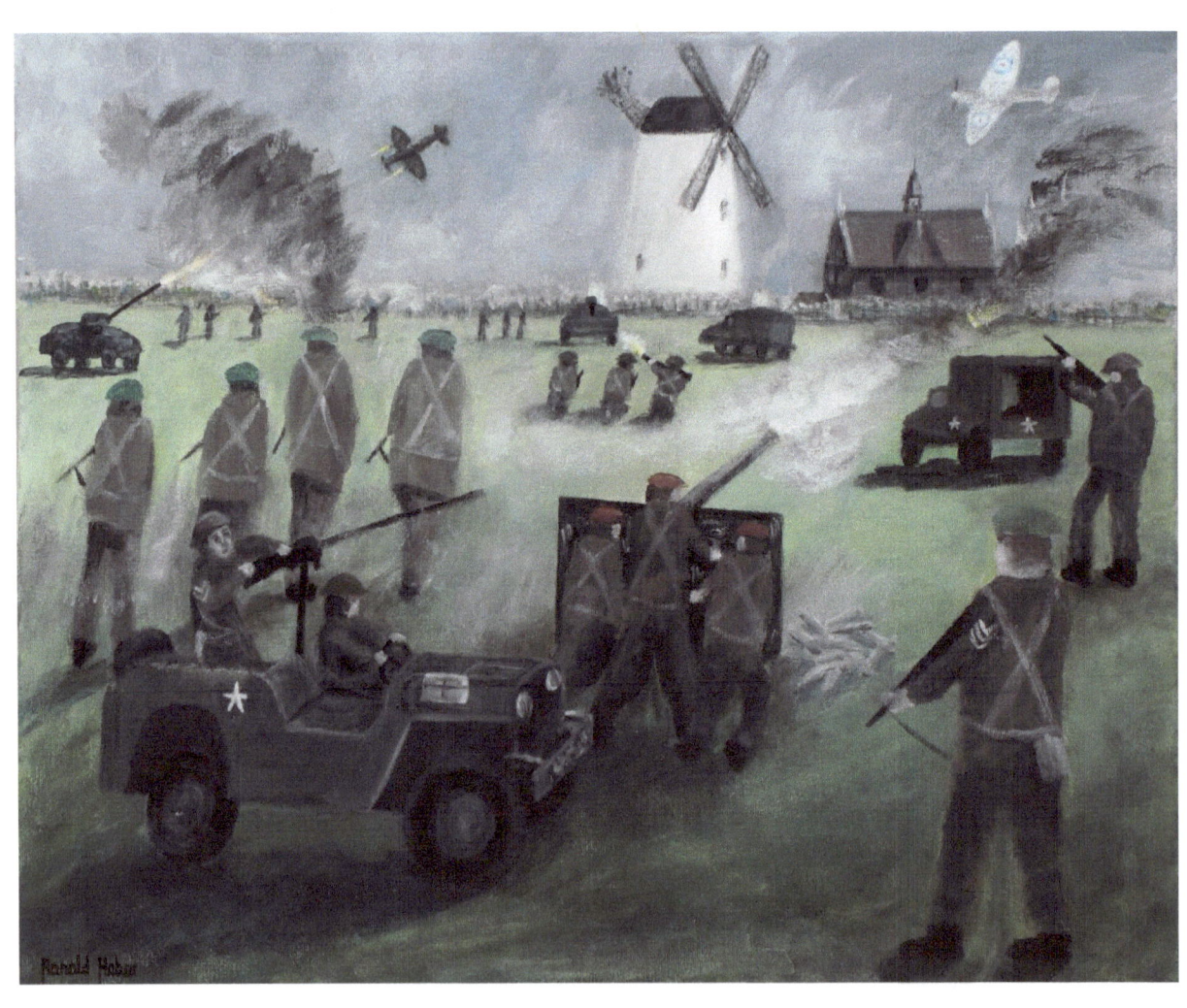

Lytham 1940's War Weekend Reenactment

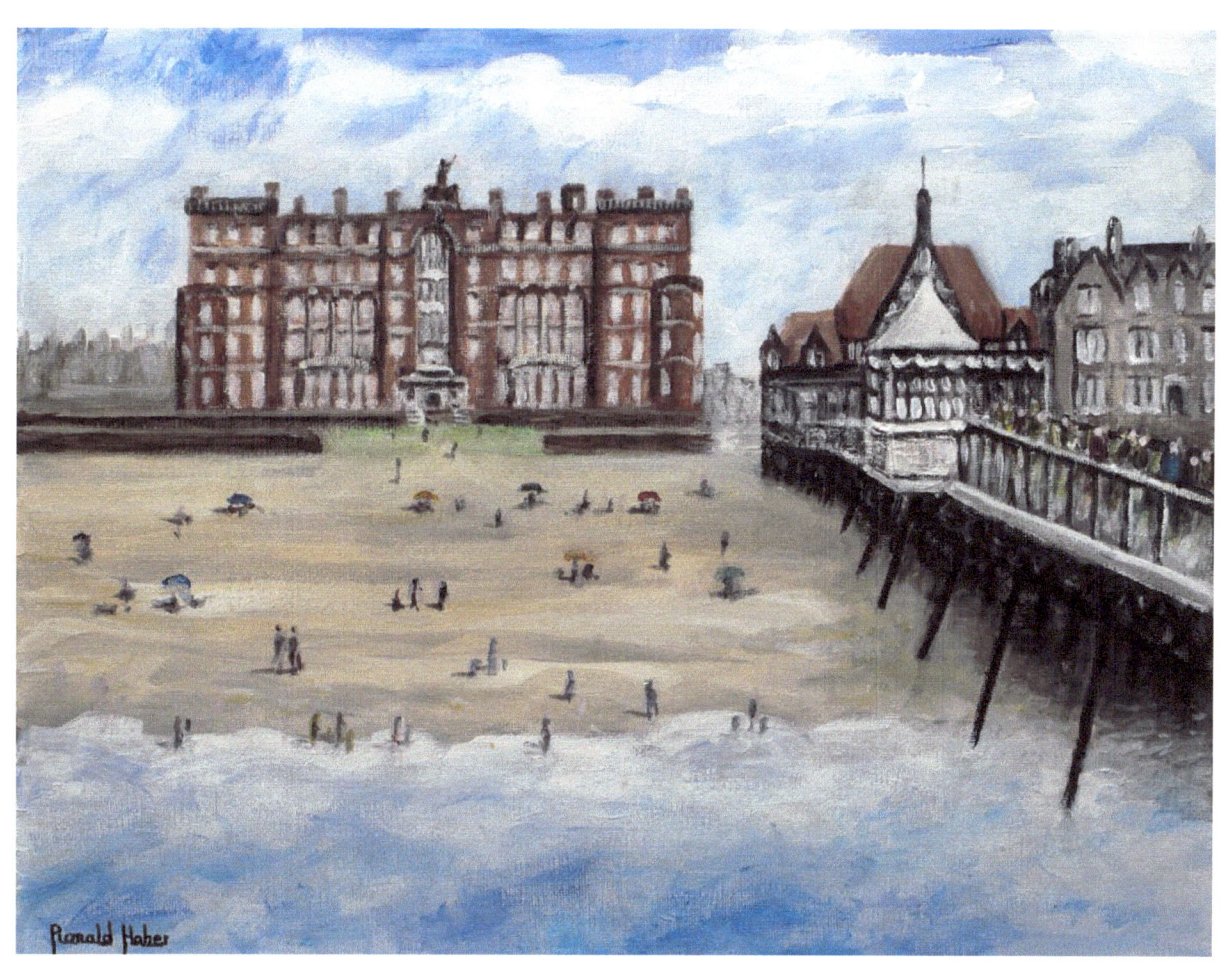

St. Annes on Sea Hotel Majestic 1925

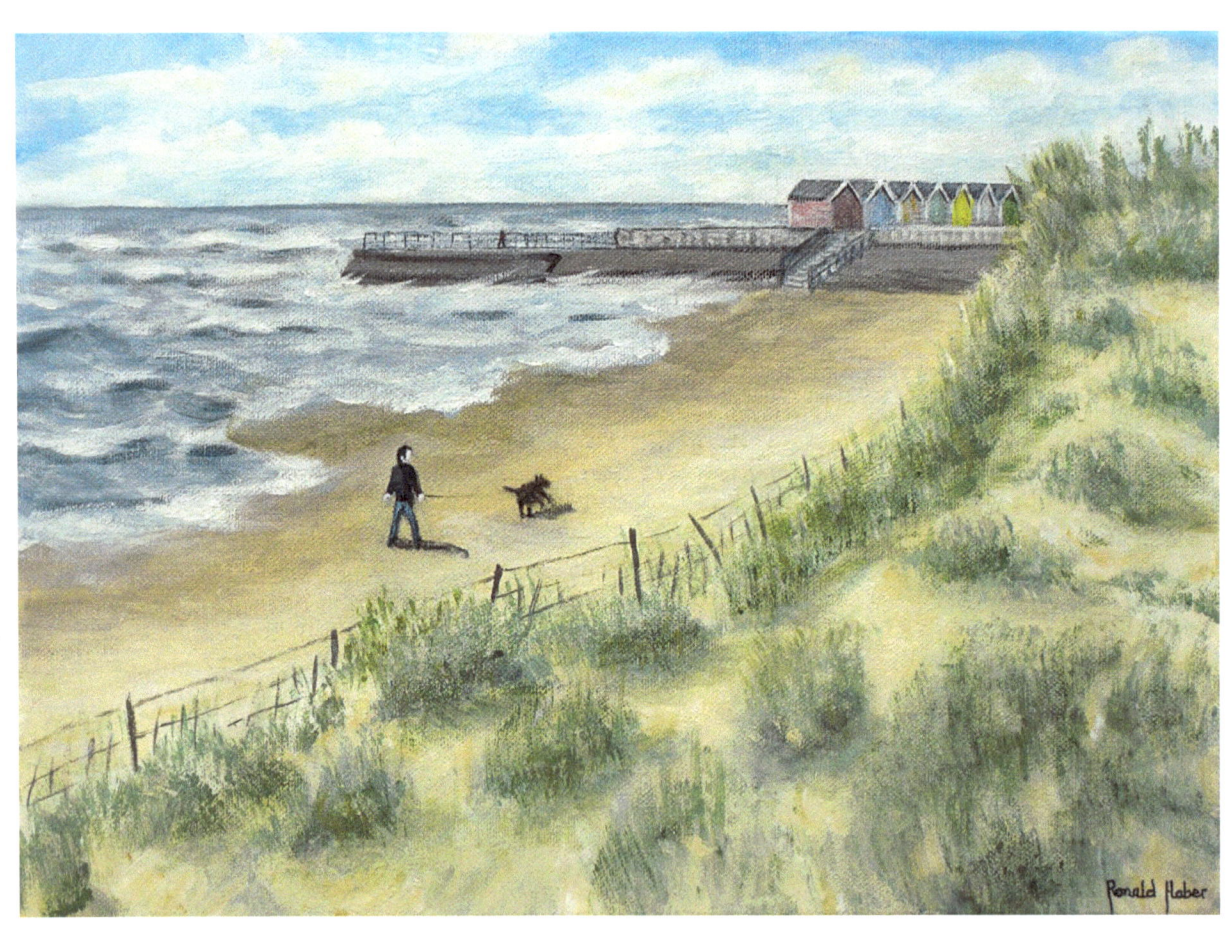

St. Annes on Sea Sand Dunes and Beach Huts

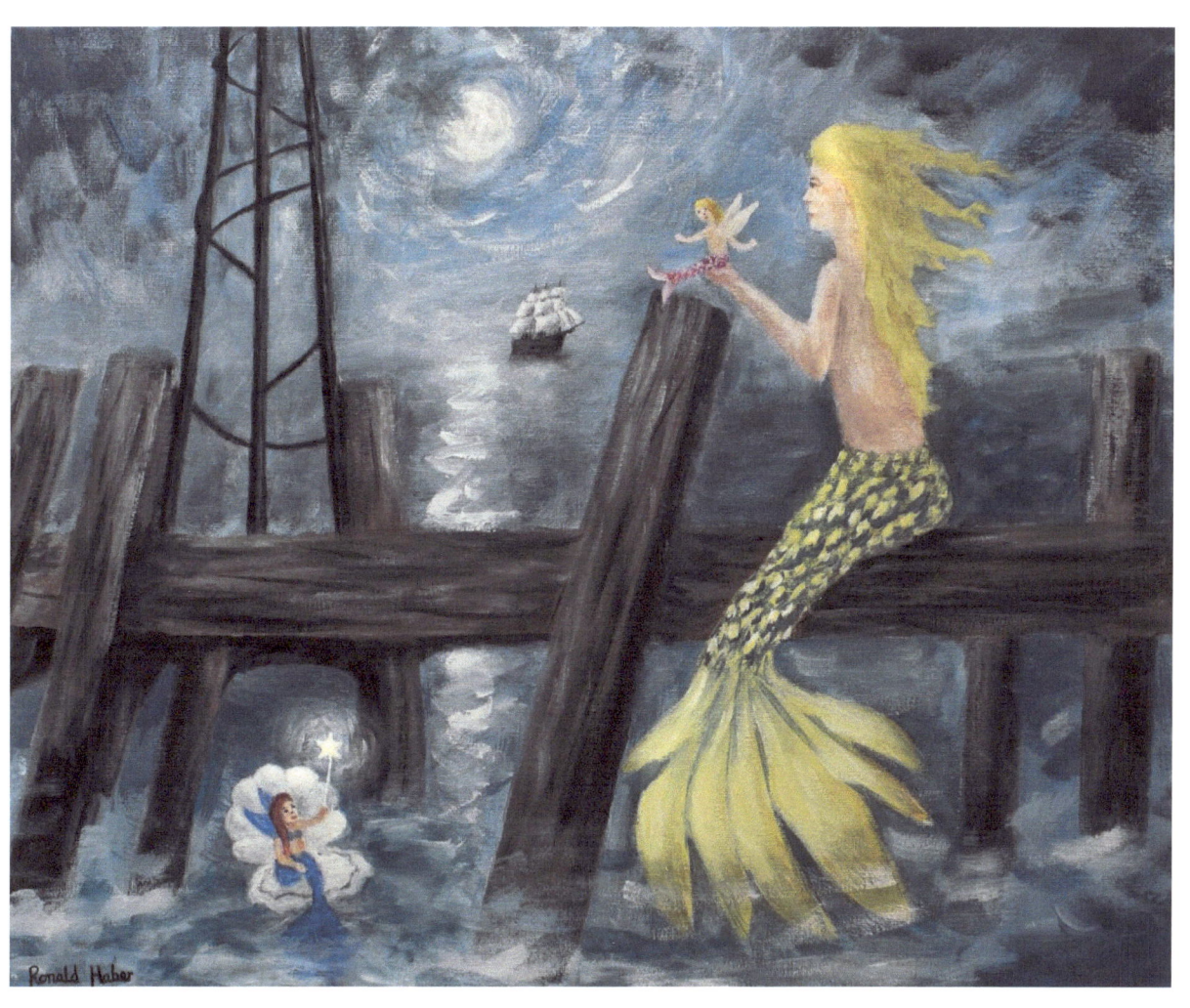

St. Annes on Sea Mermaid on the Jetty

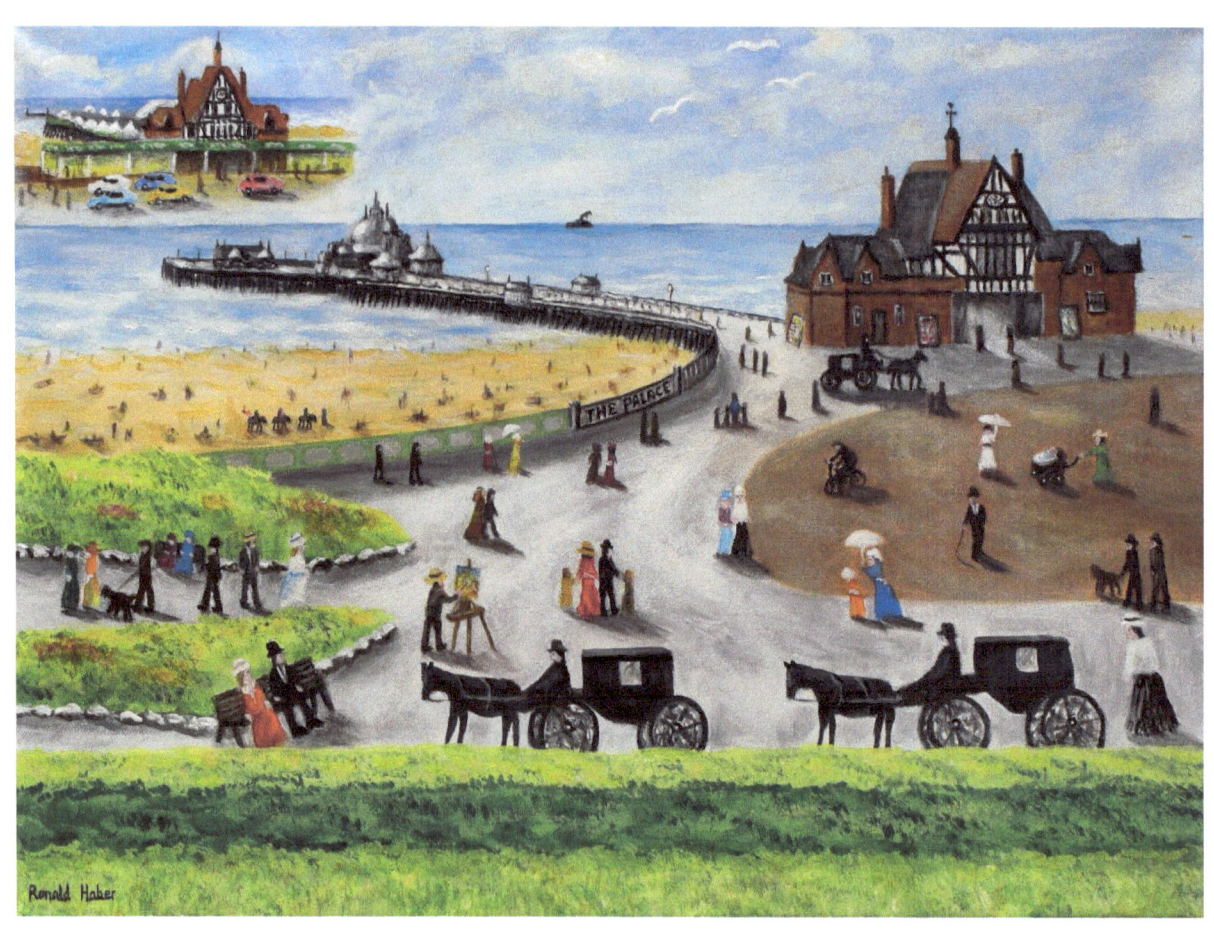

St. Annes on Sea Promenade and Pier Victorian and Modern

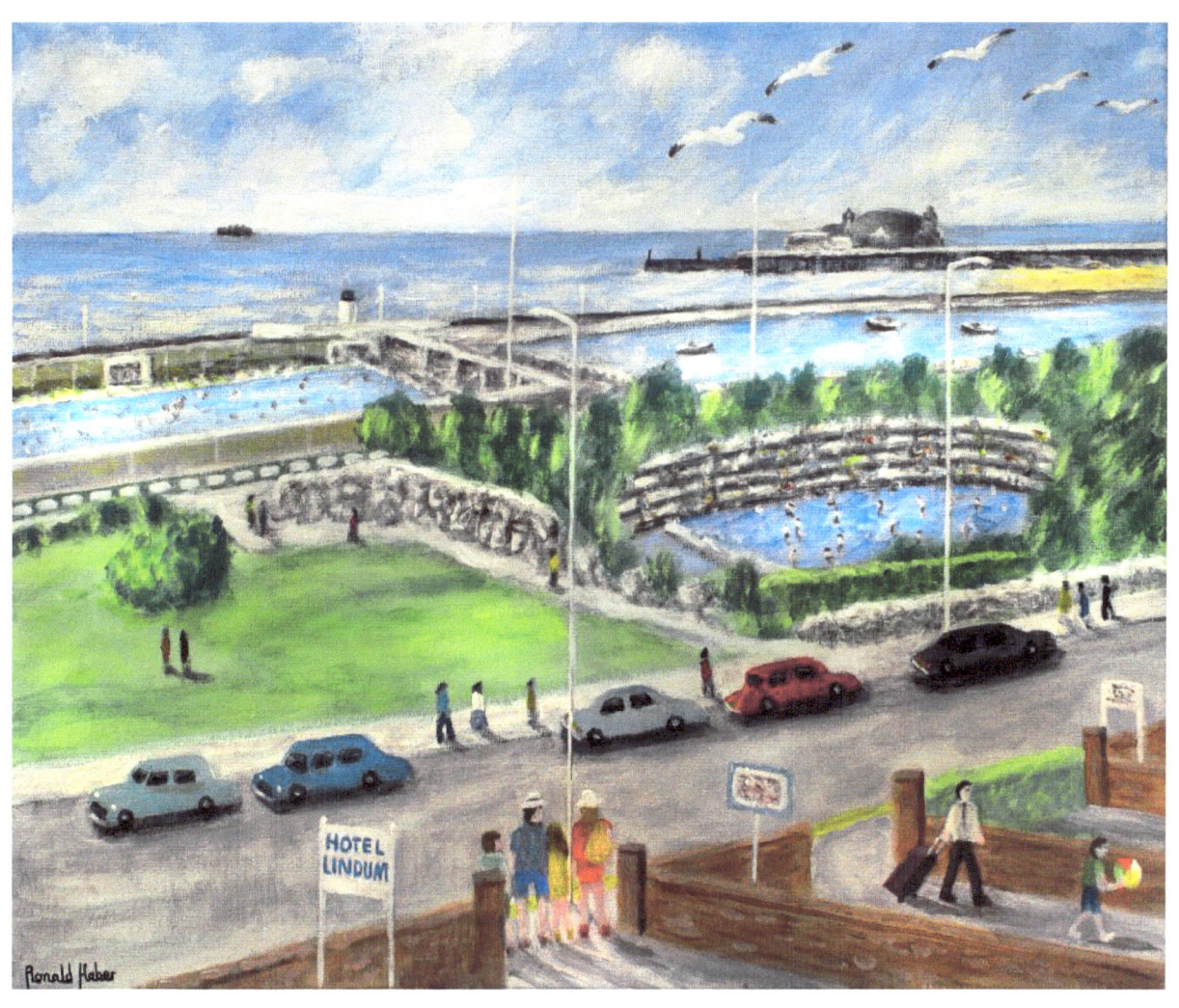

St. Annes on Sea Outdoor Swimming Pool and Boating Lake 1970's

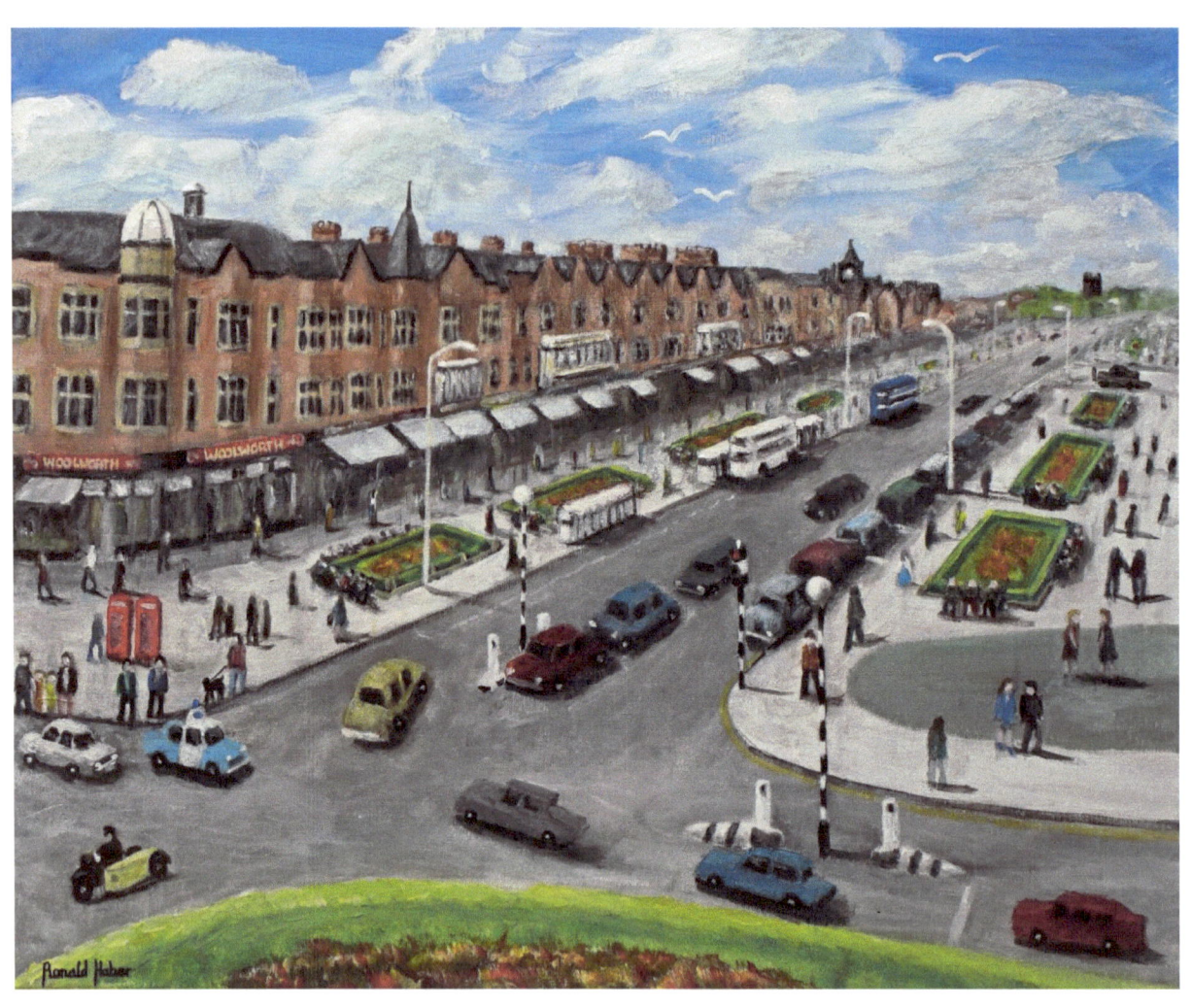

St. Annes on Sea Square 1970's

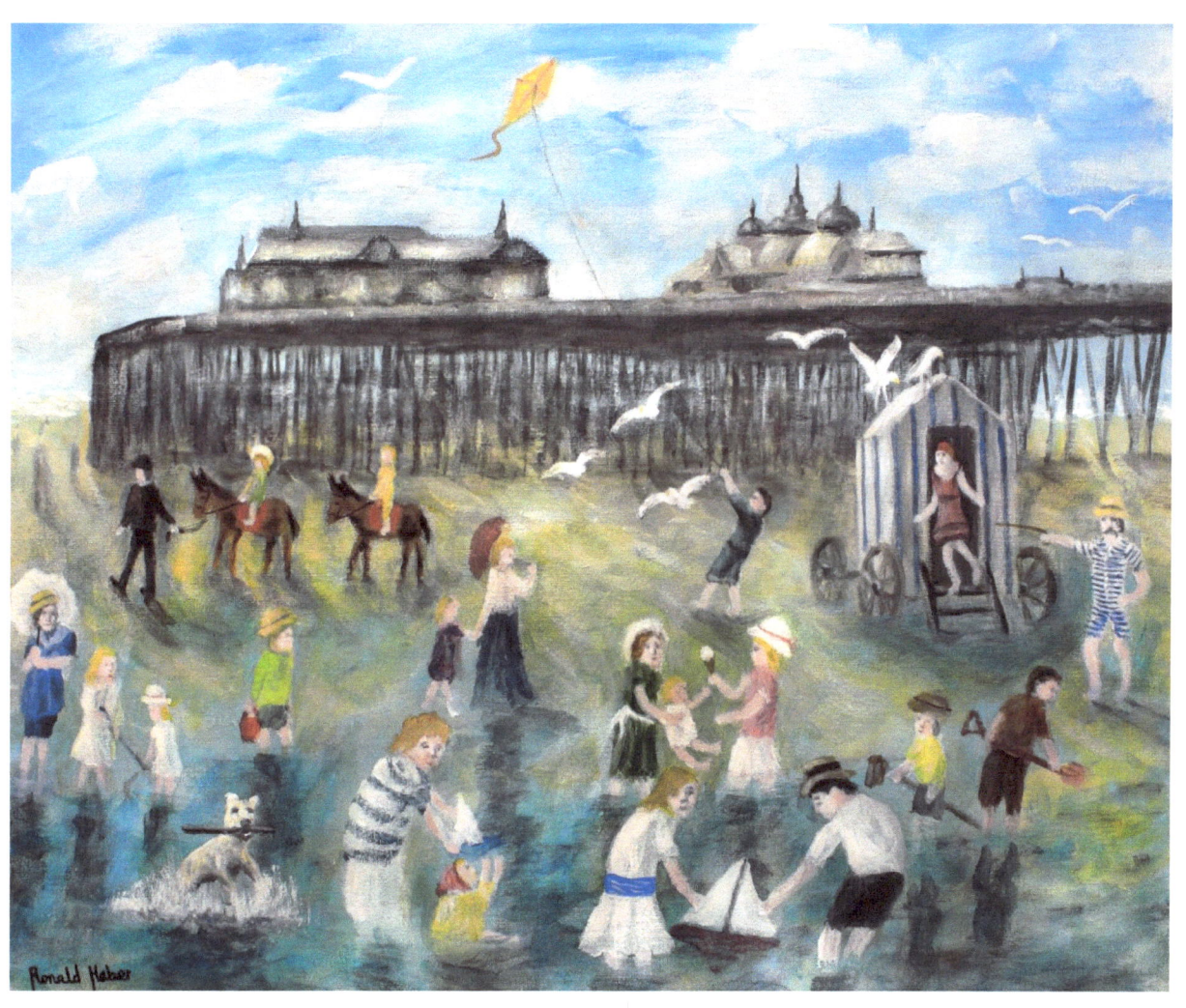

St. Annes on Sea Victorian Pier and Beach 1901

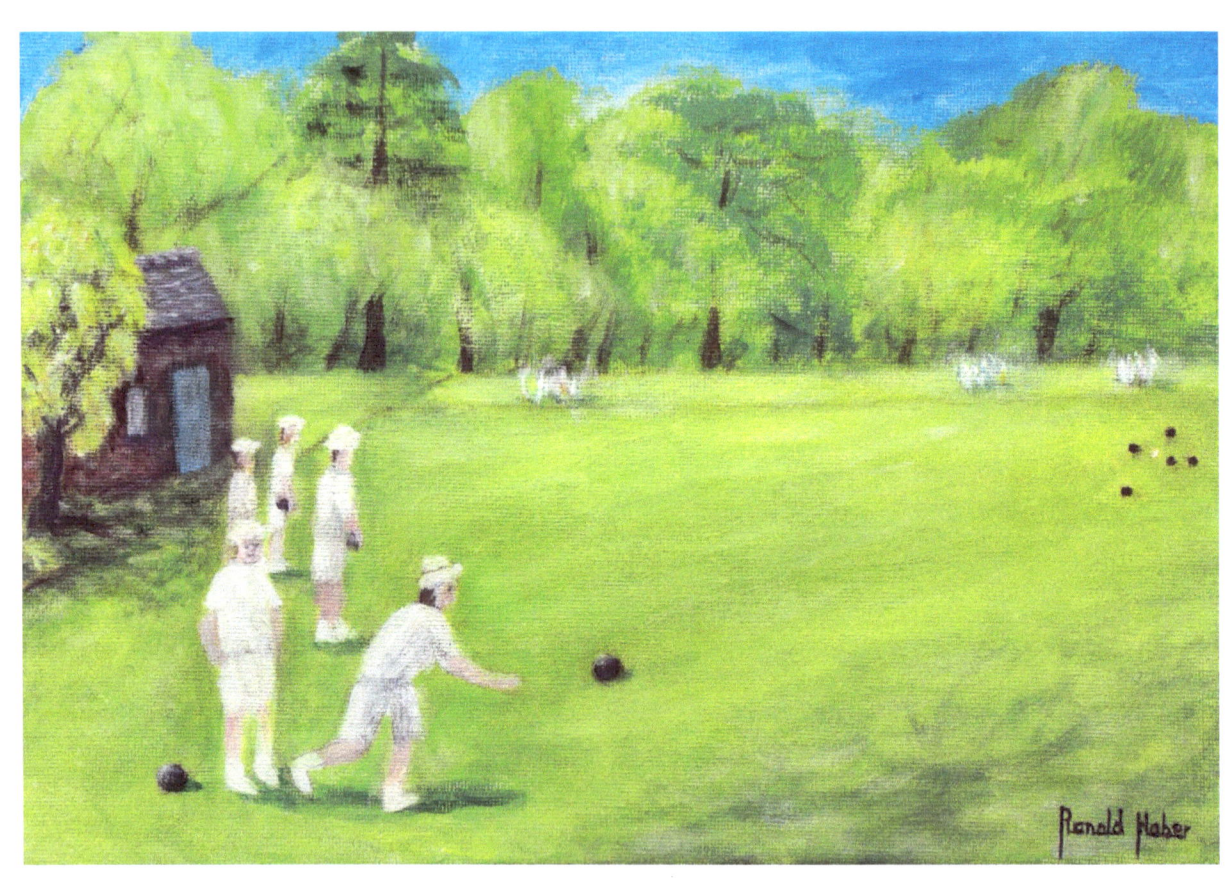

Playing Bowls in Lowther Gardens Lytham

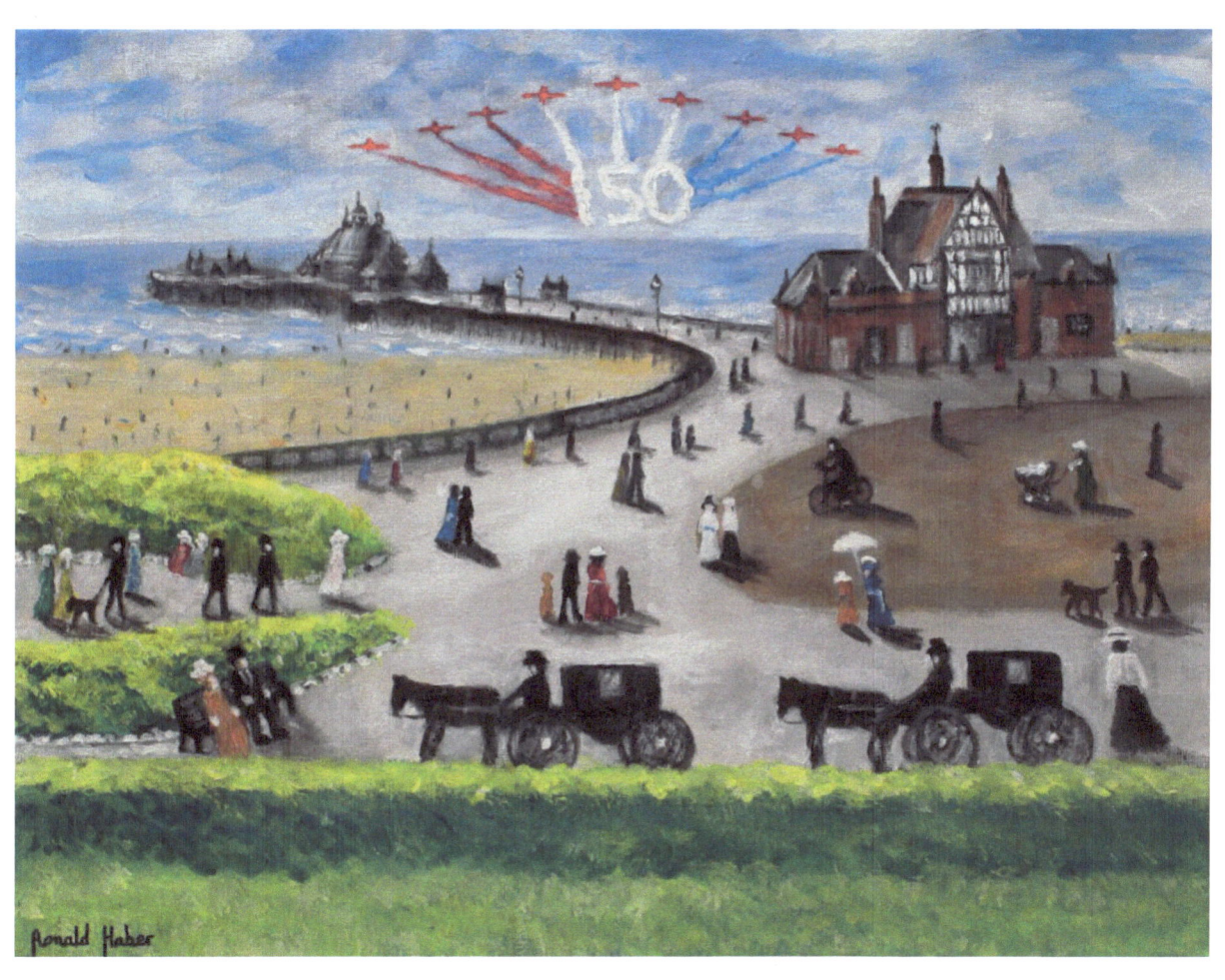

St. Annes on Sea 150th Anniversary

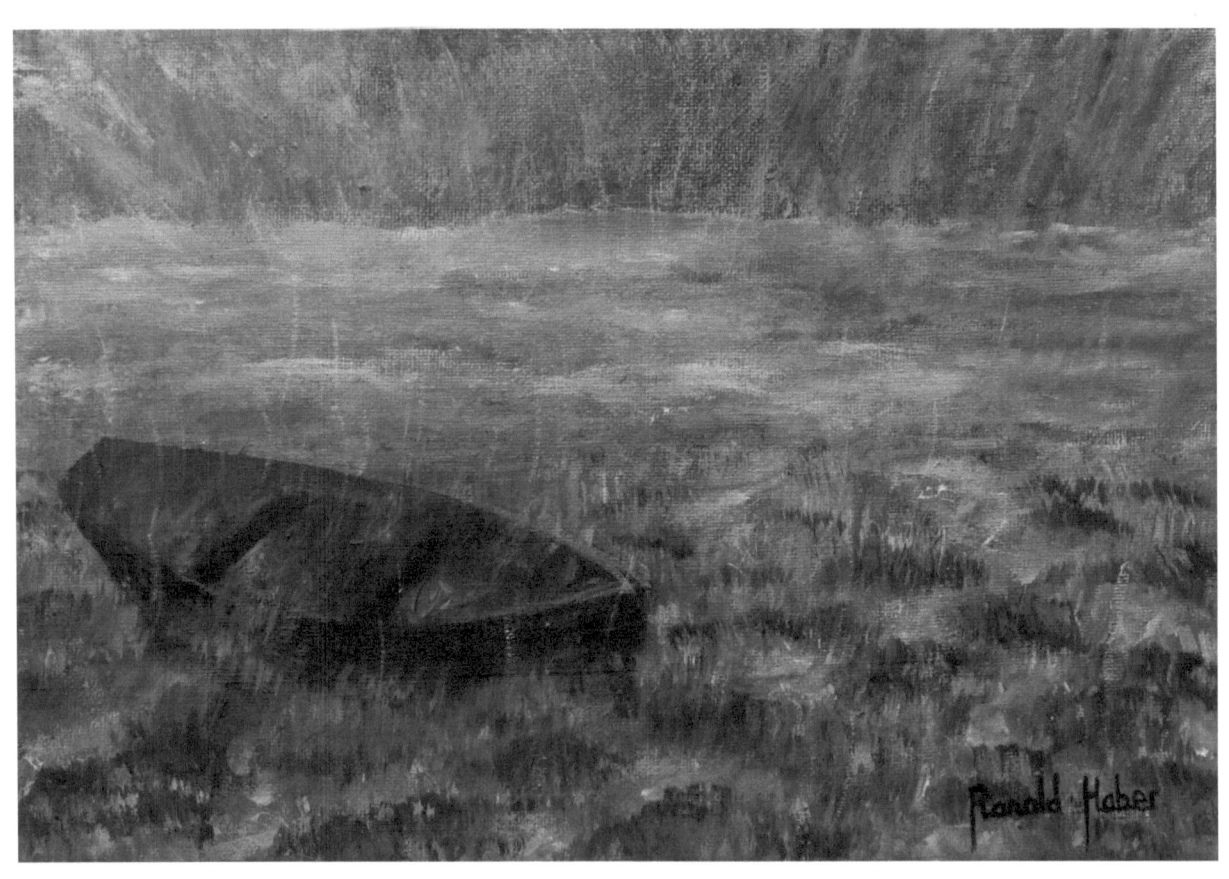

Storm over Lytham

I have included an extra chapter of my Fylde Coast Paintings

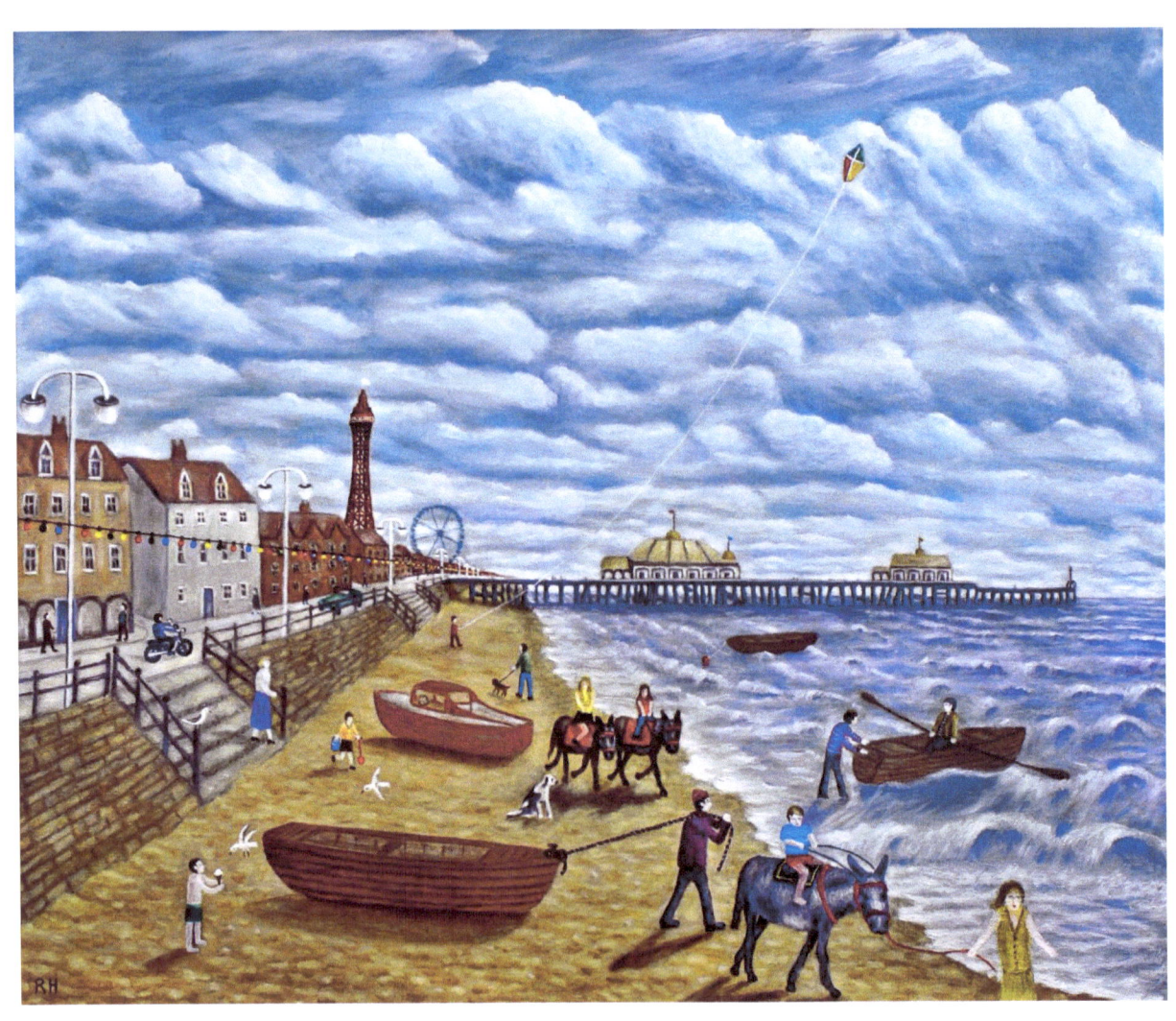

Donkey Rides on Blackpool Beach

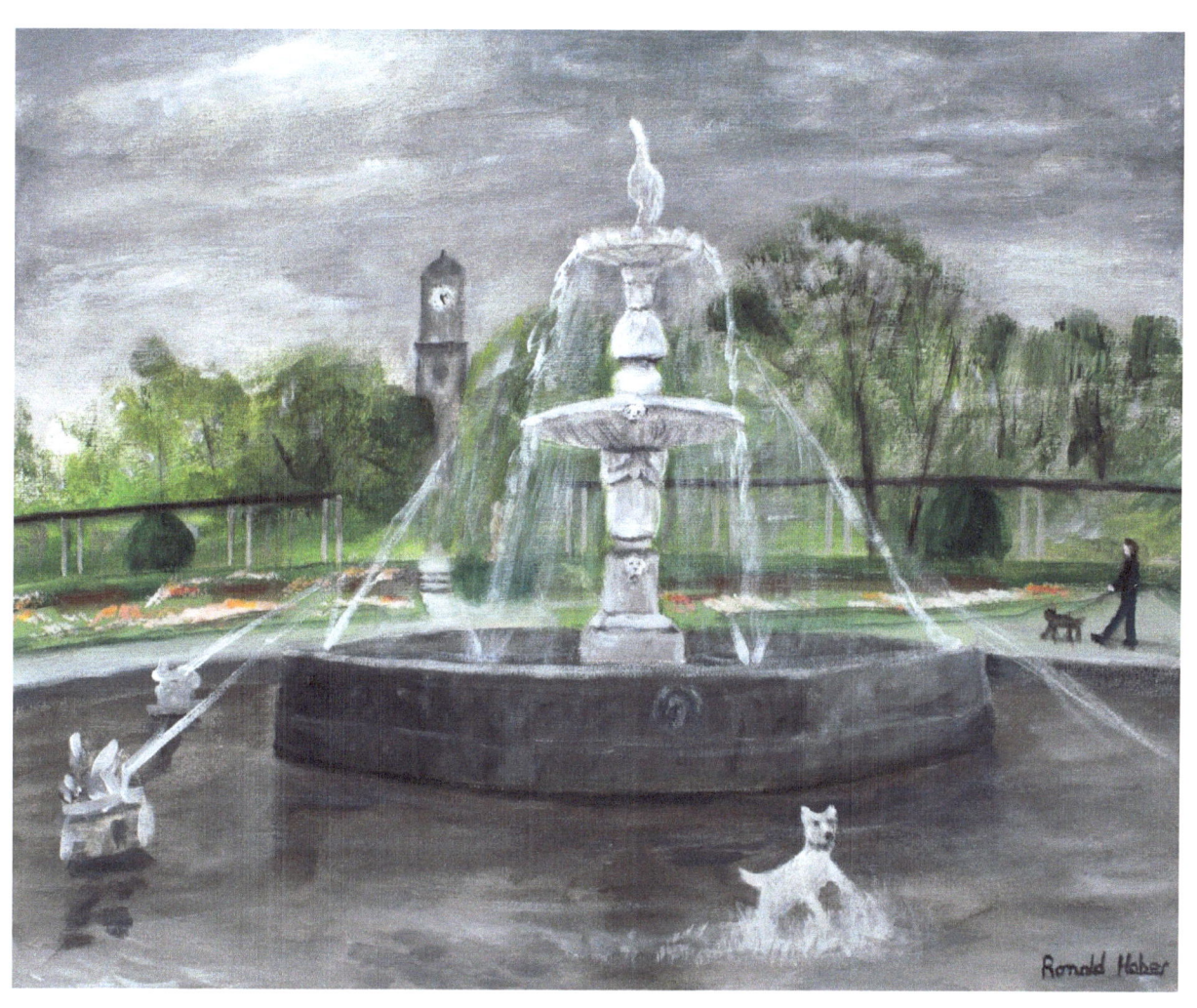

Blackpool Stanley Park Fountain

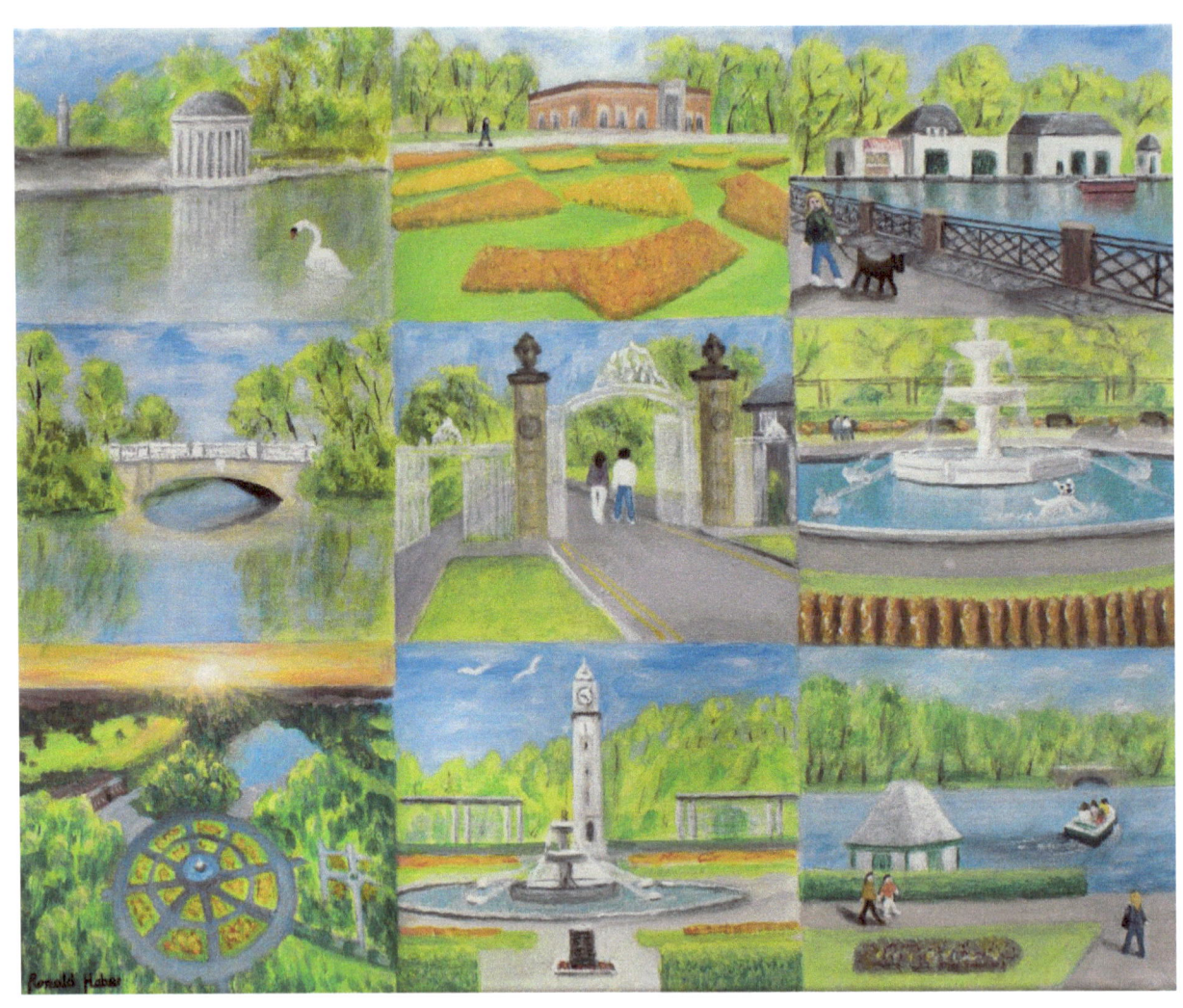

Blackpool Stanley Park Montage

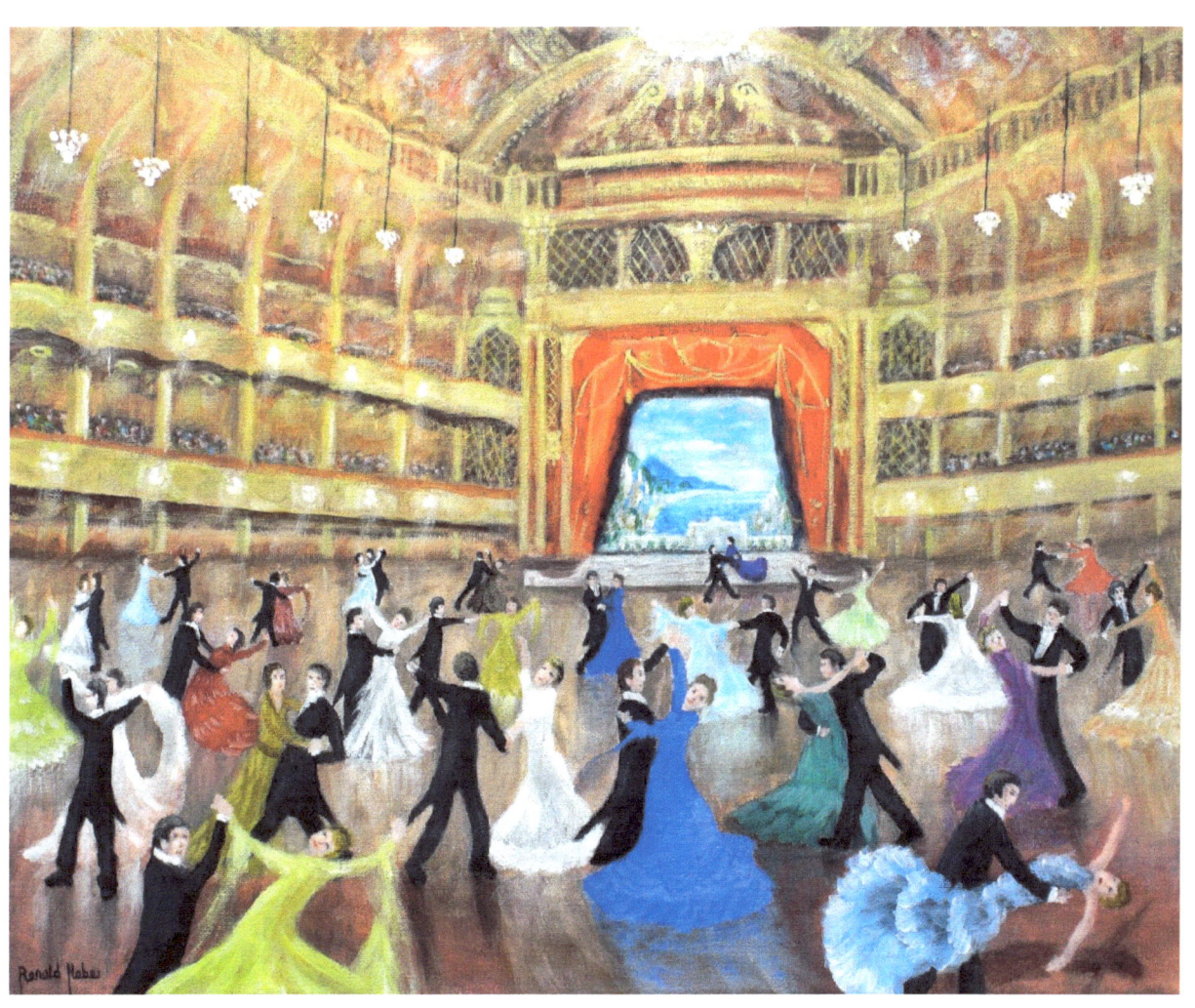

Blackpool Tower Ballroom

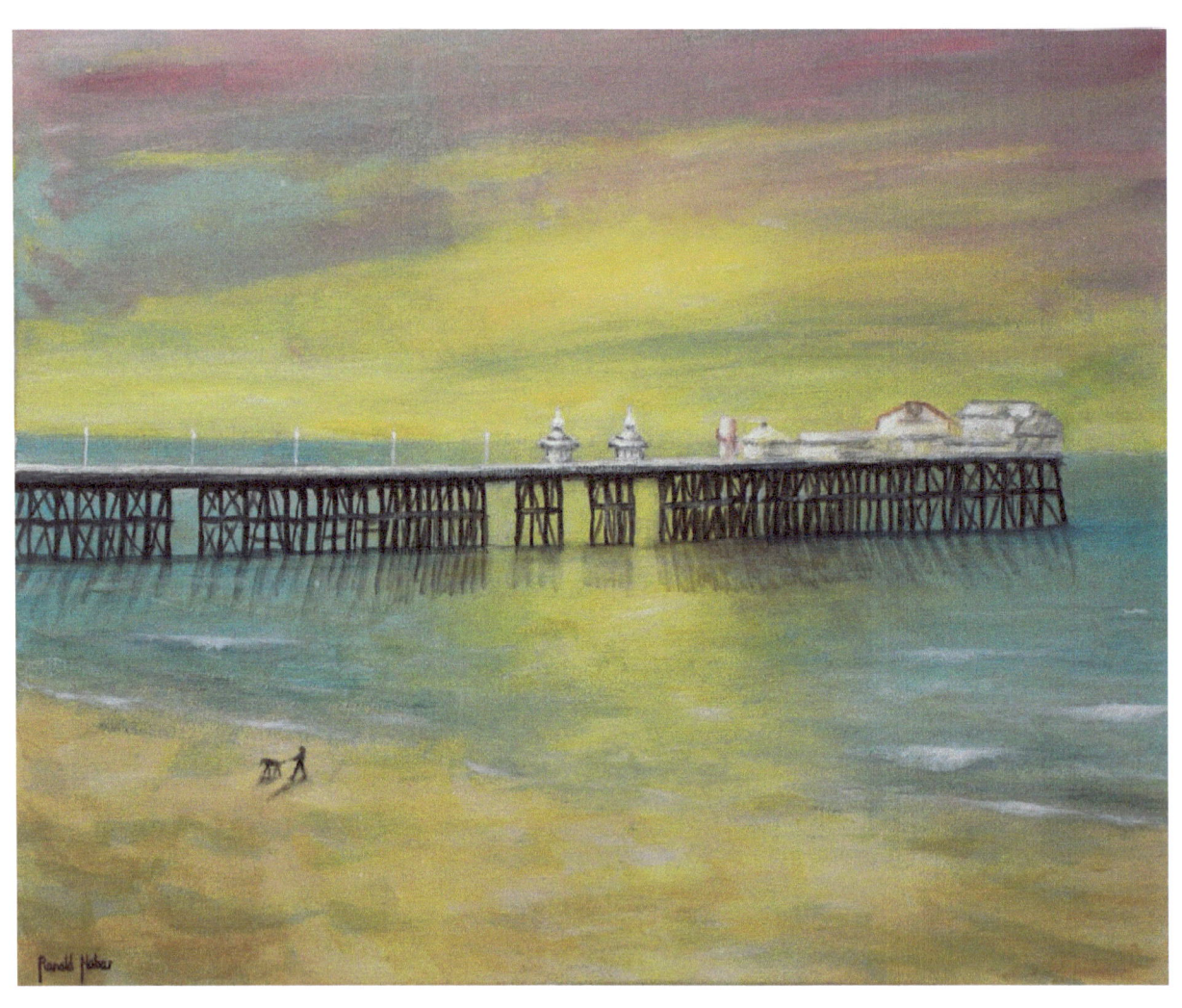

Sunset over North Pier Blackpool

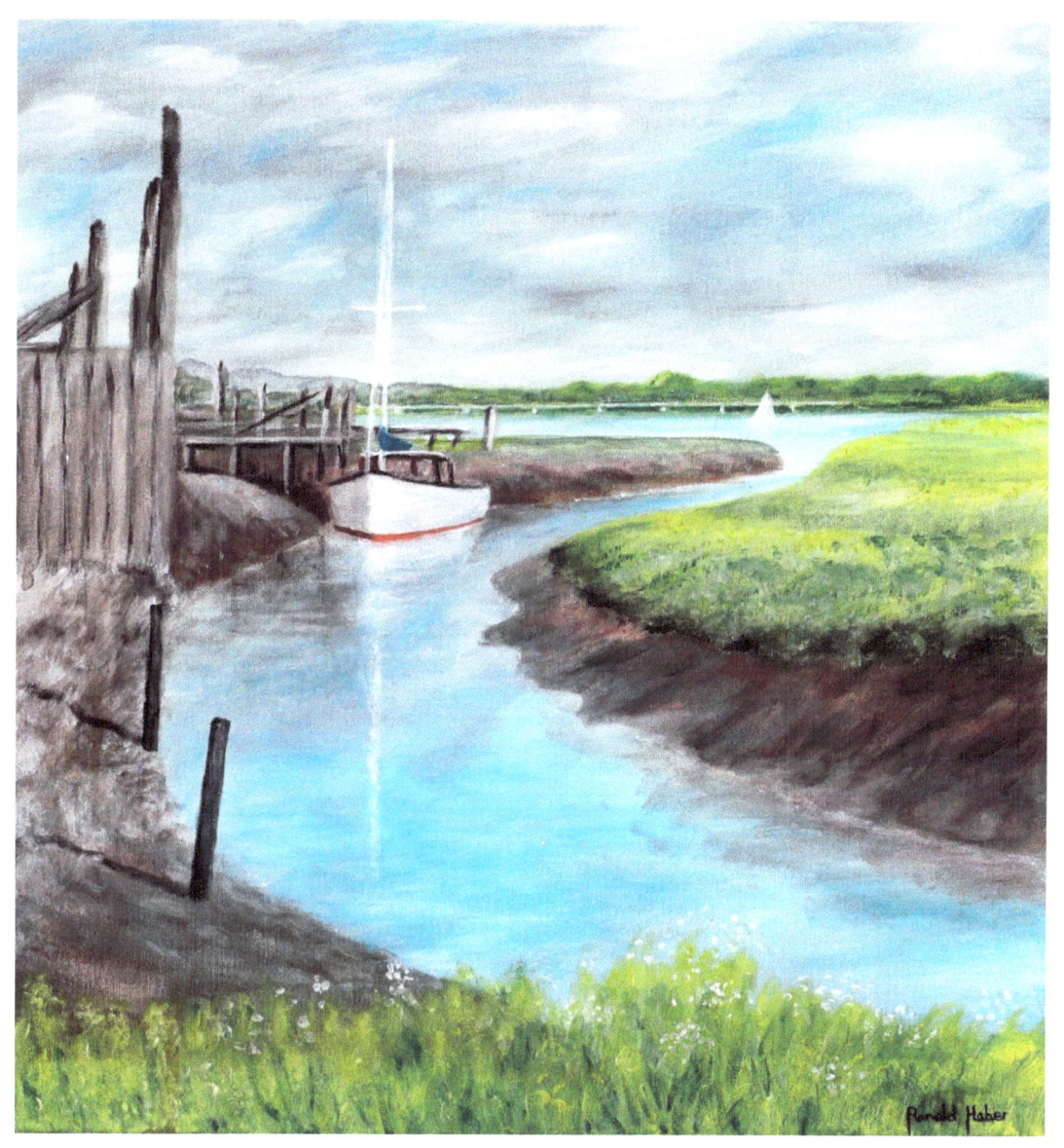

Poulton Le Fylde Skippool Creek

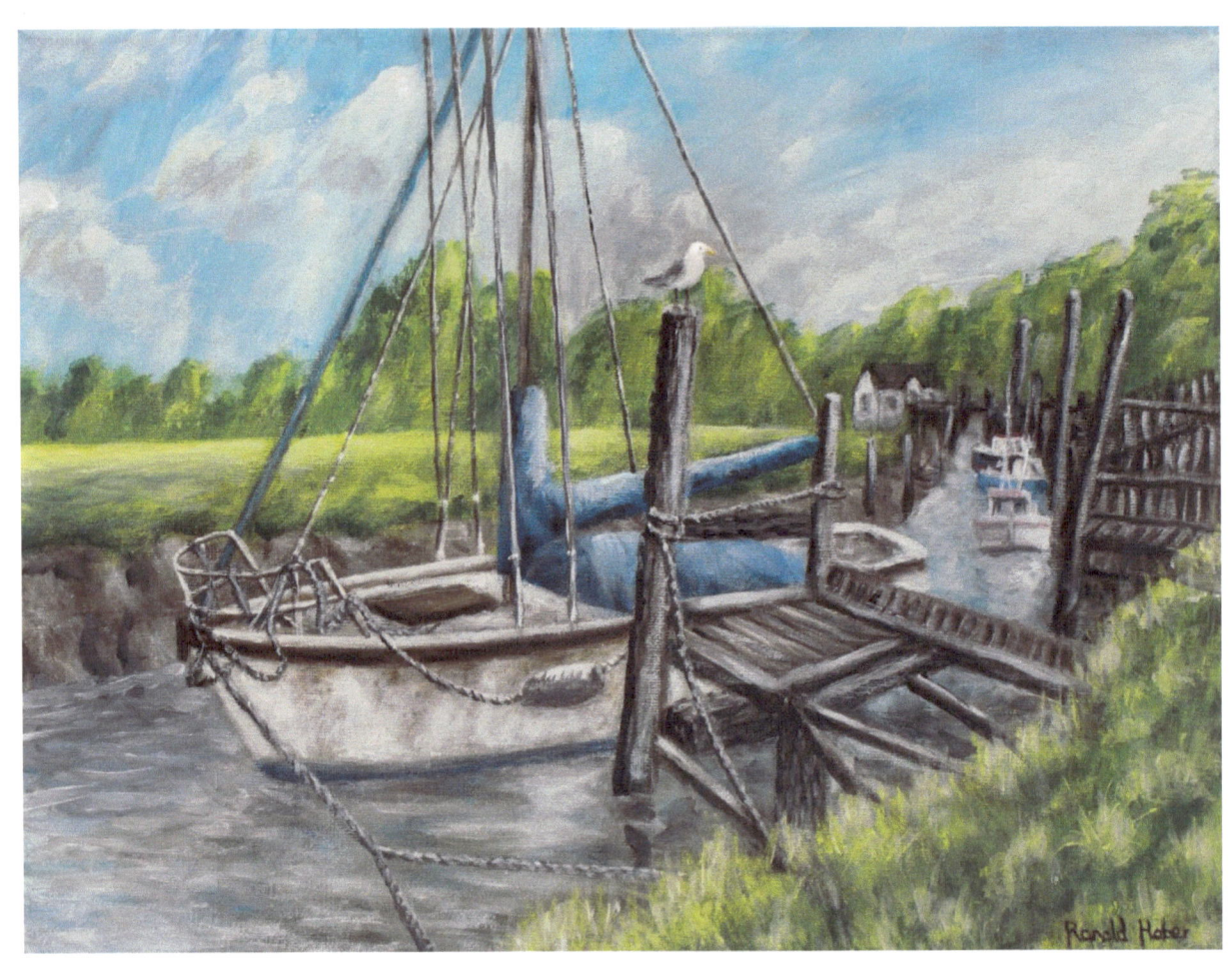

Poulton Le Fylde Skippool Creek Boats

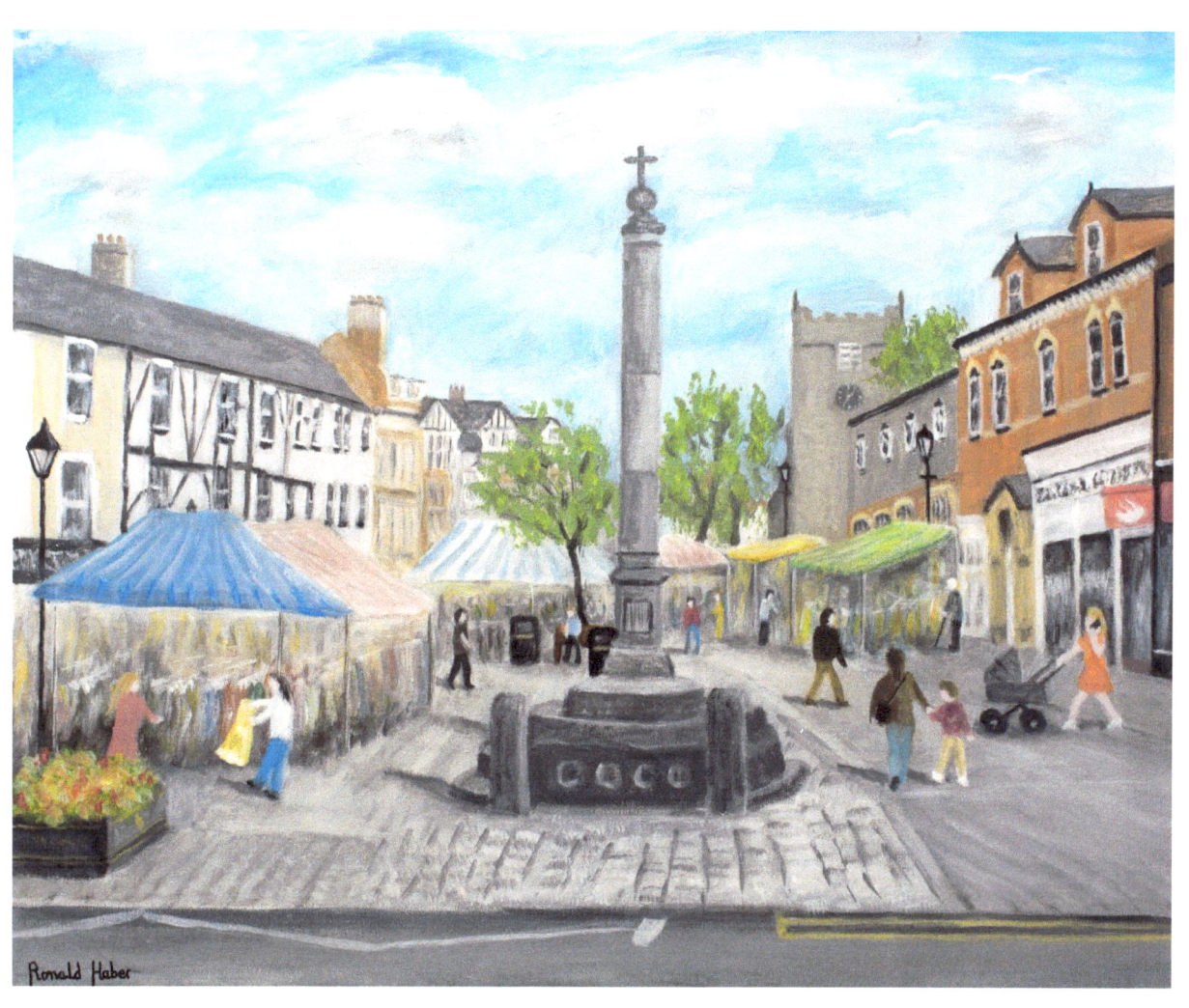

Poulton Le Fylde Market Day

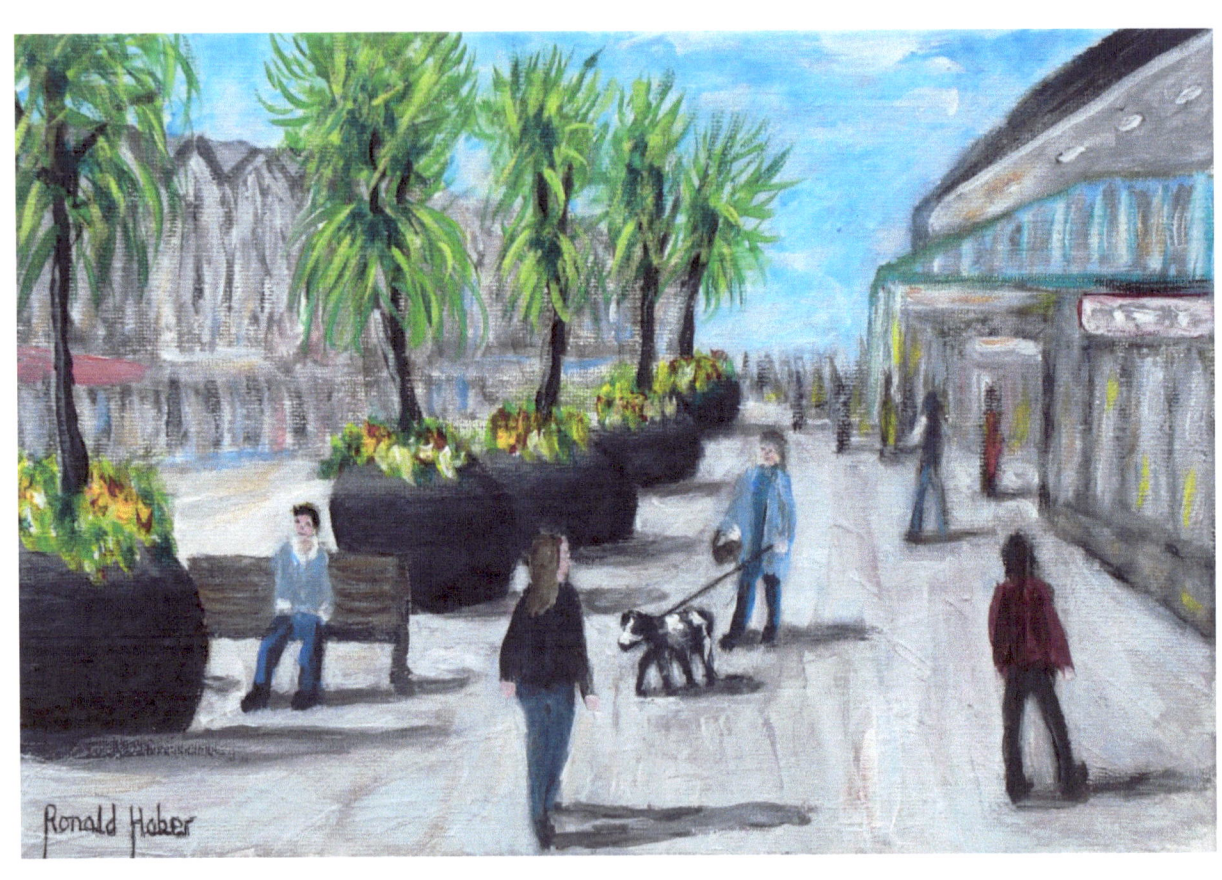

Cleveleys Town Centre

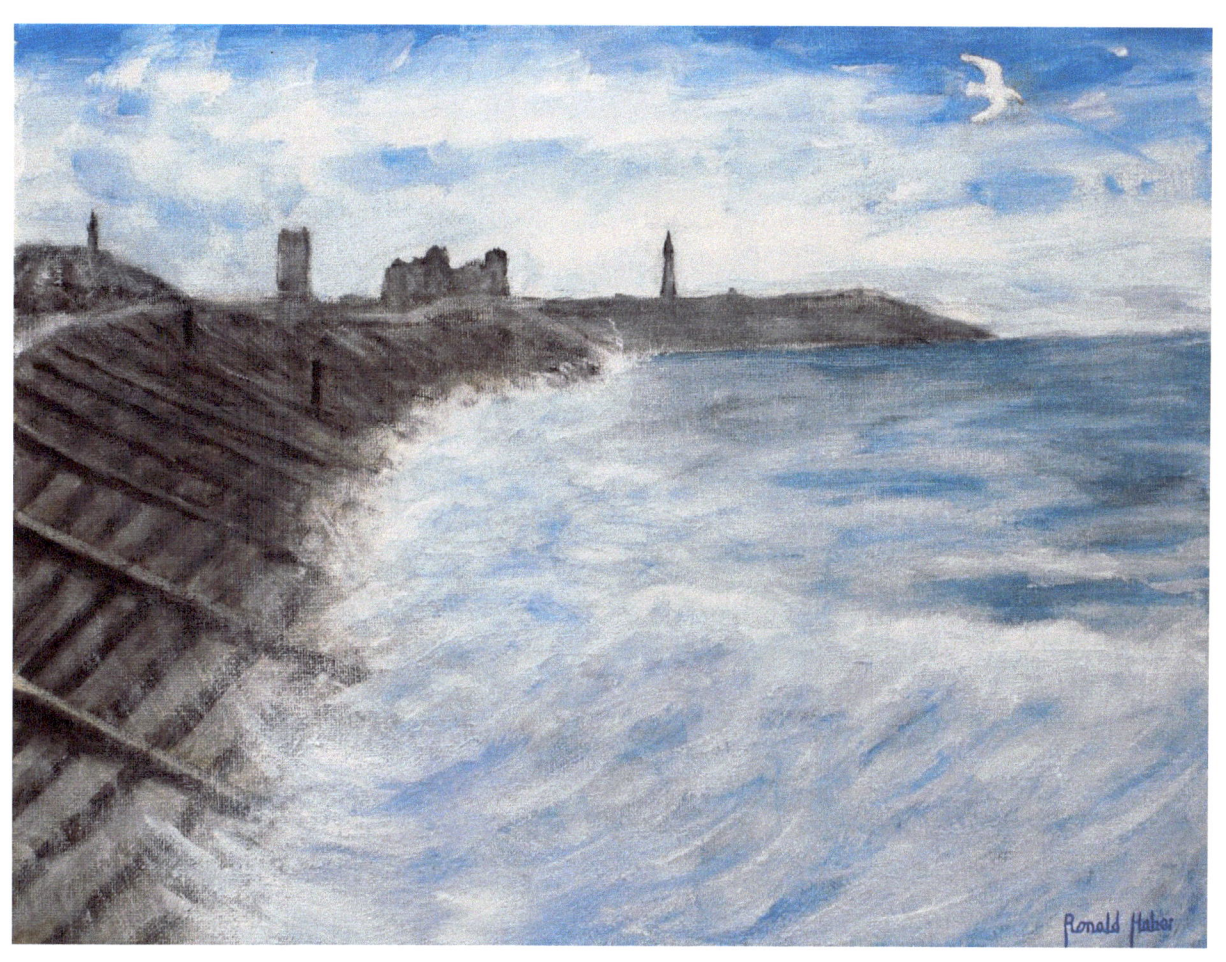

Sea at Cleveleys

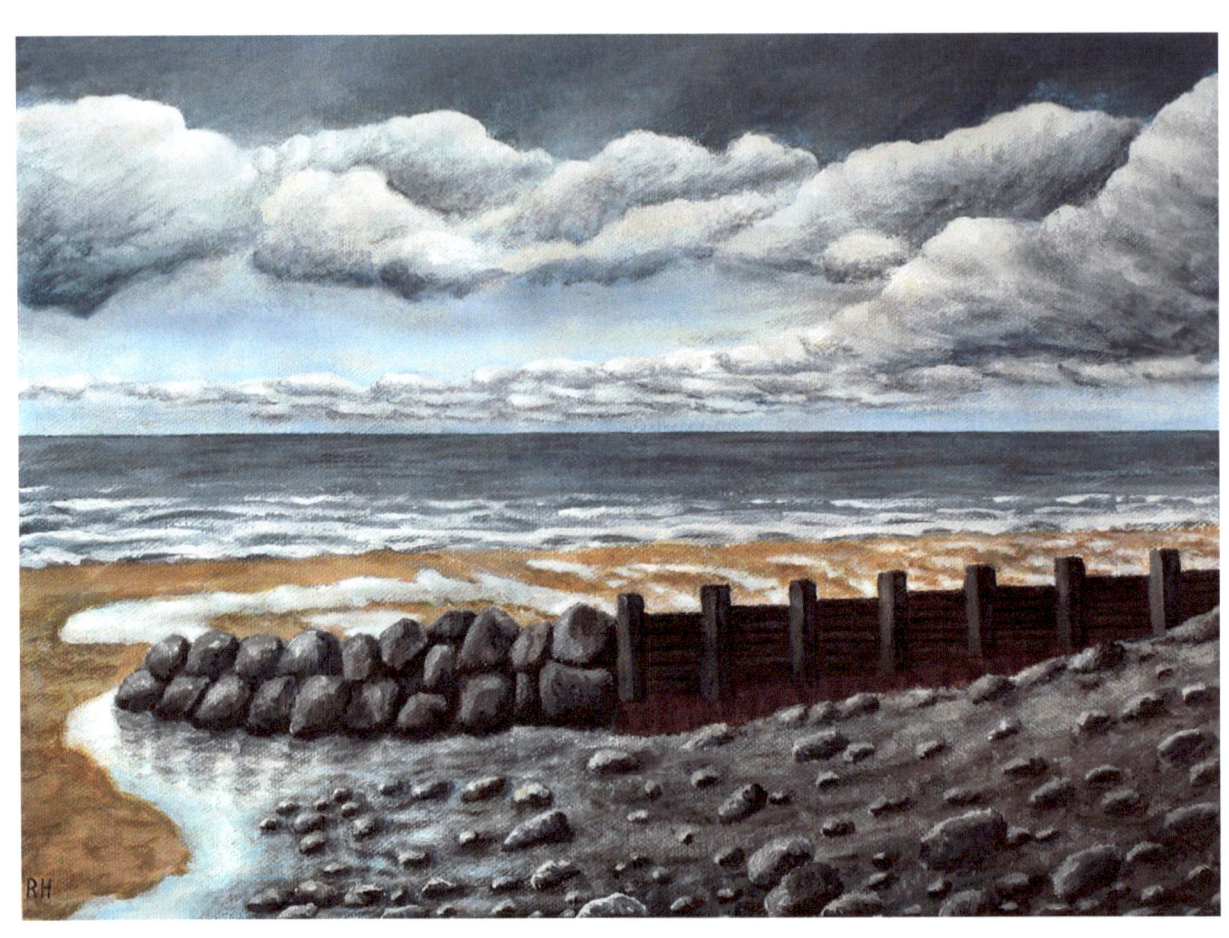

After the Rain at Cleveleys Beach

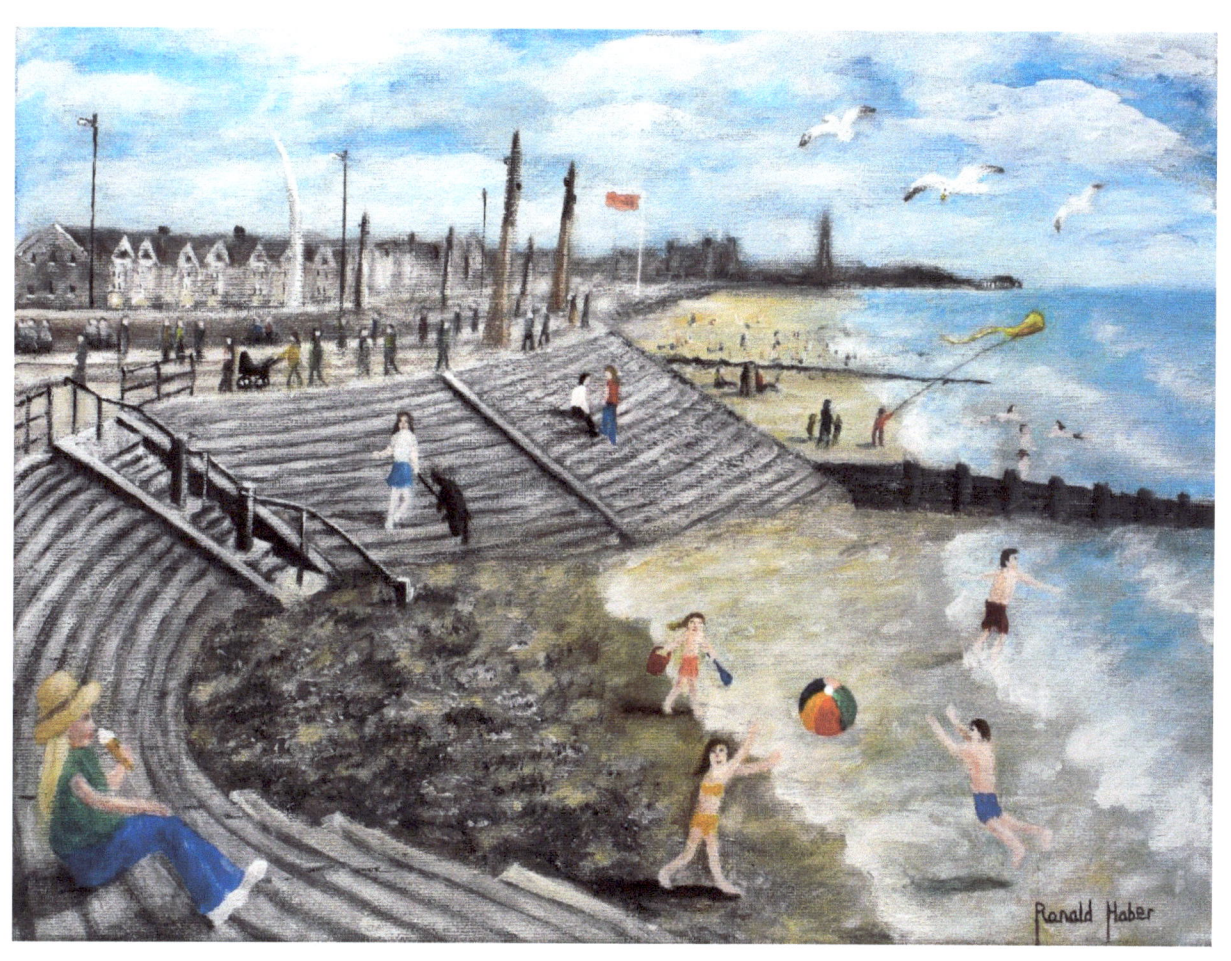

Summer Fun on Cleveleys Beach

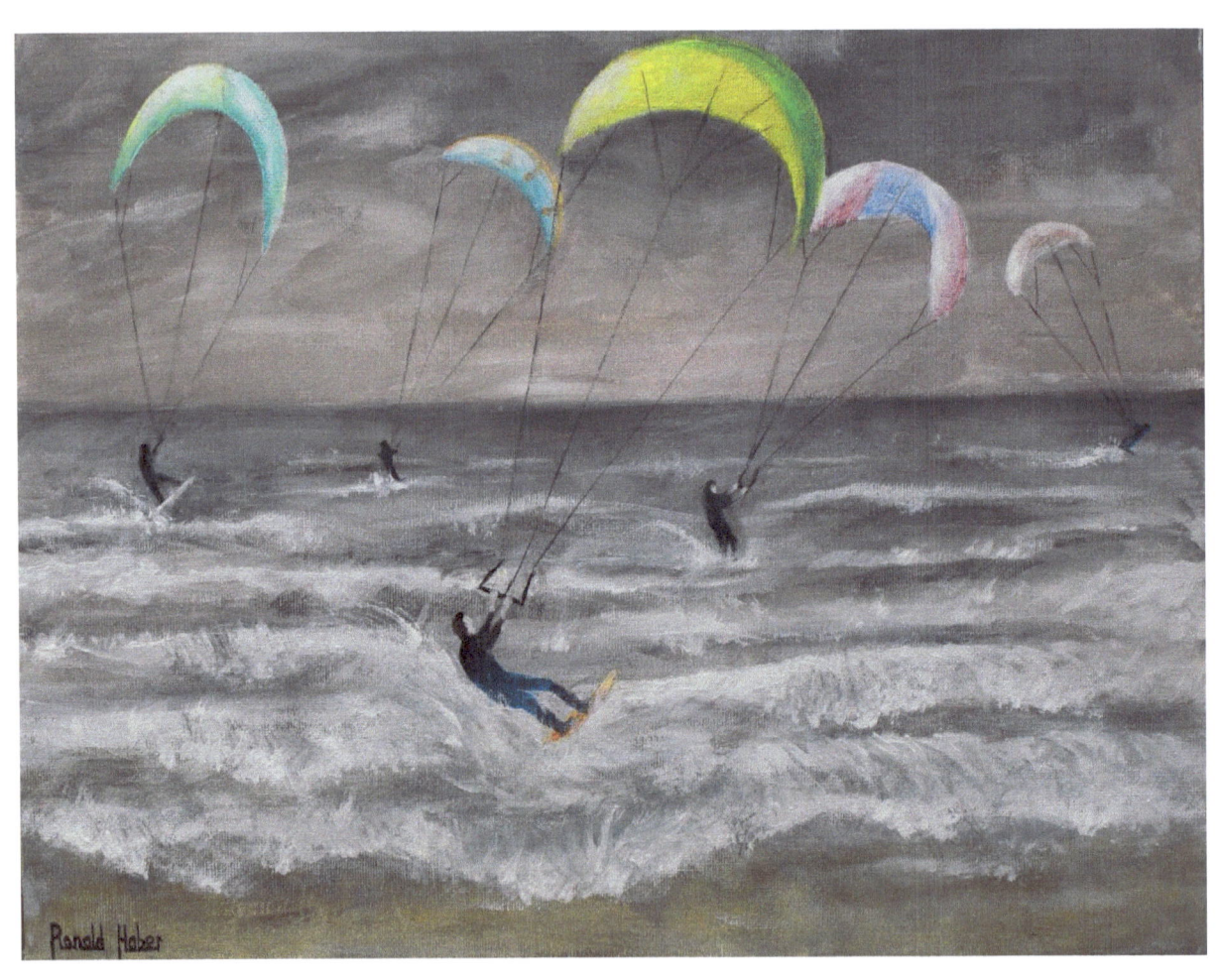

Windsurfing at Cleveleys

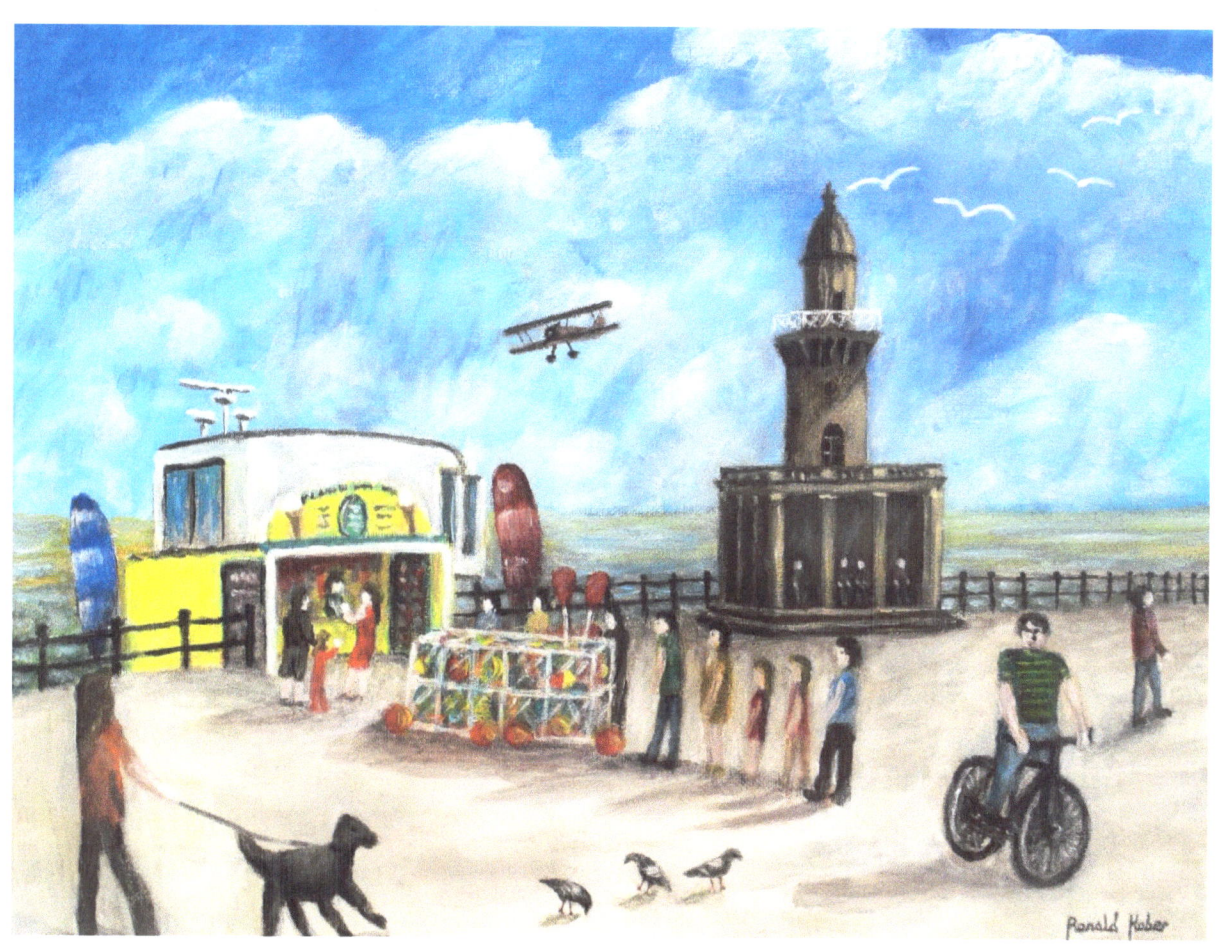

Fleetwood Promenade

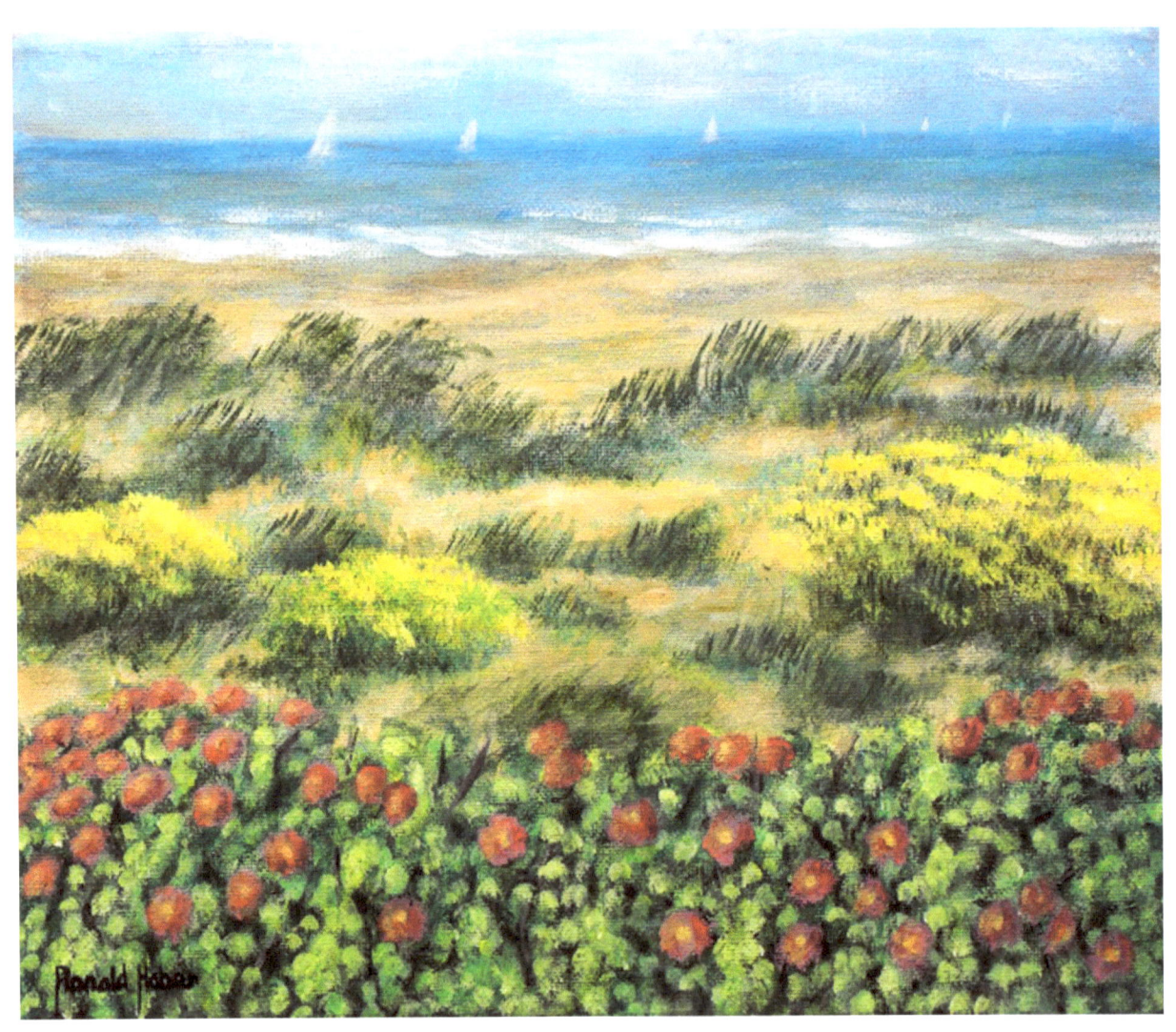

Fleetwood Beach and Flowers

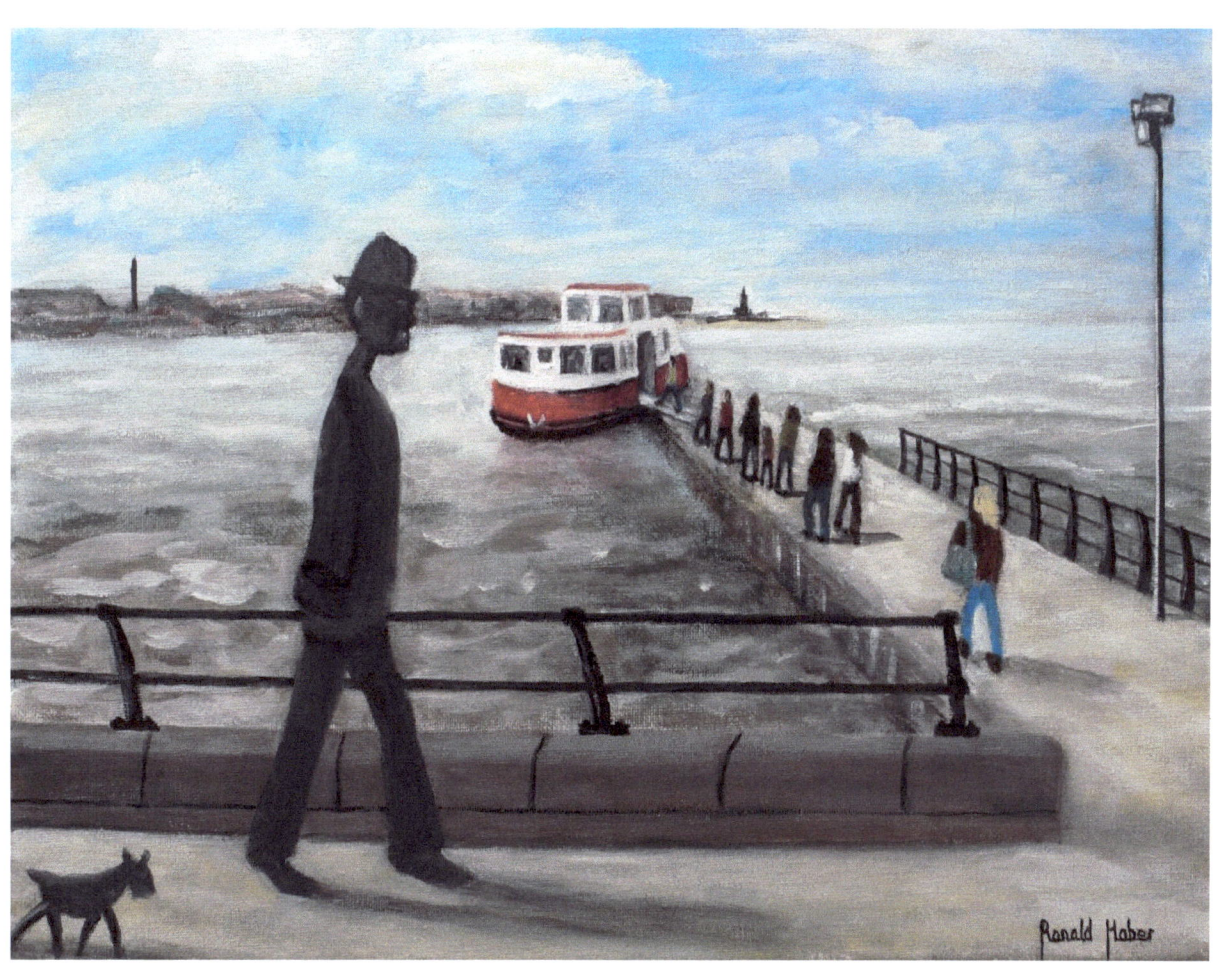

Knott End Lowry Statue

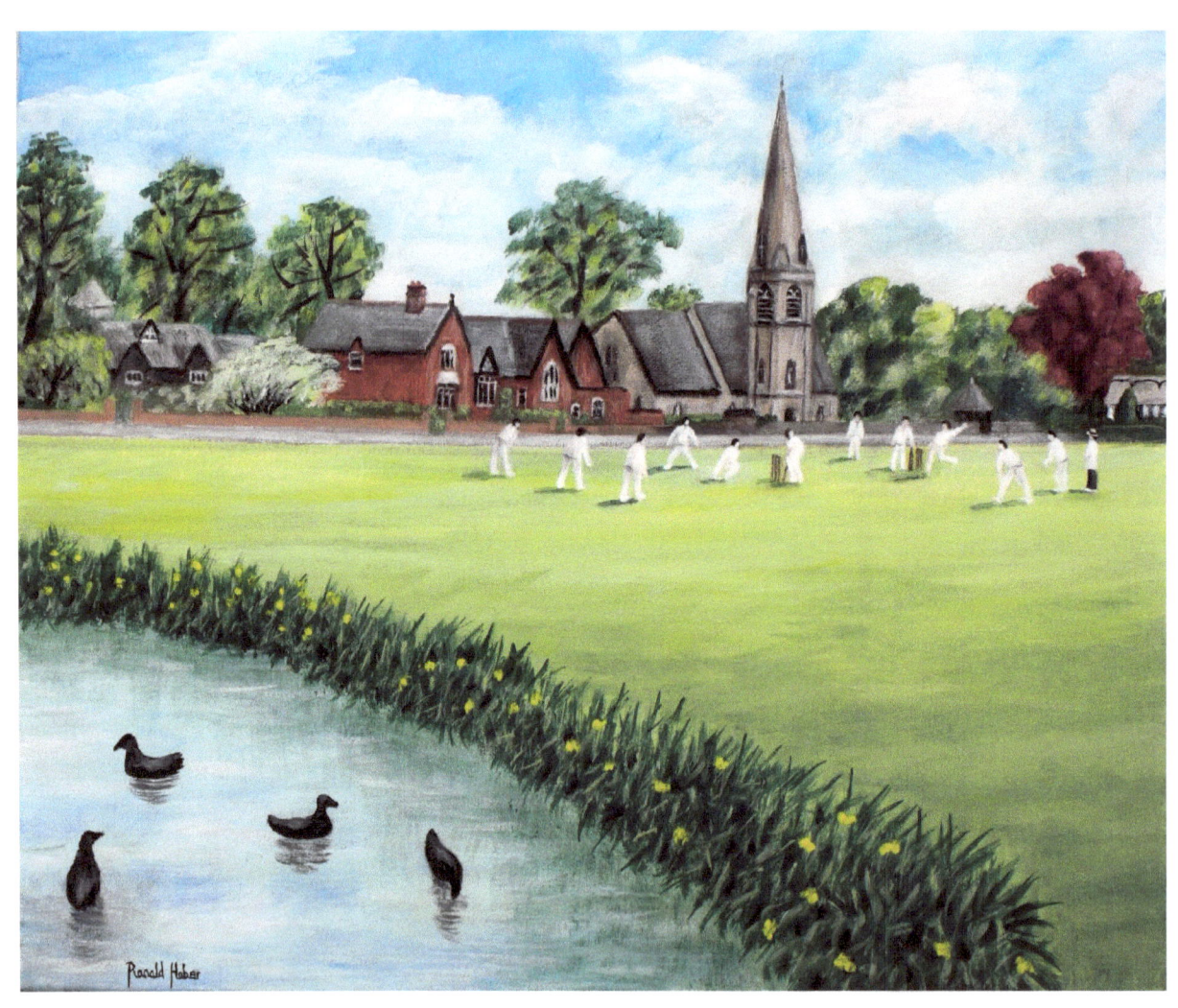

Playing Cricket Wrea Green

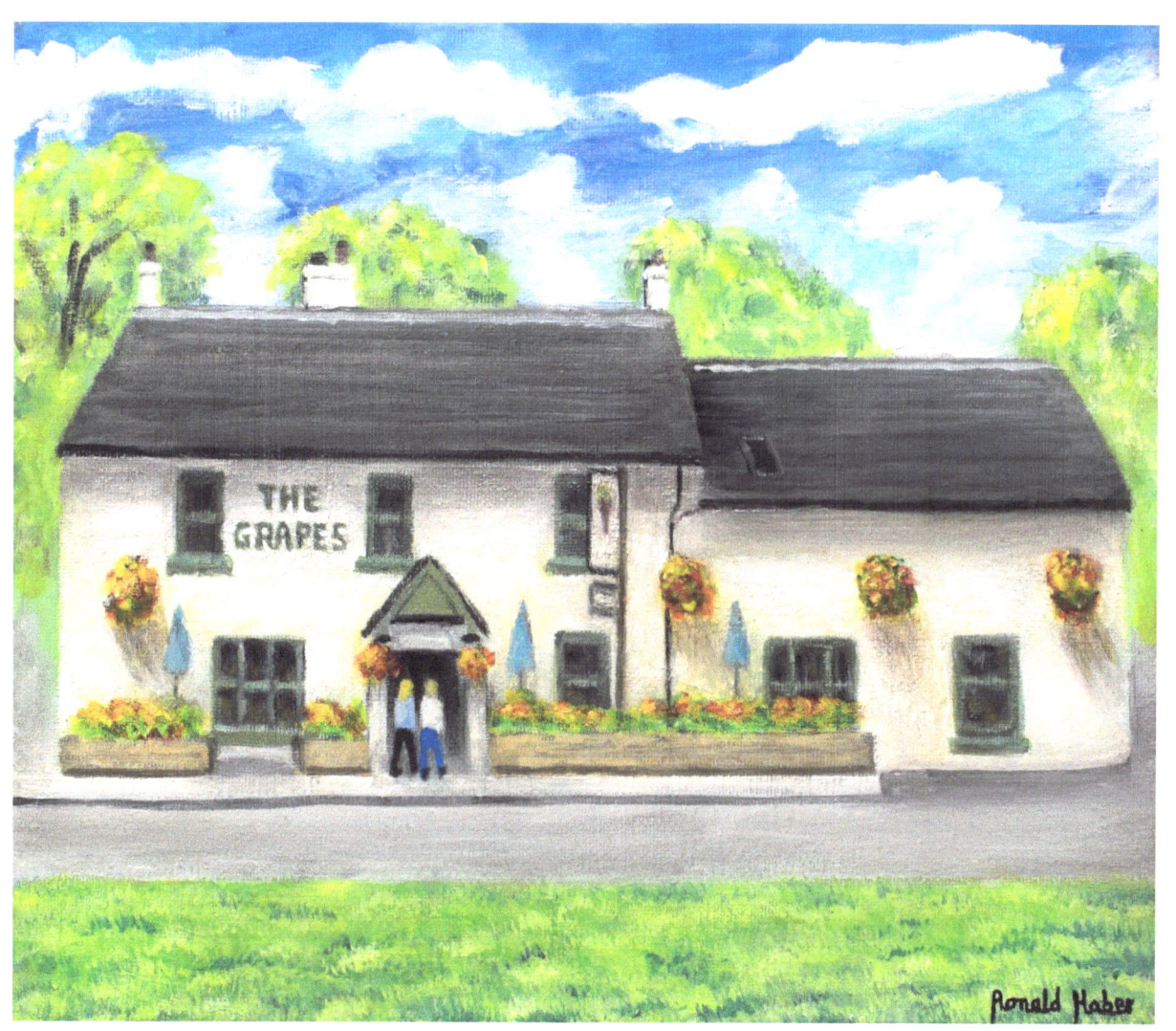

The Grapes Wrea Green

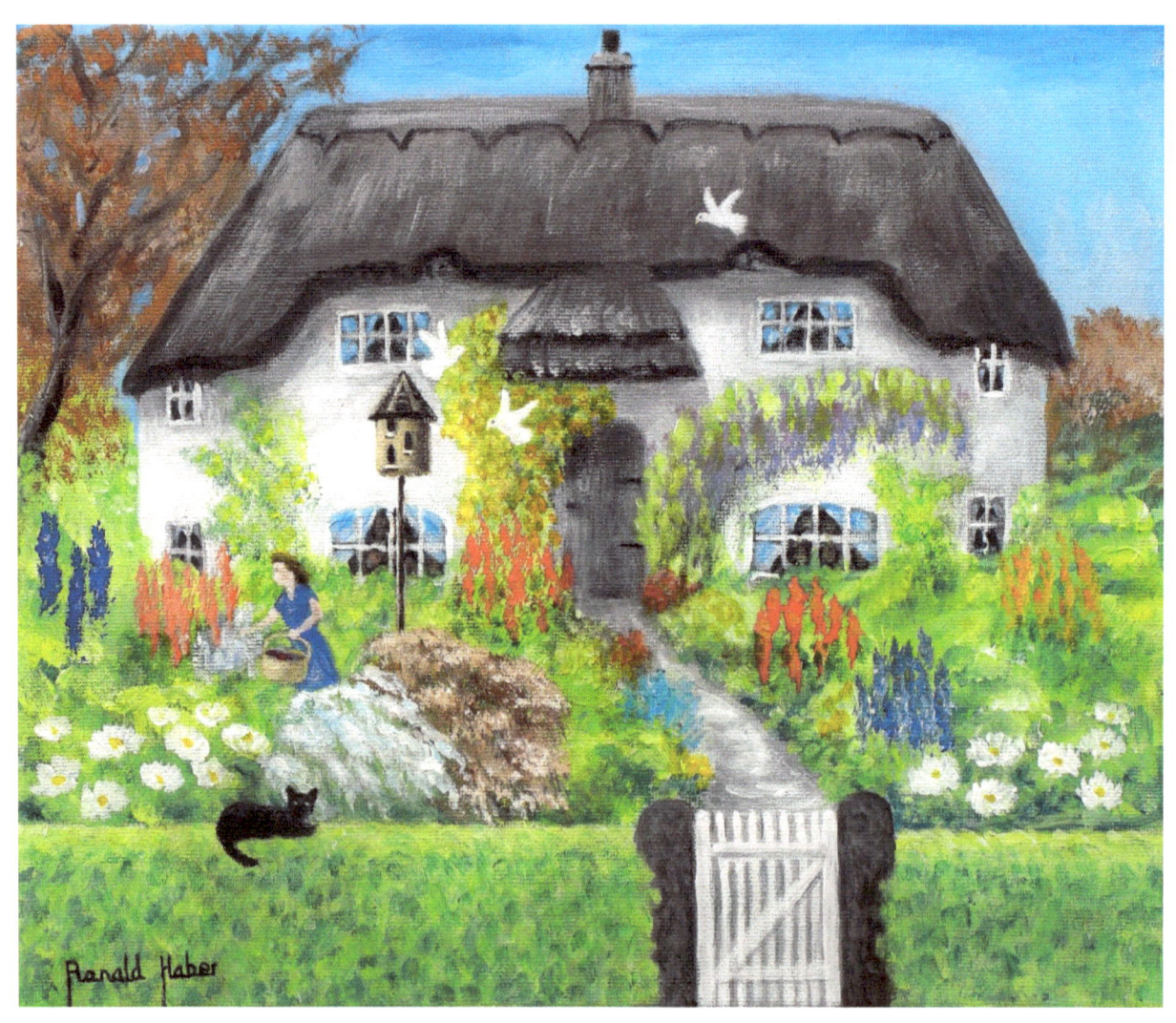

Wrea Green Thatched Cottage

116

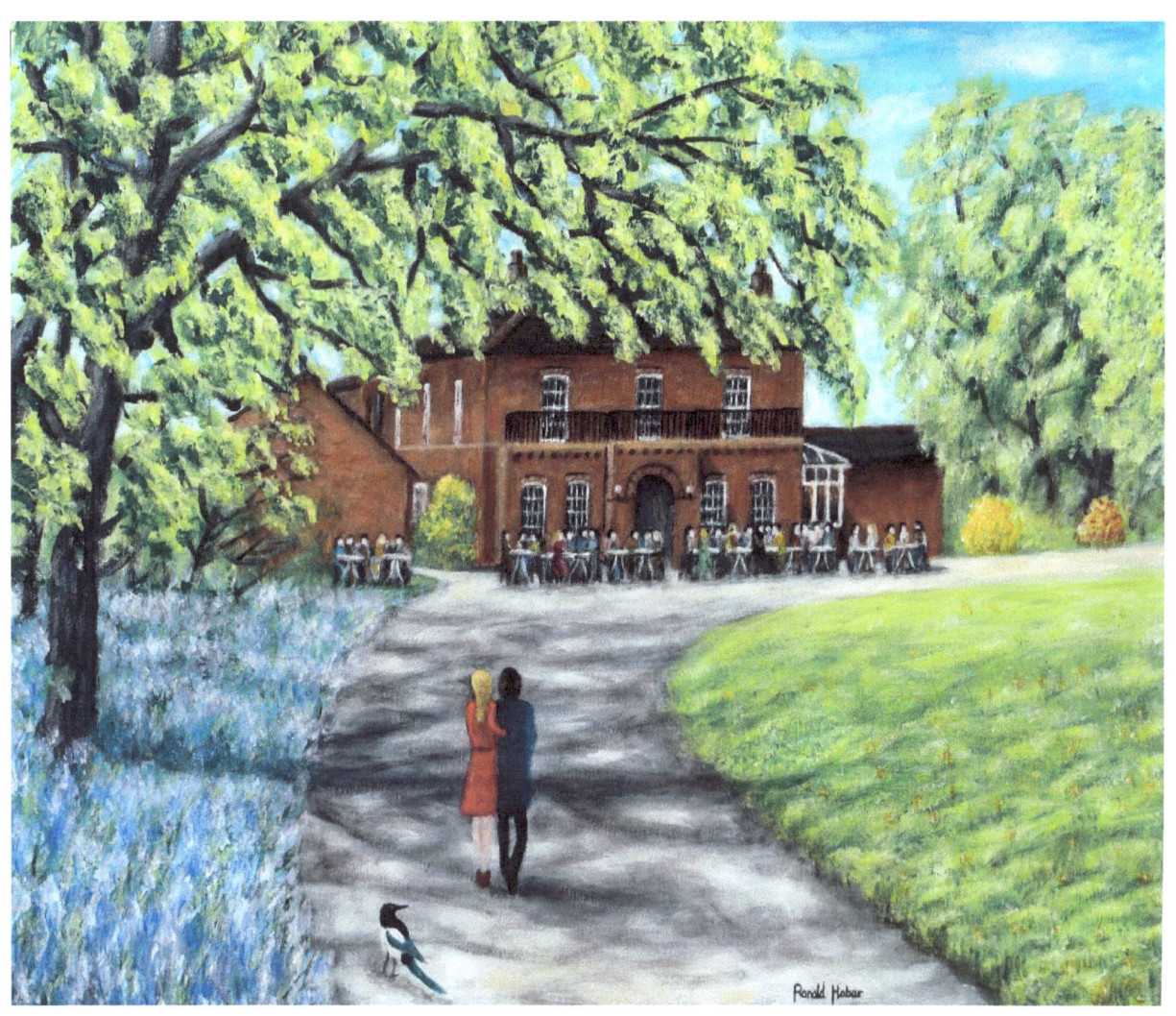

Warton Hall Bluebells

www.ingramcontent.com/pod-product-compliance
Lightning Source LLC
Chambersburg PA
CBHW051151220526
45473CB00003B/739